CALIFORNIA'S

BEST B&B_s

BE A TRAVELER - NOT A TOURIST!

OPEN ROAD TRAVEL GUIDES SHOW YOU
HOW TO BE A TRAVELER – NOT A TOURIST!

Whether you're going abroad or planning a trip in the United States, take Open Road along on your journey. Our books have been praised by **Travel & Leisure, The Los Angeles Times, Newsday, Booklist, US News & World Report, Endless Vacation, American Bookseller, Coast to Coast,** *and many other magazines and newspapers!*

Don't just see the world – experience it with Open Road!

ABOUT THE AUTHOR

Elizabeth Arrighi Borsting is the former public relations manager for the Queen Mary in Long Beach, California. Currently, she is a free-lance writer and public relations consultant for the hospitality industry. In addition to *California's Best B&Bs*, she has also authored two other books for Open Road Publishing: *Celebrity Weddings & Honeymoon Getaways* and *Southern California Guide*. Borsting has been a contributing editor for *Honeymoon Magazine,* and her work has also appeared in *National Geographic Traveler* and the *Los Angeles Times,* just to name a few. She resides with her husband Kurt, son Jake and pup Jean in Long Beach, California, just south of Los Angeles.

BE A TRAVELER, NOT A TOURIST - WITH OPEN ROAD TRAVEL GUIDES!

Open Road Publishing has guide books to exciting, fun destinations on four continents. As veteran travelers, our goal is to bring you the best travel guides available anywhere!

No small task, but here's what we offer:

• All Open Road travel guides are written by authors with a distinct, opinionated point of view – not some sterile committee or team of writers. Our authors are experts in the areas covered and are polished writers.

• Our guides are geared to people who want to make their own travel choices. We'll show you how to discover the real destination – not just see some place from a tour bus window.

• We're strong on the basics, but we also provide terrific choices for those looking to get off the beaten path and experience the country or city – not just see it or pass through it.

• We give you the best, but we also tell you about the worst and what to avoid. Nobody should waste their time and money on their hard-earned vacation because of bad or inadequate travel advice.

• Our guides assume nothing. We tell you everything you need to know to have the trip of a lifetime – presented in a fun, literate, no-nonsense style.

• And, above all, we welcome your input, ideas, and suggestions to help us put out the best travel guides possible.

CALIFORNIA'S
BEST B&Bs

BE A TRAVELER - NOT A TOURIST!

Elizabeth Arrighi Borsting

OPEN ROAD PUBLISHING

OPEN ROAD PUBLISHING

We offer travel guides to American and foreign locales. Our books tell it like it is, often with an opinionated edge, and our experienced authors always give you all the information you need to have the trip of a lifetime. Write for your free catalog of all our titles, including our golf and restaurant guides.

Catalog Department, Open Road Publishing
P.O. Box 284, Cold Spring Harbor, NY 11724

E-mail:
Jopenroad@aol.com

For Kurt & Jake – My Favorite Traveling Companions

1st Edition

Front cover photo courtesy of The Whitegate Inn, Mendocino CA. Back cover photo courtesy of Elk Cove Inn, Elk CA.

All information, including prices, is subject to change. The author has made every effort to be as accurate as possible, but neither she nor the publisher assumes responsibility for the services provided by any business listed in this guide; for any errors or omissions; or any loss, damage, or disruptions in your travel for any reason.

TABLE OF CONTENTS

6. THE BAY AREA   130

INDEXES

FEATURES INDEX 267

MAPS

California   17

SIDEBARS

CALIFORNIA'S
BEST B&Bs

1. INTRODUCTION

I remember the first time I stayed at a bed and breakfast, and I must say I was unimpressed. It was the summer of 1988, and I had just graduated college. My next three months would be spent traveling across Europe. Upon arriving in London, my first destination, I found a no-frills inn near Victoria Station. Housed in a Georgian building and run by a friendly woman with a thick accent, the accommodations were cheap and literal: bed and breakfast. As I was shown to my room, I was told that if any Polish refugees were to arrive, I would have to surrender my accommodations. Though young and naive, I was pretty sure none would come knocking; still, for the duration of my stay, I barely slept as I awaited for my impromptu eviction. It never came.

Though the bed and breakfast concept is often different abroad, here in the United States it should be an unforgettable experience. In my B&B travels, I always look for one thing: The absence of the ordinary. It could be the setting, location, accommodations, level of service or culinary efforts. California has a myriad of unique properties, from historic mansions and homesteads to contemporary inns designed for today's travelers. Many go above and beyond the call of duty with gourmet meals, en suite spa services, lessons in the culinary arts, accommodations for pets and raiding-the-pantry privileges, just to name a few. In keeping with California's innovative mindset, one Northern California B&B even offers prepared child birth classes. How's that for unusual?

This book contains 100 of the state's best inns, from Shasta to San Diego County, from the intoxicating charm of the Wine Country to the backroads of California's Gold Rush region. Each entry includes background, architectural details, accommodation overviews, a list of amenities, directions and other pertinent information to create an enjoyable and relaxing getaway. No matter which direction you choose to head first, always know that at the end of the road there is a plump bed readied for your arrival. With this book as your companion, you'll get more than a good night's rest and a delightful breakfast. You'll have memories that you won't soon forget!

2. OVERVIEW

HOW THIS BOOK IS ORGANIZED

This book is laid out in six geographical chapters, organized from north to south: Northern California, Gold Country & High Sierra, Wine Country, Bay Area, Central Coast, and Southern California.

THE INNS

No inn in this book was solicited or required to pay a fee to be included; each was selected soley by the author. Though the process was subjective, the inns were selected based upon a set of criteria that included one or more of the following: unique location or setting, sublime accommodations or outstanding amenities. With the exception of one inn, East Brother Light Station in the Bay Area, chosen because of its isolated and solitary setting, all offer private baths.

Each listing includes the establishment's name, address and county location, toll-free and local phone numbers, fax number, web and e-mail address, overnight rates, time of check-in, the year it was opened for lodging (this often differs from the year it was built) and the name of the innkeepers. Also included is its background, description of accommodations and amenities, a listing of features, directions and credit card information. Unless otherwise noted, parking is complimentary.

AIRPORT INFORMATION

Under each city name, or in some cases the region, a **major** airport is listed. In some instances, more than one airport can serve an area. For example, San Francisco is served by two major airports, as is Orange County. For the more rural areas, an inn can be located several hours away from a major airport and, most likely, a city or regional airport also serves the area. Check with your travel agent or the individual innkeeper to see if a smaller commercial airport is nearby.

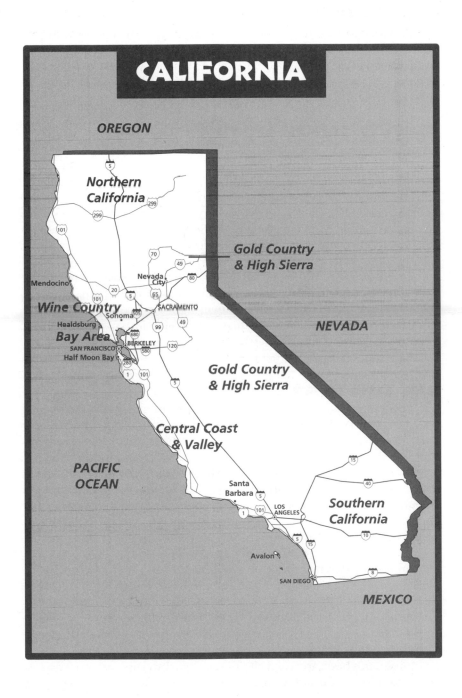

DIRECTIONS

Provided with each entry are directions for those traveling by car with the origin usually beginning near a major city or airport. It's always best to call ahead to the inn to make sure there are no road closures or detours prior to your departure. You can always call the **Caltrans 24-hotline**, *Tel. 800/427-7623*, for the latest road conditions throughout the state.

DEPOSITS, CANCELLATIONS & POLICIES

Unlike major hotels, innkeepers of bed and breakfast inns are greatly affected by last minute cancellations. When making reservations, most require a one-night deposit held with either a check or major credit card with the option to cancel three to seven days prior to your scheduled arrival. Weekends, which tend to be when occupancy is at its highest, also require a minimum two-night stay; holiday weekends often require a three-night minimum stay. Policies vary from inn to inn, so be sure to ask when making reservations.

You'll also find other restrictions set by innkeepers, such as no smoking policies and minimum age requirements for children. Although it's against the law to forbid children overnight privileges, please keep in mind that many of these inns are just not suitable for youngsters. In the Features Index, you'll find a list of family-friendly inns that allow children of all ages as well as those that prefer adults only.

BEST TIME TO GO

This depends on your interests, destination and thickness of your wallet. If none of these matter to you, carry on. But if you're planning to travel the wine trail, be sure you arrive when the tasting rooms are open, typically Wednesday through Sunday. If you want to work on your tan, maybe a December journey to Santa Monica isn't your best bet. And, if money is an issue, by all means avoid booking a room during the summer months or on the weekend, when innkeepers can fetch the highest price for even the most modest room. Budget-minded travelers can often save money mid-week and especially during the cooler months, when innkeepers have less guests and more flexibility.

And, if you arrive without a reservation and there are rooms still available, don't be shy about negotiating. Often, an innkeeper will take a lower tariff in order to fill a bed. Also, ask about AAA and senior discounts, as well as special rates for multiple-night stays.

INDEX LISTINGS

Inns in this book are listed by cities and can be cross-referenced in the Features and/or County Indexes. The Features Index lists everything from historical properties and all-inclusive retreats to inns found along the coast. You'll also find a directory of travel sources to help better plan your trip, including city and county convention and visitors bureaus, the California Division of Tourism office and the California Association of Bed & Breakfast Inns.

SPECIAL OCCASIONS

If your visit to a bed and breakfast inn coincides with a special occasion, such as an engagment, birthday or anniversary, or you're honeymooning, often the innkeepers enjoy fueling the celebration. When making a reservations, be sure to mention the reason for your visit. Frequently, though there are no guarantees, you'll find a complimentary bottle of champagne or some other thoughtful gesture awaiting your arrival – even if it's just an upgrade to a better room.

SIDEBARS IN THIS BOOK

You'll also find a list of sidebars, shaded in gray and outlined in a box like this one, dispersed throughout each chapter. These offer everything from anecdotes to practical information to alternative accommodations located in the area.

3. NORTHERN CALIFORNIA

ALBION

Served by San Francisco International Airport (SFO) or Oakland International Airport (OAK).

ALBION RIVER INN

3790 Highway One North
Albion, Mendocino County
Tel. 800/479-7944 or 707/937-1919
Fax: 707/937-2604
Web Address: www.albionriverinn.com
E-mail: ari@mcn.org
Rates: $180-280
3pm check-in
Year Opened: 1981
Innkeeper: Debbie Desmond and Doug Hynes

Profile

Along Highway 1, halfway between Elk and Mendocino, there's a bend in the road where the Albion River Inn rests. Like Elk to the south, the town of Albion boasted more than 1,000 residents during the height of its lumber-producing days. The last log was cut in 1928, right along with the town's population.

Thankfully, travelers tend to chug right through Albion, along with the logging trucks, either en route to Mendocino or heading south towards San Francisco. Hanging from a clifftop location and scattered along a gorgeous bluff is the Albion River Inn.

The inn's acclaimed restaurant was built in 1919 from first-growth heart redwood milled in the long forgotten Albion Mill. A smithy was also built to service the locals and the mill, but as needs changed the blacksmith vacated the premises. The building was first transformed into a store, then the area's first Ford dealership and, at mid-century, a restaurant. Eventually four rooms were added for the convenience of travelers and, in 1981, the present owners took this little roadside inn and eatery to an entirely new level.

Located on 10 verdant acres and shrouded by dense redwoods, the inn offers classic New England architecture and an isolated location.

Accommodations

A spray of contemporary Cape Cod-style cottages cling to the cliffside, each boasting a private garden entrance and simple elegance. Drink in the rugged ocean views while reclining in an Adirondack chair on your private balcony or through an expansive window that is slightly misted from the ocean sprays. Most rooms are equipped with soaking tubs with ample room for two, crackling fireplaces that come in handy year round, and regal king- or queen-size beds. All but two rooms offer a private balcony, so request accordingly.

As for television sets, there are none. But with such spectacular views, even the most ardent TV addict won't mind.

Amenities

Albion is a sleepy hamlet and about the only sign of civilization you'll find between Elk and Mendocino. Thankfully guests of the Albion River Inn are treated to a full cooked-to-order breakfast with regular offerings such as oatmeal and granola, eggs with seasoned potatoes, honey-cured bacon, tomato-basil benedict and apple-raisin bread pudding. Other perks include fresh-roasted coffees, teas and wine, fires laid daily and a morning newspaper delivered to your doorstep. All rooms come equipped with binoculars for spotting spouting whales, seals and seabirds just off the coast.

The inn is also widely known for its award-winning, oceanview restaurant. Under the toque is Chef Stephen Smith, who has created an innovative menu of fresh seafood, succulent meats and savory pastas. The award-winning wine list gets a nod of approval from the editors of *Wine Spectator*, who have presented the restaurant with its coveted Award of Excellence for the past eight years.

Various workshops are also hosted throughout the year. Chef Smith conducts regular cooking classes during the week, and award-winning photographer Robert Glenn Ketchum leads an annual photography workshop series. There are also winemaker dinners and other special events worth attending.

At-A-Glance Features
20 Rooms
Children Welcome
Complimentary Breakfast
Complimentary Newspaper
Cooking Classes
Full-Service Restaurant
Non-Smoking

Directions
From San Francisco, travel north on Highway 101 to Highway 128 west. When you reach Highway 1, go north for about three miles and the inn will be on your left.

Credit Cards Accepted
Visa, MasterCard, American Express, Discover.

THE RETURN OF THE FISHER HAWK
*If you're staying at the Albion River Inn during March, you'll witness the return of the magnificent **Fisher Hawk**. Each year, like clockwork, these creatures return to the Mendocino Coast and Albion Cove to mate, hunt and rear their young. With an average of 22 inches in length, a wing span of 54 inches, a dark black/brown hue, white bellies, black wrist markings, and a black bandit-like mask covering their eyes and cheeks, they're easy to spot. Mated pairs and their offspring are often heard before they're spotted, sailing high above the seas in search of fish, their only prey. It's moments like this when those in-room binoculars are much appreciated.*

ELK

Served by San Francisco International Airport (SFO) or Oakland International Airport (OAK).

ELK COVE INN

6300 South Highway One
Elk, Mendocino County
Tel. 800/275-2967 or 707/877-3321
Fax: 707/877-1808
Web Address: www.elkcoveinn.com
E-mail: elkcove@mcn.org
Rates: $128-318
2pm check-in
Year Opened: 1968
Innkeeper: Elaine Bryant

Profile

Blessed with a spectacular palisade location and panoramic ocean vistas, Elk Cove Inn is an ideal find along the Mendocino Coast. Rugged and romantic, the inn's main house was originally built in 1883 by the L.E. White Lumber Company as an executive guest house when Elk, then known as Greenwood, was a prosperous lumber producing town. Though the deed to the home has since passed through many hands, it was destined to become one of the area's first bed and breakfast inns.

The modest Victorian home reeks of long forgotten craftsmanship with 8-foot-wide dormer windows graced with built-in seats, gleaming woods and lasting details. Aside from the manor, the property also contains a quartet of cabins and a collection of newly-built Craftsman-style oceanfront suites. Together they create a seaside compound unlike anything else along Highway 1.

The town of Elk is nothing more than a few shops, restaurants, post office and deli/market. Time seems to have stopped somewhere around 1930 along this two-lane stretch of ocean-hugging highway and, for the handful of people that call Elk home, that's the way they prefer it.

Accommodations

At Elk Cove Inn, guests have a choice on where they sleep. For those with a penchant for antiques, the main oceanfront home offers half a dozen Victorian rooms on both the first and second floors. Appointments vary from gas fireplaces, panoramic ocean vistas, garden views to private entrances. The four oceanview cottages, though a bit more rustic, offer similar appointments and million-dollar panoramas.

Though I prefer the confines of the original home, the new **ocean-front suites** are the most in demand. Though newly constructed with redwood beams, stone work, copper gutters and hand railings, they embody the Arts and Crafts movement from the last century. Behind the shingled exteriors are wood-beamed supported ceilings, extra large fireplaces, wet bars with cappuccino machines and mini refrigerators, tubs with multi-jets and waterfall spouts, and private oceanfront decks.

No matter which annex you call home, each room is doused with fresh flowers, feather beds, down comforters, terry robes and flashlights for midnight beach strolls. There's even a notebook filled with restaurant menus, maps and listings of local activities.

Amenities

After checking in and being ushered to your room, guests are always a bit surprised to find a welcome basket awaiting their arrival. Inside is a piccolo of Chardonnay and a stash of freshly baked chocolate chip cookies. There's also a decanter of Australian Port and a pair of chocolates placed bedside.

Mornings begin with a savory breakfast featuring a melange of place settings served in the oceanfront dining room. Because of the owner's Alabama upbringing, usually one Southern dish makes its way to the table. Though there isn't a full-service restaurant on the premises, a cozy pub is available on the first floor of the main house. From behind the 19th-century oak bar, a menu of martinis and umbrella-laden drinks are shaken, stirred and blended. Many guests enjoy chatting it up here in the evening, and locals seem to enjoy it here as well.

If you prefer the road less traveled – in other words a chatty pub isn't your style – wander down to the cliffside gazebo and enjoy your beverage of choice there. Or pull out a good book and stake claim to a spot in the colorful garden.

At-A-Glance Features

14 Rooms
Children 12 and Older Welcome
Complimentary Breakfast
Pub on Premises
Welcome Basket
Within Walking Distance to Town

Directions

From San Francisco, travel north on Highway 101 to Highway 128 west. When you reach Highway 1, go south six miles and the inn will be on your right.

Credit Cards Accepted

Visa, MasterCard, American Express.

THE HARBOR HOUSE INN

5600 South Highway One
Elk, Mendocino County
Tel. 800/720-7474 or 707/877-1624
Fax: 707/877-3452
Web Address: theharborhouseinn.com
E-mail: harborhs@mcn.org
Rates: $205-385
3pm check-in
Year Opened: 1959
Innkeeper: Sam and Elle Haynes

Profile

There are three words that aptly describe The Harbor House Inn: location, location, location. Situated atop a dramatic cliff overlooking the Pacific Ocean, a room with a view takes on new meaning at this coastal hideaway.

Built in 1916 by the thriving Greenwood Mill, the Craftsman home, constructed from local redwood, served as a lodging refuge for the company's lumber executive and his family. For more than a decade the majestic parlor, the inviting dining room, the assembly of bedrooms and the menagerie of gardens and paths were filled with gaiety and laughter as times prospered. In 1929, the stock market wasn't the only thing to crash. In the lumber-rich town of Elk, the mill was sold, fortunes were lost and the streets grew hauntingly silent.

In 1932, during the height of the Great Depression, the bondholders of the lumber company deeded the house to the last managing partner of the mill who resided here until the 1950s. The next owner added a quartet of cottages hoping to attract anglers and passersby, and christened the new annex 'The Greenwood Motor Court.' Other owners tried to enhance the home-cum-roadside refuge, but it remained a rustic word-of-mouth retreat.

It wasn't until 1974 that The Harbor House Inn finally began to reach its potential. Then owner Patricia Corcoran added private bathrooms to each room, created sprawling suites and upgraded the furnishings. Today the present owners, who purchased the inn in 1998, have further enhanced its luxury with a total interior and exterior refurbishment. Redesigned are the gardens with herbs and greens added, many of which find their way into Executive Chef Paul Ciardiello's signature dishes. It took plenty of years and many attempts, but The Harbor House Inn has finally risen to become one of the Mendocino Coast's most regarded establishments.

Accommodations

There are six rooms and suites located in the main lodge and four adjacent cottages. While all the rooms are splendid, I can't stress enough the importance of having an ocean view at this particular inn. The craggy coast that rests below, and the spectacular rock formations that have evolved over time, are like having an original Ansel Adams masterpiece hanging on the wall. Only this work of evolving art is framed by a picture window.

In the main lodge, half of the rooms offer ocean views: **Cypress**, **Harbor**, and **Lookout**. Of the three, I found the **Lookout** to be the most romantic with a crisp, airy motif and a private deck flanked with a pair of Adirondack chairs. It isn't the largest chamber available – that would be the Cypress – but it is definitely one of the most cozy.

The cottages are rustically charming. The **Seaview** and **Oceansong** both offer stunning ocean vistas from nearly every angle, while the **Shorepine** and **Edgewood** offer glimpses of the sea from private decks. Individual appointments add to each room's ambiance with such decorative elements as fireplaces, claw-foot tubs, European antiques, and wood-burning stoves, just to name a few.

Amenities

There are no elk in Elk, or much of anything else for that matter including restaurants. Therefore, Harbor House Inn includes a full breakfast and four-course dinner for two with each stay. The dining room, with its tables cloaked in white linen and fine china, seems to carefully teeter above the ocean, providing patrons with some tantalizing views. In addition, coffee and tea are available throughout the day.

The inn's gardens are designed for both beauty and function, and are a great place to relax or lose yourself in a good book. There are pairs of

Adirondack chairs strategically placed about to maximize the ocean views, and a pathway leads past a secluded waterfall to the private beach below. Birds nibble randomly at scattered feeders, and the chicken house contains a noisy batch of hens who earn their keep by providing the kitchen with one to two dozen eggs weekly. The gardens, which sit perched high above the sea, provide hours of endless exploration.

At-A-Glance Features

10 Rooms
Children 16 and Older Welcome
Complimentary Breakfast
Complimentary Four-Course Dinner
Within Walking Distance to Town

Directions

From San Francisco, travel north on Highway 101 to Highway 128 west. When you reach Highway 1, go south five miles and the inn will be on your right.

Credit Cards Accepted

Visa, MasterCard, American Express.

FERNDALE

Served by San Francisco International Airport (SFO) or Oakland International Airport (OAK).

GINGERBREAD MANSION INN
400 Berding Street
Ferndale, Humboldt County
Tel. 800/952-4136 or 707/786-4000
Fax: 707/786-4381
Web Address: http://gingerbread-mansion.com
E-Mail: innkeeper@gingerbread-mansion.com
Rates: $140-350
3pm check-in
Year Opened: 1983
Innkeeper: Ken Torbert

Profile
If the Gingerbread Mansion Inn looks hauntingly familiar, it's probably because you've seen it grace the cover of a book, calendar or some other object. With its turreted, carved and gabled features, the inn is considered by many to be a visual masterpiece and is one of Northern California's most photographed buildings. Its elaborate icing-like trim certainly gives the illusion of an oversized gingerbread house, but the inn's exterior is elegant enough to be mistaken for a wedding cake.

Built at the turn-of-the-century for Dr. Hogan Ring, the home is an architectural blend of Queen Anne and Eastlake styles. During the 1920s, the good doctor formed a corporation and added an annex before converting the entire building into the Ferndale General Hospital. Within three years it went bankrupt, and for the next couple of decades it was transformed into a rest home, doctor's offices, and an American Legion Hall.

During the 1950s, things weren't so fabulous as the mansion underwent yet another transformation, this time emerging as an apartment building. By the time the 1960s arrived, the home was abandoned and nearly in ruins. Eventually it was purchased by a pair of landscape architects who restored the building and gardens. In 1981, Ken Torbert, the present owner, purchased the home and created one of California's most prized inns.

The Gingerbread Mansion is located in the heart of the Victorian village of Ferndale, a town that has the distinction of being listed on both the State and National Register of Historic Places. Virtually unaltered since the 1800s, Ferndale offers a postcard setting with its fleet of pitched roofs, steepled churches, bevy of boutiques, quaint eateries and collection of Victorian homes.

Accommodations

Behind the butter cream exterior you'll find 11 rooms and suites offering Victorian grandeur. For the most part, fainting couches, claw-foot tubs, stained-glass windows, French doors, canopy beds and elaborate fireplaces offer a time travel experience. The only thing that seems out of place are the guests clad in their contemporary clothing.

But not all is what it seems at the inn. The Gingerbread Mansion's two most opulent rooms, the **Empire Suite** and the **Veneto**, are anything but a Victorian secret. With a style more likely to impress The Sopranos (of TV land fame), the Empire Suite is a lofty chamber graced with Ionic columns framing a large marble-cloaked bathing area. Hardwood floors create a pathway leading to a pair of fireplaces, a living and dining area, and an alcove where the king-size bed rests. The Veneto, equally commanding and of Italian influence, boasts trompe l'oeil gardens cast upon the walls and ceiling, faux finish stone and marble floors, and an assortment of ornate Venetian mirrors.

One of the most idyllic rooms is the **Fountain Suite**, a large front corner room with a dreamy bay window overlooking the village with side views of the garden and its tiered fountain. You'll also find a tiled fireplace, canopied queen-size bed and, my favorite, his and her side-by-side claw-foot tubs.

Amenities

As the sunlight filters through the lace curtains, an early morning tray of coffee and tea is likely making its way to your doorstep. In the meantime, the elegant dining room, with its lace-covered communal tables, is being readied for a sumptuous breakfast. Enjoy the homemade specialties before heading out to explore Ferndale or the region's backroads flanked with rivers and redwood forests.

Return late in the day to enjoy the ritual of afternoon tea, served in one of the Gingerbread Mansion's four ornate parlors. Challenge a fellow guest to a game of chess, or simply smear an extra layer of Devonshire cream on a scone and help yourself to a stack of magazines. You can also tag along on a guided tour of the inn, offered daily from noon to 4pm.

At-A-Glance Features

11 Rooms
Afternoon Tours of the Inn

Children Welcome
Complimentary Breakfast
Complimentary Afternoon Tea
Evening Turndown Service
Walk to Shops, Restaurants and Sights

Directions

Head north on 101 from San Francisco, exit Ferndale and follow signs to Ferndale via Fernbridge. Travel for about five miles across dairy farms to the center of town, then turn left at Six Rivers Bank. The Gingerbread Mansion is located one block up.

Credit Cards Accepted

Visa, MasterCard, American Express.

SHAW HOUSE BED & BREAKFAST

703 Main Street
Ferndale, Humboldt County
Tel. 800/557-7429 or 707/786-9958
Fax: 707/786-9758
Web Address: www.shawhouse.com
E-Mail: bandb@shawhouse.com
Rates: $85-185
4pm check-in
Year Opened: 1860
Innkeeper: Ellen Benson and Tony Eilert

Profile

In a town that's flanked with Victorian showpieces and architectural marvels, it's hard to make an indelible mark. Yet the Shaw House Inn hasn't had much difficulty creating a buzz, considering it's Ferndale's longest standing structure and California's oldest bed and breakfast inn.

Built in 1854 by the city founder for his bride, the Shaw House Inn, listed on the National Register of Historic Places, was also the site of Ferndale's first post office and courthouse. Designed after Hawthorn's famous house of seven gables, the inn's architecture is a rare Carpenter Gothic Revival brimming with jutting gables, lacy balconies and protruding bay windows. The home is encapsulated within a one-acre parkland setting boasting more than 25 varieties of mature trees and is within walking distance to town.

Accommodations

The Shaw House Inn, with its steepled roof and lattice balustrades, looks as if it belongs inside a snow globe. Utterly romantic, yet ever so refined, the inn's eight bedrooms run the gamut from fairy tale splendor to efficiently tailored.

The upstairs rooms are quite enchanting with oddly configured rooms, hidden nooks and breathtaking views. The **Shaw Suite** is especially unique with its vaulted coffered ceiling that make you feel as if you're sleeping under the Big Top. Both the **Garden** and **Wisteria** rooms, along with the simply named **Guest Room**, are all tucked away in the upstairs gables creating a snug and cozy hideaways. The Garden and Wisteria rooms lead to an expansive balcony and, though all the rooms feature private bathrooms, these particular rooms offer the detached variety. If you prefer to stay grounded, all the first floor rooms have private entrances to create a sense of seclusion.

Amenities

Breakfast, which is presented with flair, is served in either the formal dining room or in the privacy of your guest room beginning at 8:30am. With such mouthwatering items as cheddar cheese French toast, macadamia nut pancakes, stuffed croissants and airy quiches, you might as well forget your cholesterol count for the duration of your stay.

Work off your morning meal with a stroll around town or a vigorous hike through the redwoods, then return to the inn for afternoon tea and a tray of treats. There is also a trio of parlors for reading or playing games, old-fashioned horseshoes in the garden and a gift shop. The innkeepers can also help arrange for town carriage rides, fishing excursions, horseback outings and other area activities.

At-A-Glance Features

8 Rooms
Complimentary Breakfast
Complimentary Afternoon Tea
Gift Shop
Non-Smoking
Not Appropriate for Children
Walk to Shops, Restaurants and Sights

Directions

Head north on Highway 101 from San Francisco, exit Ferndale and follow signs to Ferndale via Fernbridge. The road crossing the bridge is Highway 211. Follow it for five miles to the "Prettiest Painted Places" sign, which is now Main Street. The inn, set back from the road, will be on your right.

Credit Cards Accepted

Visa, MasterCard.

VICTORIAN INN

400 Oceanfront Avenue
Ferndale, Humboldt County
Tel. 888/589-1808 or 707/786-4949
Fax: 707/786-4558
Web Address: www.a-victorian-inn.com
E-Mail: innkeeper@a-victorian-inn.com
Rates: $85-150
2pm check-in
Year Opened: 1988
Innkeeper: Lowell Daniels and Jenny Oaks

Profile

The Victorian Inn, an ornate catercorner structure located in Ferndale's historic downtown, offers the coziness of a bed and breakfast yet resembles that of an intimate inn. Built in 1890 by wealthy banker Ira C. Russ, whose descendants still live in the area, and created entirely from local redwood, the inn stands as a testament to a forgotten era.

Embellished with magnificent detail, the Victorian Inn is a remnant from the region's long forgotten timber boom era. The building was the site of one of the town's first banks with 33 professional offices located above. It also housed a millinery shop and haberdashery at one time. Today, the inn's ground floor is home to a full-service restaurant and jewelry store with the guest rooms located upstairs, and in either direction are a collection of shops, eateries and Victorian homes.

Accommodations

Other than sharing the long second story hallway, the dozen guest rooms belonging to the Victorian Inn have little else in common. There are actually 33 doors, but only 12 are numbered. That's because these former office and apartment dwellings were combined to create larger accommodations when the building was converted into a bed and breakfast. Each is a snapshot of Victorian elegance with such bygone appointments as claw-foot tubs, bay windows, turreted sitting areas and antique armoires. Floral wallpaper, brass beds and expansive ceilings also add to the flawless surroundings.

Two exceptional rooms are the airy **Pacifica Room**, complete with wood-burning fireplace and antique armoire; and **The Ira Russ Suite**, with a sitting area tucked away in a turret and an expansive bay window, add extra light and warmth. The other 10 chambers also offer their own brand of spacious charm.

Amenities

The innkeepers, who acquired the Victorian Inn in 1999, are also gemologists and together run **Silva's Fine Jewelry** in what used to be the inn's front parlors. Before tending to their gem business, Lowell and Jenny first make sure their overnight guests are taken care of with a hot breakfast. There are often snacks available to guests as well, and the innkeepers often churn out espresso on cold afternoons.

Though Ferndale, in all its vintage splendor, offers a number of restaurants, the inn is also home to **Curley's**, a casual restaurant and tavern. Its massive bar and lofty presence is popular with both visitors and residents, and the eatery provides a convenient place to dine or enjoy a hot toddy. Should you want a picnic lunch or a carriage ride tour, the innkeepers are more than happy to make the necessary arrangements.

At-A-Glance Features

12 Rooms
Children Welcome
Complimentary Breakfast
Full-Service Restaurant and Bar
Near Shops, Restaurants and Sights
Non-Smoking

Directions

Head north on Highway 101 from San Francisco, exit Ferndale and follow signs to Ferndale via Fernbridge. The road crossing the bridge is Highway 211. Follow it for five miles to the "Prettiest Painted Places" sign, which now becomes Main Street. Take Main Street to Ocean Avenue.

Credit Cards Accepted

Visa, MasterCard, American Express.

IGO

Served by Sacramento International Airport (SMF).

BRIGADOON CASTLE
9036 Zogg Mine Road
Igo, Shasta County
Tel. 888/343-2836 or 530/396-2785
Fax: 530/396-2784
Web Address: www.brigadooncastle.com
E-Mail: inquiry@brigadooncastle.com
Rates: $188-325
3pm check-in
Year Opened: 1996
Innkeeper: Geri MacCallum

Profile
Pack your best kilt and family tartan for a stay at Brigadoon Castle. Remotely located in the northern reaches of California, the ivy-covered inn, built less than two decades ago, certainly looks the part of an Elizabethan castle. Tucked amid 86 acres of redwood forests, the only sounds that are audible are those of the babbling brook meandering through the estate and the occasional chirp of birds.

The magical gardens, with its fountained pond, rushing stream, expansive lawns and walkways, offers up solitude. Consider that there are never more than 10 guests staying here at any given time, and you've found a priceless stop on your travels.

Accommodations
If you loved fairy tales as a child, then assume the role of your favorite make-believe character while at Brigadoon Castle. The entrance is graced with a soaring three-story round tower ripped right from the pages of *Rapunzel*. Beyond the threshold lies a touch of drama with vaulted archways, a magnificent staircase, soaring ceilings and palatial surroundings.

There are five chambers offering an array of appointments. Choose from **The Swan Room** with an elegant marble bath framed by a gothic arch, the romantic **Bonny Jean Room** with its Juliet-style balcony overlooking the dense forest, or **Feona's Suite** creating a glass slipper setting with its angled four-poster bed and cozy fireplace. Perhaps the most unique of the rooms is the two-level **Tyler's Tree Top**, looking every bit like a fortress with a turreted location and circular staircase – plus faux

sandstone and ivory murals accents. Offering the ultimate in privacy is a
separate cottage located near the castle.

Amenities

The two-tiered **Great Hall**, with its plush sofas facing a brick fireplace,
is the hub of Brigadoon Castle. Because there are no television sets
available in the rooms, guests congregate here to get their TV fix. But
often the sound of chatter is more in favor than watching the evening
news, and conversations are taken to new heights in the loft-style library
located just above.

Guests are treated to a bountiful breakfast and an afternoon of snacks
and beverages. Shasta County is for nature lovers offering a myriad of
waters for fishing, trails for hiking, and fresh air for breathing.

At-A-Glance Features

5 Rooms
Complimentary Breakfast
Complimentary Afternoon Snacks and Non-Alcoholic Beverages
Non-Smoking
Not Appropriate for Children
Outdoor Hot Tub

Directions

Head north on Interstate 5 from San Francisco or Sacramento, take
Highway 299 west to Placer Road and proceed south to Igo. Continue
straight at the T-junction into Zogg Mine Road, which leads to the castle
gates.

Credit Cards Accepted

Visa, MasterCard, American Express.

LITTLE RIVER

Served by San Francisco International Airport (SFO) or Oakland International Airport (OAK).

GLENDEVEN INN

8205 North Highway One
Little River, Mendocino County
Tel. 800/822-4536 or 707/937-0083
Fax: 707/937-6108
Web Address: www.glendeven.com
E-mail: innkeeper@glendeven.com
Rates: $110-250
3pm check-in
Year Opened: 1977
Innkeeper: Sharon and Higgins

Profile

Little River is just a couple of miles south from the village of Mendocino, but don't blink for more than a second or you're likely to pass it right by. Except for a road sign, a few homes and some lodging establishments lining Highway One, there's not a whole lot going on in Little River.

Glendeven Inn is another reason to take note of Little River. An 1860s Federalist New England farmhouse and a pair of recently constructed annexes are the setting for a delightful stay. Built by Isaiah Stevens, a native of Maine who traveled the continent via the Isthmus of Panama, he and his brood were among the founding pioneers of Little River. The family remained owners of the house until the late 1930s.

Removed from the main highway, the compound sits perched on a headland meadow and is surrounded by an abundance of fields and aged trees. The original clapboard home is the epitome of New England elegance with protruding gables, an expansive balcony and long-forgotten craftsmanship. Down the road, less than a two-minute drive, is the village of Mendocino.

Accommodations

For the indecisive traveler, Glendeven offers a number of settings to ponder. There are three choices, the original farmhouse and a pair of newer annexes. This can further complicate matters for the ambivalent guest unless, of course, they know what they like.

The original **farmhouse**, created for the traveler with a passion for vintage architecture and an appreciation for detail, offers three spacious suites and two smaller rooms. The **Stevenscroft** looks as if it were part of the original estate and is a nice complement to the original 19th-century home. Added to the compound in 1984, this freestanding building features a quartet of spacious suites complete with ocean views, fireplaces, antiques and, in many cases, porches or balconies. The **Carriage House Suite** is the latest installment, having opened in 1999, and offers complete seclusion, full-service amenities, skylight ambiance, and a private balcony. Attention to detail doesn't go unnoticed with featherbeds, in-room CD players and plush robes.

Amenities

The emphasis at Glendeven Inn is on privacy. While the oceanview sun room is certainly an idyllic spot for enjoying the first meal of the day, most guests opt to dine behind closed doors. Breakfast trays typically include champagne glasses filled with fresh-squeezed orange juice, a plate of seasonal fruit cleverly prepared, a savory egg dish, warm muffins or moist coffee cakes along with tea and locally roasted coffee.

Social graces are saved for the daily wine and hors d'oeuvres gathering hosted by the innkeepers each evening in the farmhouse living room. Local wines are poured, snacks are passed and stories are swapped in front of a roaring fire.

Also on the grounds is **Partners Gallery**, created by an assembly of local artists for the purpose of exhibiting their contemporary paintings, sculptures, ceramics, jewelry and photography. New shows are mounted nearly every month and feature the works of one or two artists. The gallery also sponsors random events that run the gamut from poetry readings and concerts to lectures on a variety of subjects.

At-A-Glance Features

10 Rooms
Children Welcome
Close to Shops and Restaurants
Complimentary Breakfast
Complimentary Wine and Hors d'oeuvres

Directions

From San Francisco, take Highway 101 north to Cloverdale. Take Highway 128 west, about 60 miles, to Highway 1. Go approximately eight miles, and Glendeven Inn will be on the right-hand side of the road at the end of Little River and just past the entrance to Van Damme State Park.

Credit Cards Accepted

Visa, MasterCard, American Express, Discover.

McCLOUD

Served by Sacramento International Airport (SMF).

McCLOUD BED & BREAKFAST HOTEL

408 Main Street
McCloud, Siskiyou County
Tel. 800/964-2823 or 530/964-2822
Fax: 530/964-2844
Web Address: www.mccloudhotel.com
E-mail: mchotel@snowcrest.net
Rates: $174-163
3pm check-in
Year Opened: 1915
Innkeeper: Lee and Marilyn Ogden

Profile

Located in the shadow of Mt. Shasta, not too far from the Oregon border, rests this historic inn. Built in 1915, the inn recently was completely renovated to offer maximum comfort. Visible improvements include an expanded lobby area complemented by original details. The original registration desk, with its fleet of cubby holes, is where guests are greeted. Aged beams and a grand staircase are bathed in warm woods and a collection of plump sofas add to the comfort of the public rooms.

Accommodations

Since Americans aren't keen on cramped quarters and shared baths, the original rooms have been both enlarged and outfitted with en-suite restrooms. Each door unlocks its own amenities, whether it's a roomy four-poster bed, original and restored hotel furnishings , antique trunks that double as tables or benches, or extra roomy closets for the bogged-down traveler.

A quartet of L-shaped suites have also been added, with each offering an abundance of luxury. Queen-size canopy beds, love seats, whirlpool tubs for two, separate showers, sitting areas and balconies are just a few of the conveniences you'll find.

Amenities

Though the name may be confusing, McCloud Bed & Breakfast Hotel embraces the philosophy of both concepts offering the personal service of a bed and breakfast with added amenities you might expect to find at a boutique hotel.

A two-course breakfast is served at tables either in the lobby or, weather permitting, on the patio. If you tend to be social, you might settle on a communal table, however, if you prefer to mingle only with those you came with, there are plenty of tables for two. Guests can also request that their meal be brought to their rooms, which eliminates the need to be presentable in the early morning hours.

Weekend guests can partake in afternoon tea on Saturdays, and daily wine service is also available. In addition, the innkeepers are more than eager to make arrangements for an en-suite massage, snowmobile outings and hot-air balloon rides.

At-A-Glance Features

17 Rooms
Children Welcome
Complimentary Breakfast
Complimentary Saturday Afternoon Tea
Concierge Service
En-Suite Massage
Non-Smoking
Wine Service Available

Directions

From Sacramento, take Interstate 5 north to Mt. Shasta, and exit east on Highway 89. Travel nine miles to McCloud and follow the signs to the town's historic district. McCloud Bed & Breakfast Hotel is located on Main Street.

Credit Cards Accepted

Visa, MasterCard, American Express.

MENDOCINO

Served by San Francisco International Airport (SFO) or Oakland International Airport (OAK).

ALEGRIA OCEANFRONT INN & COTTAGES

44781 Main Street
Mendocino, Mendocino County
Tel. 800/780-7905 or 707/937-5150
Fax: 707/937-5151
Web Address: oceanfrontmagic.com
E-mail: inn@oceanfrontmagic.com
Rates: $134-219
3pm check-in
Year Opened: 1979
Innkeeper: Eric and Elaine Wing Hillesland

Profile

Rumor has it that the main house of this cliff hugging inn was built in 1861 for a seafaring captain. While not exactly the stuff urban legends are made of, it is still a point of debate for some old timers as to who built the house and for whom. What is known is that a captain by the name of John Perry and his family resided here shortly after their 1869 arrival to Mendocino.

During the 1960s, the home was owned by a sculptor and single mother who occasionally felt the need to escape. She renovated the former chicken coop into her own private hideaway and, from time to time, she'd pack up, move out and tell the kids to leave her alone for a few days. Marilyn Soloman eventually purchased the Victorian home, added a cluster of cottages and opened it up to the public as "1021 Main Street, A Unique Guest House." Upon her death the inn was sold to a couple who renamed it Captain's Cove. Then, in 1998, the present owners acquired the inn, renaming—and reinventing—it as a Yin-Yang retreat on the bluff.

Accommodations

The Alegria Inn may have begun life as a proper Victorian manor, but this palisade getaway has been reincarnated as a bohemian retreat. It has none of the trappings you'd expect from a home built during this era, such as dainty wallpaper or period antiques. Instead it's completely funky and Zen-like; a place you might feel inclined to practice yoga or meditation.

While Mendocino's other bed and breakfast inns boast of ocean vistas, this is the only one that actually sits on an oceanfront bluff overlooking a serene estuary. With sweeping views at every turn, guests have a choice of varying settings. There are two rooms located upstairs in the main house, a pair of adjacent cottages, and a second floor room in the carriage house.

One of the most popular rooms is the Craftsman-style **Cove Cottage**, which offers the most scenic water views. Creating an eclectic feel are the Asian accents complete with a Japanese soaking tub and private deck overlooking the beach. Another innovative chamber is the split-level **Driftwood Cottage** resembling a bachelor's pad. All rooms offer private baths, either a fireplace or wood stove, private entrance, deck, television and VCR along with coffee and tea makers.

Amenities

Begin your day with the morning paper at your door and breakfast in the solarium-style dining room overlooking the breathtaking estuary. The innkeepers are committed to supporting sustainable agriculture, and therefore their philosophy spills over — or into — their culinary creations. A sample breakfast may include a veggie frittata, pumpkin ginger pancakes or a delicious slice of blueberry cream cheese coffee cake. Of course, the coffee, Thanksgiving Organic, is locally roasted in Fort Bragg. If you prefer, a tray can be delivered to your room.

If you find your stomach growling later in the day, the intimate lobby usually has a stash of homemade cookies and tea. Ask the innkeepers to prepare a picnic basket for you, and then wander down the private footpath to the beach and enjoy an al fresco lunch in one of Northern California's most breathtaking settings. The inn also has an outdoor hot tub for guest's enjoyment.

At-A-Glance Features

5 Rooms
Children Welcome
Complimentary Breakfast
En-Suite Massage
Outdoor Hot Tub
Within Driving Distance to Wineries
Within Walking Distance to Shops, Restaurants and Attractions

Directions

From the Bay Area, take Highway 101 north to Cloverdale. Take Highway 128 west, about 60 miles, to Highway 1. Go nine miles north to

Mendocino, and after crossing the bridge over Big River turn left at the first entrance to the village. The inn will be the third property on your left.

Credit Cards Accepted
Visa, MasterCard, American Express, Discover.

MENDOCINO - HOLLYWOOD NORTH!
While I don't recommend the Blair House Inn, fans of the long-running television show **Murder She Wrote** *may want to take a peek, if only from the outside. The exterior of this 1888 Victorian home was the backdrop for Jessica Fletcher's abode, portrayed by Angela Lansbury. While most of the series was shot at Universal Studios in Los Angeles, nine episodes were actually filmed in Mendocino. The town has also been used in a number of feature films including* **East of Eden**, **The Summer of '42**, **Same Time Next Year**, **Dying Young** *and* **Forever Young**, *just to name a few.*

WHITEGATE INN
499 Howard Street
Mendocino, Mendocino County
Tel. 800/531-7282 or 707/937-4892
Fax: 707/937-1131
Web Address: www.whitegateinn.com
E-mail: innkeepers@whitegateinn.com
Rates: $149-249
3pm check-in
Year Opened: 1980
Innkeeper: George and Carol Bechtloff

Profile
Bed and breakfast inns are a dime a dozen in Mendocino, but few are deserving of a recommendation. The Whitegate Inn, a Victorian home built in 1883, is one that shouldn't be overlooked. The home was built for a lumber entrepreneur, who quickly rented it to a doctor and his family. It then doubled as both homestead and the town's hospital during their tenure.

Situated in the heart of village with peekaboo ocean views, the manor has been meticulously restored by its new owners. Past the creaking white gate is the entrance, and beyond the threshold is a stately 19th century dwelling that is warm and inviting. The decor is elegant without being ostentatious and, with only a half-dozen rooms, the ambiance is cozy yet extremely private.

Surrounded by verdant gardens and within earshot of crashing waves, the Whitegate Inn is one of the town's loveliest establishments.

Accommodations

Old world charm runs rampant here at the inn. The rooms, located on both the first and second floors, are regal and striking with a scattering of antiques, fireplaces, European featherbeds, concealed television sets and roomy baths.

My personal favorites are the **French Rose Room**, with its bold crimson color, stately French antique bed, and distant ocean views; and the **Enchanted Cottage**, with its secluded garden entrance, French doors revealing a private deck, and dark collection of furnishings. The **Garden Path Room** is another alluring choice with its canopy bed and literary-style wing chairs.

Amenities

After a peaceful night's rest, roll out of your rumpled bed and make your way to the dining room for an exhausting supply of edibles. There is also an outdoor table sheltered by a pergola that offers a nice dining alternative on warm days, though those are few and far between in Mendocino.

The inn's drawing room is an inviting enclave for chatting it up with fellow guests, enjoying a sherry or just relaxing with a book. The snug grounds are filled with an abundance of ancient cypress trees and colorful flora, which grow extremely well in Mendocino's cool climate. A garden deck offers lounge chairs, and there are swinging benches placed about.

The nice thing about staying at the Whitegate Inn is that once you park the car, you'll rarely have to move it. Everything is generally within walking distance and, should you have to climb behind the wheel, most points of interest are easily reached within 30 minutes.

At-A-Glance Features

6 Rooms
Children Welcome
Complimentary Breakfast
Complimentary Evening Wine and Snacks

Complimentary Welcome Baskets
Concierge Service
En-Suite Massage
Within Walking Distance to Shops & Restaurants

Directions

From the Bay Area, take Highway 101 north to Cloverdale. Take Highway 128 west, about 60 miles, to Highway 1. Go nine miles north to Mendocino, and turn left at the first stop light, which is Little Lake Road. The second street on your left will be Howard; go two blocks to the inn.

Credit Cards Accepted

Visa, MasterCard, American Express, Discover, Diners Club.

GET WHITEGATE'S RECIPE SECRETS

Take a slice of the Whitegate Inn home with you in the form of a cookbook. The innkeepers have put together a collection of recipes that are easy enough to duplicate at home. When you have a craving for a slice of the inn's coffee cake or homemade cookies, simply whip up a batch at home. The book, protected by a crisp white cover and graced with watercolor rendering of the inn, is available for $14.95.

POINT ARENA

Served by San Francisco International Airport (SFO) or Oakland International Airport (OAK)

COAST GUARD HOUSE HISTORIC INN

695 Arena Cove
Point Arena, Mendocino County
Tel. 800/524-9320 or 707/882-2442
Fax: 707/882-3233
Web Address: www.coastguardhouse.com
E-mail: coast@mcn.org
Rates: $115-175
3pm check-in
Year Opened: 1992
Innkeeper: Mia and Kevin Gallagher

Profile

California certainly offers some unusual hostelries, and the Coast Guard House Historic Inn is among the more unique. It was built in 1901 for the U.S. Life-Saving Service, later to be renamed the Coast Guard, and was officially known as Station Number 314 at Arena Cove. The lifeboats that were stored and maintained here were manned by resident Surfmen and launched during many daring rescues. The craggy Mendocino coast, with its jagged shores and protruding rock formations, sent enough vessels to the bottom of the sea that the station was rarely idle.

Though the post closed in the 1950s, the two-story Cape Cod home, listed on the National Register of Historic Places, is a symbol of the honorable service performed here for more than five decades.

Accommodations

At the turn-of-the-century, the Mendocino coast was littered with Victorian homes. But when the Coast Guard was constructing its residence, it must have figured that such a dainty style wouldn't fare well with the heroic men that would have to live here.

Instead, classic lines and an overall simplicity are the results of this Arts and Crafts manor. The five rooms, located in the main house, offer either ocean vistas or canyon views and an uncluttered approach with comfortable furnishings, artwork commissioned from local artists, and a collection of maritime history. The **Boathouse** is an intimate cottage and within an ocean spray of the pounding surf. A replica of the original boathouse where the Surfmen launched their rescue missions, guests who slumber here have total privacy and unbelievable seaside vistas coupled with a tandem whirlpool spa, fireplace and private patio.

Amenities

Aside from an Art Deco movie theater, a few shops and strolls along the pier, there's not much to do in Point Arena, and that's precisely the reason for coming to Coast Guard House Historic Inn. After a hearty breakfast served in the oceanview dining room, guests can retreat to a garden chair and watch the seascape unfold. The inn and its grounds offer an ideal vantage point for spotting the California gray whale, whose annual migratory path skims the shoreline.

Though the area is semi-remote, there is golfing nearby as well as the fascinating **Point Arena Lighthouse** and museum. In the late afternoon, try soaking in the al fresco hot tub or warming up by the living room fireplace with a glass of wine.

At-A-Glance Features

6 Rooms
Children Welcome
Complimentary Breakfast
Outdoor Hot Tub
Near Shops, Restaurants and Attractions

Directions

Travel north on Highway 101 from San Francisco, take the East Washington Street/Bodega Bay exit near Petaluma. Turn left, and proceed west to Bodega Bay to Highway 1 north. Travel Highway 1 north to Point Arena, and turn left at the Coastal Access sign onto Iversen Avenue. Travel one mile west to the wharf, and before you arrive at the pier you'll see the Coast Guard House on your right on the hill. Travel around the red structure and up the driveway leading to the inn.

Credit Cards Accepted

Visa, MasterCard.

4. GOLD COUNTRY & THE HIGH SIERRA

AHWAHNEE
Served by San Francisco International Airport (SFO).

THE HOMESTEAD
41110 Road 600
Ahwahnee, Madera County
Tel. 800/483-0495 or 559/683-0459
Fax: 559/683-8165
Web Address: www.homesteadcottages.com
E-mail: homesteadcottages@sierratel.com
Rates: $125-209
3pm check-in
Year Opened: 1992
Innkeepers: Cindy Brooks and Larry Ends

Profile
The Homestead is a very different kind of experience. The cottages are less than a decade old, but offer none of the trappings of a typical bed and breakfast. Common rooms don't exist, the accommodations are comfortably spaced apart, and everything you could ever yearn for is found within the confines of your room. There's little reason to interact with other guests, unless, of course, you choose to.

Constructed in 1992, the results combine the expertise of both innkeepers, from carpentry skills to a flair for style. The real perk is that

The Homestead is located just 21 miles from Yosemite, making it a convenient base for exploring the park's natural wonders.

Accommodations

Usually The Homestead is booked to capacity, but every once in a while there's a chance you could be the only one enjoying the grounds. There are just four cottages and one suite offering a rustic yet stylish escape on 160 wooded acres.

Beyond each threshold are beamed ceilings, paver tile floors, wicker and pine furnishings, separate living rooms with fireplaces, fully equipped kitchens and dining areas. Separate bedrooms offer queen-size beds and an adjoining bathroom. The **Star Gazing Loft** is a studio room with a combined living area, kitchenette and bedroom and is located upstairs in a raised center barn that overlooks the landscape. All units feature satellite television.

Amenities

With no common dining room or set gathering place for meals, guests create their own agenda. Cottage kitchens are stocked daily with coffee, tea, juice, muffins and fruit. For lunch or dinner, you can opt to use one of the outdoor barbecues. Daily maid service is scheduled according to your timetable, and, by the time you return home, the dishes are done and the place spotless.

The innkeepers are active in the community and can recommend everything from dinner reservations at a local restaurant to the best hiking trails to how to navigate about Yosemite to arranging for an in-room massage. A special feature of The Homestead is its ability to board not only guests but their horses, too. Nearby the Star Gazing Loft are 12' x12' partially covered corral stalls that can accommodate up to five horses. The innkeepers have graciously mapped out trails that wander through the nearby Sierra National Forest as well as Yosemite to make your equestrian adventure a bit more manageable.

At-A-Glance Features

5 Rooms with Kitchens
Children Welcome
Close to Restaurant, Shops and Galleries
Complimentary Edibles
Horse Stalls Available
In-Room Spa Services
Close to Restaurant, Shops and Galleries

Directions

From San Francisco head south on Highway 101 to Highway 580 east. Take Highway 580 east to Highway 205, and continue to Highway 120. Follow Highway 120 to Manteca and take Highway 99 south. When you reach Merced, take Highway 140 east heading towards Yosemite/Mariposa and continue until you reach Highway 49 heading towards Oakhurst.

Take Highway 49 for about 22 miles, and turn right on Road 600 heading toward Raymond. The Homestead is 2 1/2 miles ahead on the right side.

Credit Cards Accepted

Visa, MasterCard, American Express, Discover.

CROWLEY LAKE

Served by Reno/Tahoe International Airport (RNO).

RAINBOW TARNS BED & BREAKFAST

P.O. 79, Box 55-C
Crowley Lake, Mono County
Tel. 888/588-6269 or 760/935-4456
Fax: none
Web Address: www.rainbowtarns.com
E-mail: info@rainbowtarns.com
Rates: $90-140
3pm check-in
Year Opened: 1988
Innkeepers: Brock and Diane Thoman

Profile

Every bed and breakfast inn has something, at least in most cases, that makes it special. It could be the plush accommodations, the outstanding cuisine or abundance of amenities. For Rainbow Tarns, it's all about location.

Situated in the Eastern High Sierras, sandwiched between the small town of Bishop and the rugged resort community of Mammoth Lakes, guests come here to get reacquainted with the great outdoors. Located at an altitude of 7,000 feet, Rainbow Tarns is ultra-secluded and wonderfully rustic. The amenities around here are mostly the doings of Mother Nature, with three acres of ponds, open meadows and soaring mountains.

This is a manly man's place, the kind of establishment that would appeal to the likes of Clark Gable and Ernest Hemingway. But the ladies will enjoy the slow pace and peaceful surroundings, not to mention the abundance of recreation offered. The dress is strictly plaid shirts and Levis, and cell phone reception is fuzzy at best. This inn is not for the well connected, but rather for the person eager to go it unplugged.

Accommodations

Rustic and weathered is what you can expect at Rainbow Tarns, and that's simply part of the charm. Rawhide rockers totter back and forth on the front porch and rusty wagon wheels sit propped against scattered logs. The great room, where guests congregate, is part of the original 1920s log cabin. Its worn log walls, stone fireplace and vaulted log-trussed ceiling create a sturdy presence.

There are only three rooms to choose from: **The Rainbow Room, The Gemini Room** and **Grandma's Room**. Except for the Tiffany lamps and double whirlpool baths, the overall look is simple, with antiques and pine tree views. Snuggle beneath a plump down comforter and enjoy the dense forest vistas. Reality, and everything that goes along with it, will return soon enough.

Amenities

The hearty country breakfast is strictly no frills, but it's filling and delicious . As the sun goes down, wine and snacks are shared in the great room.

Shaded by leafy willows and aspens, the trio of tarns – or ponds – are just a few steps from the inn's front porch. Originally used as "u ketch'm" trout farms, schools of rainbow trout from neighboring Crowley Lake still pass through the waters at springtime to spawn.

For the angler, there's fishing at nearby **Hot Creek, Lake Crowley, Mammoth Lakes, June Lake Loop** and **Rush Creek**. For the horseman, there's plenty of stables and trails to explore; you're even welcome to board your horse while at Rainbow Tarns. For the snow skier, **Mammoth Mountain**, one of California's best ski resorts, is just minutes away. And, for the hiker, the **John Muir Trail** is within striding distance.

At-A-Glance Features

3 Rooms
Children 12 and Older Welcome
Complimentary Breakfast
Complimentary Evening Wine and Refreshments
Horse Stalls Available
Near Ski Resorts, Fishing and Horse Trails

Directions

The inn is about a six hour drive from Los Angeles. Take Interstate 15 north to Highway 395. Follow Highway 395 to the Rock Creek exit (between Bishop and Mammoth Lakes), and go west past Tom's Place on Crowley Lake. Drive for approximately 3/4 of a mile to Rainbow Tarns Road. Take a right and follow the dirt road to the inn.

Credit Cards Accepted

None.

GROVELAND

Served by San Francisco International Airport (SFO).

THE GROVELAND HOTEL

18767 Main Street
Groveland, Tuolumne County
Tel. 800/273-3314 or 209/962-4000
Fax: 209/962-6674
Web Address: www.groveland.com
E-mail: peggy@groveland.com
Rates: $125-195
3pm check-in
Year Opened: 1990
Innkeepers: Peggy and Grover Mosley

Profile

Ladies and gentlemen, Elvis has left the building. Well, he actually never stayed here, but the innkeeper is proud of the fact that she and The King were classmates back in Tennessee. In fact, each August the Groveland Hotel is transformed into a Graceland of sorts to commemorate Elvis' birthday. It's a quirky, sell-out event featuring a true-to-life impersonator along with a room full of die-hard fans who are perhaps convinced that The King is alive and well.

For the rest of the year, this 1849 adobe building and the adjacent 1914 Queen Anne Victorian, originally built to house VIP guests visiting San Francisco's nearby Hetch Hetchy water project, make up the Groveland Hotel. Slated for demolition in 1990, the owners not only saved these historic relics but they returned them to their original splendor. The two-story adobe echoes its former self, from the wraparound verandahs to the casement windows, and the Victorian looks as fit as one might expect.

The American flag flies high above the Groveland Hotel, which is less than 25 miles from Yosemite National Park's main gate. Located in California's historic Gold Country, there are plenty of attractions nearby, **including Pine Mountain Lake**, whose private facilities are open to guests of the inn.

Accommodations

With sprays of floral wallpaper and an eclectic mix of antique furnishings, guests may feel as if they have been transported back to the 19th century. But with plush terry robes dangling from hooks in the closet, private baths with running water and a common lounge housing a television set, we can still enjoy our modern pleasures.

While all rooms offer queen beds and full baths, the suites are perhaps the nicest and definitely the largest of the lot having been created from two rooms. Cuddle up on the floral tapestry sofa facing a carved wooden fireplace in the **Lillie Langtry Suite**, where a massive turn-of-the-century brass bed dominates the decor. **Hetch Hetchy Suite** is another enchanting room with a spray of antiques including a French bed, and a private entrance leading to the courtyard. The **Julia Bulette Suite** is filled with sunlight and wicker and also has a wood-framed fireplace.

Amenities

Each morning guests are served a continental breakfast consisting of baked goods, cereals, fresh-brewed coffee, tea, juices and fruit. In the evening guests mull over their days with a glass of wine and conversation. Pets, dogs and cats mostly, are welcomed here as well.

A plus when staying at the Groveland Hotel is its **Victorian Room restaurant**, a recipient of *Wine Spectator's* Award of Excellence. Open for dinner and Sunday brunch, the restaurant, which also has an inviting umbrella-dotted patio, serves classic fare with an emphasis on beef. The saloon, an authentic Gold Rush variety, pours an extensive wine list and microbrewed beers.

At-A-Glance Features

17 Rooms
Children Welcome
Close to Shops and Restaurant
Complimentary Continental Breakfast
Complimentary Evening Wine
Limited Room Service
Near Yosemite National Park
Pet-Friendly

Directions

Head south from San Francisco and take the Interstate 80 east ramp towards Bay Bridge/Oakland. Merge onto Interstate 80 east to Interstate 580 east towards Downtown Oakland/Hayward-Stockton. You'll travel 45 miles before merging onto Interstate 205 east towards Tracy/Stockton. Take Interstate 205 north and exit onto Highway 120 heading towards Manteca/Sonora. Next, take the Highway 99 north/Highway 120 east exit on your left. Continue on Highway 120 east and at Yosemite Junction exit towards Sonora. At the fork in the ramp keep to your right, turning right onto Highway 120. You'll travel Highway 120 for approximately 25 miles. Highway 120 turns into Main Street in Groveland. The hotel is located at 18767 Main Street.

Credit Cards Accepted

Visa, MasterCard, American Express, Discover, Diners Club.

IONE

Served by Sacramento International Airport (SMF)

THE HEIRLOOM INN

214 Shakeley Lane
Ione, Amador County
Tel. 888/628-7896 or 209/274-4468
Fax: 209/274-6716
Web Address: www.theheirloominn.com
E-mail: piccadillycatering@prodigy.net
Rates: $75-115
2pm check-in
Year Opened: 1980
Innkeepers: Sherry and Rich Scagliola

Profile

With the discovery of gold in 1849, fortune hunters and those with inflated optimism headed to California in hopes of striking it rich. Few did, yet they continued to arrive in droves. The town of Ione was a supply center to the gold camps in nearby Jackson, Sutter Creek and Amador City, and today is a remnant of small town America.

The Heirloom Inn, a two-story brick manor hailing from the early 1860s, was built long after the mad rush. Its design is reminiscent of an antebellum manor with gracious columns, ornate balustrades and breezy balconies. Century-old trees outline a spacious English garden. Its location, nestled among the sweeping folds of the Sierra Nevada Mountains, creates an idyllic hideaway for the weary traveler.

Accommodations

There are only six rooms at The Heirloom Inn with four located in the main house and a pair of cottages just a stone's throw away.

Rooms are named for the seasons and each color scheme forecasts a very different mood. The **Summer Room** is cloaked in soft pastel hues of mostly creams and blues with a hint of gold, while the **Winter Room** is adorned in blues and whites with a private entrance leading from the balcony. The **Spring Room** offers a wisteria-draped balcony with an Eastlake bed and wicker accents, while its **Autumn** counterpart features hues of plum and gold along a balcony framed by French doors.

The two cottages offer maximum privacy along with in-room televisions. The rustic **Early American** bungalow, dominated by hand-hewn cedar, redwood and pine, has the feel of an alpine retreat. A roomy couch, positioned near the wood-burning stove, seems made for curling up with a good book. The **Carriage House**, with its pitched roof and simple decor, offers a pair of bedrooms joined together by a jack-and-jill bathroom. One room features a queen-size bed, while the other contains twin beds, an ideal setting for couples with children.

Amenities

The inn's living room, with its cozy fireplace, picture windows and conversational nooks, is the setting for afternoon tea. The rosewood piano, which tempts guests to take to the ivories from time to time, once belonged to entertainer Lola Montez. Guests are also treated to a full breakfast each morning in either the dining room or the blooming gardens when weather permits.

Nearby is an abundance of recreation and activities including wine tasting, fishing and antique hunting. If you yearn for a taste of urban living, the inn is located a mere 40 miles from Sacramento, California's capital city.

At-A-Glance Features

6 Rooms
Children Welcome
Close to Restaurants, Shops and Historic Sites
Complimentary Breakfast
Complimentary Afternoon Tea
Pet-Friendly

Directions

From Sacramento, take Sunrise Avenue south off Highway 50 to Highway 16 towards Jackson to the Ione turnoff. Continue to Highway 104 and into Ione. Turn right on Shakeley Lane.

Credit Cards Accepted

Visa, MasterCard, American Express.

JACKSON

Served by Sacramento International Airport (SMF).

THE GATE HOUSE

1330 Jackson Gate Road
Jackson, Amador County
Tel. 800/841-1072 or 209/223-3500
Fax: 209/223-1299
Web Address: www.gatehouseinn.com
E-mail: info@gatehouseinn.com
Rates: $110-155
2:30pm check-in
Year Opened: 1981
Innkeepers: Keith and Gail Sweet

Profile

Tucked behind a white picket fence and illuminated by a single gas lamp, The Gate House is a handsome Victorian mansion. Listed on the National Register of Historic Places, the inn recalls a gentler style of living in the heart of California's Mother Lode.

The home was built by the son of an Italian immigrant, who came to the gold fields of Jackson in 1849 with his 10-year-old brother. The tike later went on to become the first president of the Bank of Italy, while the elder brother settled down in this gorgeous manor. After serving as a private residence for more than a century, the home was transformed into a bed and breakfast during the early 1980s.

Accommodations

The Gate House offers four rooms in the main house and a pair of cottages tucked in the back. A life-size mural of an angel graces the home, and the motif is subtly carried throughout. The historic chambers in the original Victorian manor reflect the era in which the inn was built, and are all beautifully decorated with antiques, intricate wall coverings and fine details from a bygone era.

The **Master Suite**, located upstairs, features a collection of period furnishings, a fireplace and a delightful turreted sitting room overlooking the gardens. The **French Room**, named for its splash of Louis XIV-style furniture, is elegant and opulent, while the two-room **Woodhaven Suite** will appeal to the male persuasion with its study-like setting and secret passageway leading to the downstairs porch. The downstairs **Parlor**

Room is simple and streamlined with a queen bed, Victorian dresser and garden views.

The two cottages are a bit more contemporary and not half as charming as the rooms found in the main house. However, if privacy is a factor or you're traveling with children, these will be your best bet.

Amenities

The smell of baked French toast, homemade muffins, sausage and quiche work as an alarm clock to rouse guests out of bed. The hearty breakfast is served in the elegant dining room, and afternoon tea lures visitors back home with an assortment of fresh-baked cookies.

As for unwinding, there's a swimming pool on the premises for cooling off on those hot summer days. In-room massages and relaxation therapy are administered by the innkeeper who is a trained nurse. Services range from acupressure and reflexology to music therapy and guided imagery.

The inn is located just a short jaunt from downtown Jackson, where an abundance of restaurants, shops and historic sites are found. The innkeepers will even take you on guided tours of City Hall, where a historical exhibit is housed.

At-A-Glance Features

6 Rooms
Close to Restaurants, Shops and Historic Sites
Complimentary Afternoon Tea
Complimentary Breakfast
Guided Tours
In-Room Spa Treatments
Near Wineries
Non-Smoking
Not Appropriate for Children Under 12
Swimming Pool

Directions

From Sacramento, take Highway 50 to Highway 16 towards Jackson. Head south on Highway 49, and after leaving Sutter Creek, approximately two miles, turn left on Jackson Gate Road.

Credit Cards Accepted

Visa, MasterCard, American Express, Discover.

LAKE TAHOE

Served by Reno/Tahoe International Airport (RNO).

BLACK BEAR INN

1202 Ski Run Boulevard
South Lake Tahoe, El Dorado County
Tel. 877/232-7466 or 530/544-4451
Fax: 530/544-7315
Web Address: www.tahoeblackbear.com
E-mail: info@tahoeblackbear.com
Rates: $150-350
3pm check-in
Year Opened: 1999
Innkeepers: Jerry Bidwell and Kevin Chandler

Profile

Realtors often use certain adjectives and jargon in order to mask a more accurate description of a property. Charming can often equal antiquated, vintage usually means old, and rustic is another way of saying rundown. Enter the Black Bear Inn, one of Lake Tahoe's most prized retreats, where *rustic* is finally getting the respect it deserves.

Though short on history – the inn was only built in 1999 – it's destined for greatness. This luxe retreat is found adrift on a wooded acre overlooking Tahoe's mountainous beauty. If you enjoy skiing, paradise has been found with 19 champion resorts all within a snowball-toss from here, including the renowned **Heavenly** less than a mile away. The warmer months offer another type of nirvana, one where fishing, golfing, hiking and sailing are the primary pleasures. Cross the California stateline, just a short drive down the road, and you're surrounded by a crop of casinos on the Nevada side.

The Black Bear Inn is centrally located, comfortably appointed and unabashedly luxurious. Even if you lose at the craps tables, at least you've hit the jackpot at the end of the night.

Accommodations

Choose to slumber in the **main lodge** where five ample-size guest rooms await, or reserve one of three **cabins** shaded by towering pines. Let yourself be spoiled by such conveniences as king-size beds, river rock fireplaces, televisions and VCRs (some rooms even offer DVD players), and telephone and data ports.

The five rooms in the main lodge offer varying appointments from wet bars and sitting areas, as found in the **Sequoia Room**, to vaulted log beam ceilings and balconies as illustrated in the **Fallen Leaf Room**. Beyond the inn are the trio of cottages: **Bonanza Trail**, **Sutter** and **Snowshoe Thompson**. The Bonanza Trail is actually a duplex containing two separate rooms, the Stagecoach and Black Bart chambers. Snowshoe Thompson and Sutter cabins offer spacious digs with more than 900 square feet, separate bedrooms, kitchenettes and exceptional views. From the three cabins you can also expect open floor plans coated in hardwood with roomy bathrooms and a generous dose of privacy.

Amenities

The slopes in the distance might be enticing, but it's hard to pull yourself away from the comfy confines of the Black Bear Inn. Before venturing outside, if you can muster up the energy to leave these luxurious confines, fill your tummy with a heaping batch of freshly baked muffins presented on an old grocery counter, or grab an ice-cold bottle of orange juice from the well-worn washbasin. Entrees may include a brie omelet, eggs benedict or blueberry coffee cake. If you're residing in one of the cabins, you can request to have your meal brought to your room.

The three-story Great Room is an architectural marvel with a magnificent river rock fireplace, a soaring cathedral ceiling, chunky log beams and a sweeping staircase. Later in the day, as the sun fades to black, guests gather here to sample wine and cheese. Suddenly, as you gaze out from this sublime setting from one of the plush sofas, you realize that being labeled a couch potato isn't really so bad after all. The inn also has a steaming outdoor hot tub, a perfect spot to end the day.

At-A-Glance Features

9 Rooms
Close to Casinos
Complimentary Breakfast
Complimentary Evening Wine
Near Ski Resorts and Lake
Non-Smoking
Not Appropriate for Children
Outdoor Hot Tub
Within Walking Distance to Shops and Restaurants

Directions

From Reno, head south on Highway 395 before merging onto Highway 50 at the Carson City juncture. Remain west on Highway 50 until you reach South Lake Tahoe. Turn left onto Ski Run Boulevard, and the inn is a half mile down on the right-hand side.

Credit Cards Accepted
Visa, MasterCard.

COTTAGE INN AT LAKE TAHOE
1690 West Lake Boulevard
Tahoe City, Placer County
Tel. 800/581-4073 or 530/581-4073
Fax: 530/581-0226
Web Address: www.thecottageinn.com
E-mail: cottage@sierra.net
Rates: $149-245
3pm check-in
Year Opened: 1938
Innkeeper: Susanne Muhr

Profile
Crossing the threshold of the Cottage Inn, you get a sense of what Lake Tahoe must have been like during the first half of the 20th century. Lots of knotty pine and oodles of coziness come into play, as does the notion of time travel.

The fleet of cottages were built by the Pomin family in 1938, when Tahoe was a fledgling resort community. Though modern amenities are now part of the package with televisions and fax machines readily available, quaintness has not been lost at the Cottage Inn. Just a few steps from one of the lake's best beaches – and private at that – the inn is a perfect place to retreat after a day of mogul jumping or fishing.

Lake Tahoe, with its abundance of corporate lodging, can still feel like the Tahoe of your great grandparent's generation, at least within the confines of the Cottage Inn.

Accommodations
The Cottage Inn has accommodations ranging from one-bedroom studios to cottage and deluxe suites. The **Kitchen Suite** is a tidy upstairs apartment complete with kitchen, dining area, living room and separate sleeping quarters with private balcony. The **Loft Suite** offers up a large sitting area warmed by a fireplace, open-beam ceilings and sleeping loft.

For a little something out of the ordinary, why not try a theme room? Take your pick with the **Old Fishin' Hole**, a lakeview room that will appeal to anglers, or the **Tahoe Teepee** done in a Native American motif. Other choices include the **Hunter's Hideout**, **Stagecoach Stop**, **Rustic Retreat** and **Bird Nest**, just to name a few.

All rooms enjoy private entrances and original knotty pine paneling, plus fireplaces, televisions and VCRs.

Amenities

For some reason fresh mountain air creates ferocious appetites and, of course, the sound of sizzling bacon and freshly brewed coffee wafting from the inn's kitchen can only perpetuate matters. The morning meal is served either in the dining room or, when weather permits, on the picturesque outdoor deck.

A private sauna, nestled among the pines, is available après ski or anytime of day. There is also a private lakeside beach that guests are privy to, as well as lounging privileges in the lodge's sitting room, where you're usually greeted with a roaring fire, morning coffee, cookies and wine.

For those in search of seclusion, hunker down beneath an oversized comforter and request that your breakfast be left at your doorstep. Ask that your messages be held as you spend time sequestered behind your cottage door with a stash of books and videos borrowed from the lounge's library.

At-A-Glance Features

14 Rooms
Access to Private Beach
Children 12 and Older Welcome
Complimentary Breakfast
Complimentary Evening Wine
Near Ski Resorts and Casinos
Non-Smoking
Outdoor Hot Tub

Directions

From Reno, take Highway 395 north to Interstate 80 west. At Truckee, take Highway 89 south and travel for 13 miles. At the first stop in Tahoe City, turn right. The inn will be two miles south of Tahoe City on the left side.

Credit Cards Accepted

Visa, MasterCard.

MURPHYS

Served by Sacramento International Airport (SMF).

DUNBAR HOUSE 1880

271 Jones Street
Murphys, Calaveras County
Tel. 800/692-6006 or 209/728-2897
Fax: 209/728-1451
Web Address: www.dunbarhouse.com
E-mail: innkeep@dunbarhouse.com
Rates: $135-195
3pm check-in
Year Opened: 1984
Innkeepers: Barbara and Bob Costa

Profile

Innkeepers Bob and Barbara Costa are more ambitious than most. When the pair first arrived at the Dunbar House as guests in 1986, they were unimpressed with the overgrown foliage and collection of plastic furniture cluttering the porch. The one thing that did catch their eye was the "For Sale" sign impaled in the front lawn. Soon they were on the phone to the realtor, redecorating the inn in their minds, and surprising themselves by making an offer.

That was nearly 15 years ago, and the inn has since morphed into a stunning retreat. Guests no longer arrive mumbling about the bushes, frowning at the collection of porch clutter, or moaning about having to share a bathroom with strangers. Thankfully, these nuisances have been banished with the addition of manicured gardens, outdoor wicker furniture and private bathrooms for all.

As the name indicates, the Dunbar House, an Italianate beauty, was built in 1880 by Willis Dunbar for his bride Ellen Roberts. Willis was the superintendent of the Union Water Company, a precursor to Pacific Gas & Electric, as well as a state assemblyman and owner of the Dunbar Lumber Company in Murphys.

The inn is close to Murphys' historic Main Street, where a you'll find shops, galleries and restaurants.

Accommodations

The American flag waves proudly at the entrance to the Dunbar House, and the sound of a trickling fountain assures you that something special is afoot. Located in the heart of Gold Country, the Dunbar House may well indeed be the mother lode of accommodations.

Air conditioning, central heat and private bathrooms, amenities unknown to the original owner, have been installed for the comfort of guests. Hanging in each closet are soft terry-lined robes, thick oversized towels and a stash of aromatherapy candles. You'll also find such conveniences as direct dial telephones, as well as radios and CD players.

The five rooms are named for woods and are the former sewing room, sun porch, library, master bedroom and attic. Imagine cast iron beds, gas burning stoves, French doors leading to private decks, exceptional views and claw-foot tubs – all presented with a dash of preserved history.

After a night at Dunbar House 1880, you'll wish you could move in permanently.

Amenities

There's nothing like a warm welcome and, at the Dunbar House, they go a little bit over the top to ensure all guests feel at home. Upon arrival, no matter what the time, you'll find an appetizer tray placed in your suite along with a cooler containing a bottle of regional wine and mineral water.

Breakfast is served by candlelight in the dining room or century-old garden, and expect a feast of culinary masterpieces. Begin with coffee and a homemade muffin, move on to fresh fruit, a delicious main entree, juice and perhaps an edible flower or two. The inn's breakfasts have become so highly regarded that the innkeepers have published *The Best Recipes We've Ever Stolen*. For those with a serious case of bedhead, request that a tray to be brought to your room.

The grounds are lush, serene and inviting. Sneak a smooch on the two-person hammock, escape to the gazebo with trashy novel in hand, contemplate amid the rose garden, or rock back and forth on the swing. Come evening, the crisp sheets on your bed are turned back and a chocolate is placed atop plump pillows. If only every day could end so sweetly.

At-A-Glance Features

5 Rooms
Children 10 and Older Welcome
Close to Wineries
Complimentary Breakfast
Near Restaurants and Shops
Non-Smoking
Welcome Appetizers, Wine and Mineral Water

Directions

From Sacramento, take Highway 99 south to Highway 4 east. Continue on Highway 4 to Highway 49 east and go east again on Highway 4 to Murphys. Turn left on Main Street, go two blocks and turn left on Jones Street. The inn is located ahead.

Credit Cards Accepted

Visa, MasterCard, American Express.

JUMPING FROG JUBILEE

The California Gold Rush initially put Calaveras County on the map, but Mark Twain boosted the region's image when he penned his short story "The Celebrated Jumping Frog of Calaveras County" in the mid-1860s. It was his first published work, and it made Twain a household name. To pay homage to the literary genius, the first Jumping Frog Jubilee was held in 1928 at nearby Angels Camp. Today tradition continues every May when the annual Jumping Frog Jubilee gets underway at the Calaveras County Fair.

THE REDBUD INN

402 Main Street
Murphys, Calaveras County
Tel. 800/827-8533 or 209/728-8533
Fax: 209/728-1451
Web Address: www.redbudinn.com
E-mail: innkeeper@redbudinn.com
Rates: $90-245
3pm check-in
Year Opened: 1994
Innkeepers: Pamela and Steve Hatch

Profile

The pitched roof, shingled structure and stone chimney have all the earmarks of a vintage home, but The Redbud Inn, built in the early 1990s, was the first new inn to grace the town of Murphys in the last 136 years.

Taking its name from the tree that spawns a flurry of pink and burgundy blooms, The Redbud Inn is a classic country abode that embraces the history of the Gold Country. While most new structures seem to be made from the same mold, this inn takes its cue from an eclectic mix of old-world designs, which account for the high ceilings, ornate fireplaces, snug window seats, and wood stoves. Who says they don't build 'em like they use to?

Accommodations

The inn offers a dozen rooms bordering on contemporary yet, at the same time, manages to incorporate vintage qualities. You'll discover rocking chairs alongside double-sided fireplaces, four-poster beds and claw-foot tubs placed near overstocked wet bars. It's a mix of romantic Victorian coupled with five-star convenience.

Some of the more notable chambers are the **Fireside Room** with its impressive fireplace and four-poster bed. If you enjoy prancing horses, the **Carousel Room** is appealing and offers a private balcony and intimate surroundings. The **Sycamore** is another find with pine floors, interesting nooks and a private balcony. Antique fixtures lend charm to an already cozy existance.

Amenities

Begin your morning with fellow guests in the sun-filled dining room while you converse over pots of hot coffee, a selection of entrees, moist pastries and a smattering of fruit. Come evening there's an assortment of regional wines and hors d'oeuvres displayed in the parlor, then it's off to dinner at one of the local restaurants.

The region offers lots of day tripping opportunities. Explore the local wineries, take in a round of golf or head downriver on a rafting expedition. Of course, hunting for treasures along the streets of Murphys is another way to pass time.

If you're a smoker, look elsewhere as the inn has a strict no-smoking policy. Those found smoking on the premises are asked to leave and are charged an additional night's stay. Don't say we didn't warn you.

At-A-Glance Features

12 Rooms
Close to Wineries
Complimentary Breakfast
Complimentary Evening Wine and Hors d'oeuvres
Near Restaurants and Shops
Non-Smoking

Directions

From Sacramento, take Highway 99 south to Highway 4 east. Continue on Highway 4 to Highway 49 east and go east again on Highway 4 to Murphys. Turn onto Main Street, and proceed to the inn at 402 Main Street.

Credit Cards Accepted

Visa, MasterCard, Discover.

NEVADA CITY

Served by Sacramento International Airport (SMF).

THE EMMA NEVADA HOUSE

528 East Broad Street
Nevada City, Nevada County
Tel. 800/916-3662 or 530/265-2815
Fax: 530/265-4416
Web Address: www.emmanevadahouse.com
E-mail: mail@emmanevadahouse.com
Rates: $105-160
3pm check-in
Year Opened: 1984
Innkeepers: Laura Du Pee

Profile

This once modest bungalow was the childhood home of opera diva Emma Nevada, who went on to travel the world performing. But it was local politician Nathaniel P. Brown, founding owner of the *Nevada Daily Transcript*, who built this home in 1865 and lived here until 1909.

In 1991 the home was on the brink of being condemned until a local contractor began to work his magic on the dilapidated house. He painstakingly restored it to its original beauty, rescuing many of the original fixtures such as gas-lit chandeliers, claw-foot bathtubs, windows and doors. The four bedroom, two bath home was expanded to include six rooms and an equal number of private bathrooms.

In 1986, two years after making its debut as a bed and breakfast inn, The Emma Nevada House was granted historical landmark status by the county of Nevada. Finally, the fat lady had sung.

Accommodations

There are six elegant rooms coated in pleasing neutral tones and furnished with period antiques. The ambiance is that of casual elegance with grand ceilings offsetting snug rooms, feathery comforters shielding French antique beds, and claw-foot tubs competing with Jacuzzi spas.

The **Empress' Chamber** is a regal find with a color scheme of ivory and burgundy, a bank of windows overlooking the gardens, and an inviting sitting area. **Nightingale's Bower** is another keeper located on the main floor with bay windows, a dangling chandelier and antique stove.

The remaining rooms are a bit more simple, but still worthy of a night's rest. For adventure, reserve **Emma's Hideaway**, a charming upstairs room with a pair of attic niches.

Amenities

Breakfast is typically served in the dining room, but if you can finagle a table in the circular sun room, with its fleet of picture windows, I highly recommend it. If weather permits, take your plate of fresh fruit, oversized scones and airy quiche out on the deck. Come afternoon, retreat once again to the sun room for a cuppa fresh-brewed or iced tea and a pile of homemade cookies.

At-A-Glance Features

6 Rooms
Children 10 and Older Welcome
Complimentary Afternoon Tea
Complimentary Breakfast
Near Wineries
Non-Smoking
Walk to Shops, Restaurants and Historic Sites

GO BACK IN TIME TO NEVADA CITY

A visit to Nevada City is like traveling back in time. The display of Victorian homes is the result of an economic downturn when the prospecting of gold started to fade. There wasn't much need for building or even refurbishing what remained of the old structures, so the architecture was simply spared urban renewal because of circumstances. The WPA projects during the 1930s explain the Art Deco influence given to both city hall and the court house.

During the 1960s a demand for preservation got underway, and city ordinances were revised to create a more aesthetically appealing landscape. Banned were historically inaccurate storefronts; the labyrinth of power lines were buried beneath the ground; and gas lights were made from the original 19th-century molds and installed along Broad Street. In addition, the Nevada City Theatre was meticulously restored as were private homes and estates. Clearly Nevada City has emerged a museum sans walls, recapturing an almost forgotten era in California's history.

Directions

From Sacramento, take Interstate 80 north to Auburn, and head east on Highway 49/20. Take the Broad Street exit, and turn left onto Broad Street proceeding up the hill. The inn will be on your right.

Credit Cards Accepted

Visa, MasterCard, American Express.

RED CASTLE INN HISTORIC LODGING

109 Prospect Street
Nevada City, Nevada County
Tel. 800/761-4766 or 530/265-5135
Fax: none
Web Address: www.historic-lodgings.com
E-mail: none
Rates: $110-155
3pm check-in
Year Opened: 1960
Innkeepers: Conley and Mary Louise Weaver

Profile

The stories of California's Gold Rush are often sad tales of those whose hopes and dreams were dashed in the shadow of the Sierra Nevadas. But, by golly, thar were gold up in them hills! At least for some.

In 1849 John and Abigail Williams, along with their son Loring, traveled across the nation's great plains by wagon with the same hopes and dreams. While Abigail taught school in Napa, John and Loring were searching for gold in Nevada County. Their mining efforts at nearby Deer Creek and Gold Run paid off as they collected enough precious nuggets to build two ranches. Abigail rejoined her men, and before long John helped to develop Nevada City's first water company while Loring went on to became the district attorney.

With such good fortune and plenty of money, John's dream to build a mansion atop Prospect Hill became a reality. The grand four-story brick estate was begun in 1857 and completed in 1860, and is now a California State Historic Landmark. Its Gothic Revival architecture was a rare site in California, and homes of this grandeur failed to exist Nevada City.

The home eventually fell into disrepair during the 20th century and was rescued sometime during the 1950s. It has the distinction of being one of the first historic bed and breakfast inns in California.

Accommodations

From atop Prospect Hill it's easy to imagine what life might have been like during the mid-1800s in this part of California. After the gold dust had settled, those who stuck around most likely enjoyed a tranquil existence among the wooded setting.

Leave your laptop locked inside your trunk and silence your cell phone for an enjoyable journey back in time. Behind the gingerbread facade are a collection of seven lavishly appointed rooms scattered across four floors boasting high ceilings and embellishments from a bygone era. The rooms on the first and entry levels are charming offering private verandahs, queen-size beds and access to the gardens. Mid-level accommodations feature a trio of suites complete with a private parlor and floor-to-ceiling French doors revealing treetop views.

The top level, two-room suite is perhaps the most intriguing of the lot. Tucked beneath the eaves and sloping ceilings, floor-level windows create vertigo-like views. Christened the **Garret Suite**, a pair of mahogany sleigh beds, once owned by the Williams family, adds a sense of history. Gothic arched windows and a parlor separating the two bedrooms creates an idyllic retreat for couples traveling in tandem.

Amenities

Nothing is subtle at the Red Castle Inn. Breakfast isn't merely a meal, it's a five-course feast consisting of fresh juices and coffee, homemade breads and muffins, a delectable entree that might feature a three-cheese soufflé or a ham and cheese blintz.

You might consider skipping lunch knowing that afternoon tea is on the horizon. Elegant and refined, guests are served a fine spread of savories and sweets on heirloom china and crystal. Gab with other guests while sipping a cup of Earl Grey inside the inn's formal parlor, or grab the closest book and go it alone.

Walk off the weight with a stroll along the inn's footpaths, past the koi pond or near the fringes of the forest. Or head down the hill towards town where a selection of restaurants can be found interspersed with a nice collection of shops.

At-A-Glance Features

7 Rooms
Children 12 and Older Welcome
Complimentary Afternoon Tea
Complimentary Breakfast
Near Wineries
Non-Smoking
Walk to Shops, Restaurants and Historic Sites

Directions

From Sacramento, take Interstate 80 north to Auburn, and head east on Highway 49/20. Take the Sacramento Street exit, cross the intersection and go past the gas station then turn right up the hill. Turn immediately left onto Prospect Street, and continue to the end where you'll find parking for guests on the left.

Credit Cards Accepted

Visa, MasterCard.

OAKHURST

Served by San Francisco International Airport (SFO).

CHATEAU DU SUREAU
48488 Victoria Lane
Oakhurst, Madera County
Tel. 559/683-6800
Fax: 559/683-0800
Web Address: www.elderberryhouse.com
E-mail: chateau@chateausureau.com
Rates: $325-2500
2pm check-in
Year Opened: 1991
Innkeepers: Erna Kubin-Clanin

Profile
There are times when an innkeeper feels the need to add a full-service restaurant to enhance a lodging establishment, but Austrian-born Erna Kubin-Clanin, owner of Chateau du Sureau, took the opposite approach. After opening her award-winning restaurant in 1984, the acclaimed chef soon discovered that an inn would be needed to accommodate the growing number of faraway visitors who came to sample both her food and the beauty of nearby Yosemite National Park.

In 1990 she broke ground on Chateau du Sureau, named for the thatches of elderberry bushes that blanket the rolling estate. The compound was finally complete in 1999 with the addition of the ultra-private Villa Sureau, a two-bedroom estate emulating the elegant manors found along the rues of Paris.

The Sierra Nevada region is filled with cozy inns, often recalling the days of the Gold Rush era. Not the case with Chateau du Sureau. This is by far one of the more opulent inns in the area, if not the state. Celebrities, who are known to lounge poolside in big, splashy hotels with little character, are drawn to this elegant European-style estate. Famous faces have included Robert De Niro and überchef Wolfgang Puck.

Accommodations
The imposing wrought-iron gates, graced with the inn's regal crest, can be a little intimidating for first-time guests. Like magic, they swing

back to reveal the stately 9,000-square-foot manor in all its architectural glory with a stone turret, Parisian-style balconies and shuttered windows.

Inside are 10 gallant rooms, named for the abundance of herbs and flowers found on the property. The **Lavender** is a cozy corner room with a king-size sleigh bed and a snug balcony overlooking the grounds. The dramatic **Saffron** contains an 1834 ebony bedroom set, a tapestry draped from floor to ceiling, and a black marble fireplace and matching bath. The **Sweet Geranium** is a tidy chamber with a king-size canopy bed, cozy sitting area and garden views. All rooms, with the exception of the **Ciboulette**, offer fireplaces. As for televisions, they are thankfully absent.

If money is no object, consider sequestering yourself inside the **Villa Sureau**. With its own gated entrance and a secluded setting among aged oaks and overgrown pines, this 2,000-square-foot estate is a masterpiece. There are a pair of grand bedrooms featuring marble bathrooms with oversized whirlpool tubs and steam showers, fireplaces, a parlor, a library/drawing room, and a private outdoor Roman spa.

Throughout the villa is a collection of Empire-period antiques and original 19th-century artwork. You'll also find cupboards stocked with fine china, cutlery and European crystal for en-suite dining. Guests of Villa Sureau also enjoy the complimentary use of the inn's Jeep Cherokee Ltd. Other special touches, such as food trays, flower baskets and favorite books placed bedside, can easily be arranged.

Amenities

As chamber maids scurry past in their crisp black dresses and pressed white linen aprons, guests are enjoying all the inn has to offer. The public rooms, though stately, are for your enjoyment and can almost be likened to miniature galleries. Filled with fine antiques, tapestries and 19th-century art, **the Grand Salon**, with its floor-to-ceiling fireplace, and the circular **Music Room**, are wonderful places to unwind.

A two-course breakfast is served each morning in the breakfast room, and wine and hors d'oeuvres are enjoyed in the salon come afternoon. Hidden among the winding footpaths and spouting fountains are a swimming pool, bocce court and a life-size chess set. There's also a menu of spa treatments that can be administered behind chamber doors. And let's not forget the inn is just a 20-minute scenic drive from Yosemite's south entrance.

Because the area is somewhat remote, **Erna's Elderberry House** is a convenient place to enjoy an elegant dinner. Reminiscent of a European country estate, the restaurant offers a trio of dining areas replete with French provincial furnishings and oil paintings. It also doubles as a culinary school with three 8-hour courses creating a session. Hosted by

Erna and Executive Chef James Overbaugh, class begins each day with a steaming cup of coffee and a half-hour of theory regarding the day's menu, concluding with a sit-down, six-course dinner.

The only thing the inn is apparently missing is a front desk and any formal check-in procedures. This is a deliberate oversight on the part of the innkeeper, whose only desire is to make guests feel at home. Instead, a simple hand-written bill is presented at the end of your stay.

At-A-Glance Features

11 Rooms
Complimentary Two-Course Breakfast
Complimentary Evening Wine
Complimentary Jeep for Guests of Villa Sureau
Cooking School on the Premises
Full-Service Restaurant
Near Yosemite National Park
Not Appropriate for Children
Swimming Pool

Directions

From San Francisco, head south on Highway 101 towards San Jose. Exit onto Highway 92 east towards Hayward (signed 'San Mateo Bridge') and continue until reaching Interstate 880 north. Follow 880 north and exit onto Highway 238 south, which becomes Interstate 580 east in approximately three miles. Continue for 30 miles, merging onto Highway 205 east for 13 miles until reaching Interstate 5. Follow Interstate 5 north, then merge onto Highway 120 east. Travel for about six miles, then exit onto Highway 99 south. Continue on Highway 99 until reaching Merced, and exit onto Highway 140 east towards Mariposa/Yosemite. Continue east for 35 miles, and turn right onto Highway 49 south into Oakhurst.

Once in Oakhurst, turn right onto Highway 31 south. The estate is on Victoria Lane, about a half-mile south of the Highway 49-Highway 41 intersection.

Credit Cards Accepted

Visa, MasterCard, American Express, Discover .

SACRAMENTO

Served by Sacramento International Airport (SMF).

THE SAVOYARD

3322 H Street
Sacramento, Sacramento County
Tel. 800/772-8692 or 916/442-6709
Fax: 916/442-6709
Web Address: www.savoyard.com
E-mail: info@savoyard.com
Rates: $95-130
3pm check-in
Year Opened: 1995
Innkeepers: Bruce and Pat Ansel

Profile

When the opera would let out at the Savoy Theatre during the 1890s, the doting audience would gather at the legendary Savoy Hotel for a late-night supper. Though Sacramento and London's West Side are divided by more than just an ocean, the term Savoyard was – and still is – used to refer to fans of Gilbert and Sullivan. Innkeeper Bruce Ansel is a self-confessed Savoyard, and therefore his establishment also bears the moniker.

The two-story home was built in 1925 by J.O. Boyd. The plot of land belonging to the estate, as well as much of the surrounding area, was part of the original land grant awarded to John Sutter by the Mexican Government during the mid-1800s. The low pitched roof, wide overhanging eaves and classical Greek columns define the Italian Renaissance style. Located across the street from McKinley Park, one of Sacramento's most pristine greenbelts, guests of the inn are close to many of the city's historical attractions. Though the inn sits on a busy thoroughfare, it's set far enough back from the street that noise doesn't pose too much of a problem.

Accommodations

With only four rooms, all located on the upper floor, visitors are more likely to feel like invited guests rather than patrons. Each room offers some conveniences, like phones and televisions, along with plenty of reading material. The antiques are part of the owners' personal collection, one that started more than a quarter of a century ago.

Named for the works of Gilbert and Sullivan, each room offers its own brand of enchantment. The **Mikado** is wildly eastern with an oversized brass bed and Japanese wedding gown gracing the wall. The **Penzance** is more subtle with a large four-poster canopied bed and big picture windows. Both chambers overlook the park and, while the views are delightful, light sleepers may want to request the rear-facing **Iolanthe** or **Pinafore** rooms. The Iolanthe offers one of the largest bathrooms, though it is detached, and the Art Deco tub is great for a long soak.

Amenities

The public rooms consist of a parlor and dining area, both creatively eclectic blending American, European and Asian touches. The parlor features floor-to-ceiling bookshelves and oversized couches, and is a perfect place to mingle with guests or just lounge. Each morning the communal dining room table is where a no-fuss breakfast is served. Frou-frou is replaced with hearty fare such as juice, cereal, eggs and waffles, and you'll always find an overstocked cookie jar.

The front garden is part of **Azalea Row**, a three-block stretch of eye-catching flora. You'll also find a collection of well-tended camellias, tulips and a garden table with benches readied for your enjoyment. The rear yard is filled with more of the same including a leafy sycamore tree.

Historic **McKinley Park**, located just across the street, is known for its stunning rose gardens and camellia grove. Bill Clinton chose the park's jogging track for an early morning workout while in Sacramento, and there is also a swimming pool, tennis courts, baseball diamond, playground, duck pond and library too. During the summer, the park hosts a free weekly concert series in the evening.

At-A-Glance Features

4 Rooms
Children Welcome
Close to Downtown Sacramento and Historic Waterfront
Complimentary Breakfast
Within Walking Distance to Park and Recreation

Directions

Head south on Interstate 5, then take the 80 Freeway east heading towards Reno. Exit at H Street and head east. The inn is directly across the street from McKinley Park.

Credit Cards Accepted

Visa, MasterCard, American Express, Discover, Diners Club.

SUTTER CREEK

Served by Sacramento International Airport (SMF).

GREY GABLES INN

161 Hanford Street
Sutter Creek, Amador County
Tel. 800/473-9422 or 209/267-1039
Fax: 209/267-0998
Web Address: www.greygables.com
E-mail: reservations@greygables.com
Rates: $100-160
3pm check-in
Year Opened: 1994
Innkeepers: Roger and Sue Garlick

Profile

The land that the inn sits on, along with quite a few other parcels, was purchased in the late 1870s by Bishop Patrick Monogue of Sacramento for the Catholic Church. On this site the church erected a Catholic school, and after the Bishop's death some 20 years later it was willed to Patrick Riordan, the Archbishop of San Francisco. While the original building was retained during a major remodel some years back, it bears little resemblance to the modest schoolhouse that once stood here.

Bringing a touch of English refinery to what was once California's bawdy Mother Lode region are British transplants and innkeepers Roger and Sue Garlick. Beneath the pitched roof and series of jutting gables, the Garlicks have created a country manor any anglophile would be proud to call home...even if only for a few days.

Accommodations

Dainty lace table coverings and floral wallpaper create a formal yet inviting ambiance behind each chamber door. Guest rooms, named for such celebrated poets as Keats and Byron, are blanketed in plush carpeting and each features an impressive fireplace, antique armoire for hanging clothes, roomy beds and tiled baths all equipped with showers – some even offer deep claw-foot tubs.

The **Browning** room, located on the main floor overlooking the impressive gardens, is a mid-priced room with lace curtains framing the expansive bay window. The **Shelley** chamber, one of the least expensive and handicapped accessible, can be a cozy choice with its Eastlake bed and

Victorian loveseat. While the rest of the rooms can accommodate a maximum of two guests, The **Tennyson** room, cloaked in Laura Ashley wall coverings, has both a queen bed and day bed making it available for families of three. Its tiptop location creates a secluded escape, which can be good if you're traveling with children.

Amenities

The parlor, the pulse of the inn with wingback chairs and a glowing fireplace, is where guests gather each afternoon for traditional English tea and return again in the evening for a glass of wine and hors d'oeuvres. The dining room is where mornings begin with a full breakfast served on bone china, or a tray can be delivered to your room upon request.

Sometime during the day take a moment to stroll along the red-brick pathway that meanders through the garden, under arbors and past a tiered fountain. Nearby are shops and restaurants, as well as an array of family-operated wineries.

At-A-Glance Features

8 Rooms
Children Welcome
Close to Wineries
Complimentary Breakfast
Complimentary Evening Wine & Hors d'oeuvres
Traditional Afternoon Tea
Near Shops, Restaurants and Attractions

Directions

From Sacramento, take Highway 50 east towards Lake Tahoe. Take the Bradshaw Road exit and head south to Highway 16. At Highway 16 turn left and head east to Highway 49. Travel south on Highway 49 to Sutter Creek. The inn is located in town on Highway 49.

Credit Cards Accepted

Visa, MasterCard.

SUTTER CREEK'S GOLD FRENZY

Sutter Creek is one of the Gold Country's most charming towns, a place where dot-com zillionaires come for weekend getaways. But during the mid-1800s, the only thoughts prospectors were computing was the hope of striking gold.

Sutter Creek, founded in 1844 by Captain John Sutter, has a firm place in California's history. The original settlers arrived in search of timber, but when gold was discovered in 1848 it created quite an international frenzy – not unlike what's taking place today just a few miles away in Silicon Valley. Overnight, homes and businesses sprang up along what is now Highway 49 and, while many of the wood-framed buildings were destroyed by fire, the brick and greenstone variety were spared.

A fleet of century-old Victorian, New England, and Greek Revival buildings are now home to antique shops, restaurants and galleries located along Main Street and neighboring avenues.

HANFORD HOUSE BED & BREAKFAST INN

61 Hanford Street, Highway 49
Sutter Creek, Amador County
Tel. 800/871-5839 or 209/267-0747
Fax: 209/267-1825
Web Address: www.hanfordhouse.com
E-mail: bobkat@hanfordhouse.com
Rates: $99-185
3pm check-in
Year Opened: 1984
Innkeepers: Bob and Karen Tierno

Profile

The Hanford House Inn can be considered both old and new. Built over a 1929 cottage, the visible edifice was only erected in 1984 and was fashioned after a Gold Rush-style building.

The ivy-covered edifice is close to all Sutter Creek has to offer: restaurants, shops, galleries and wine tasting rooms. The nearby foothills provide added recreation such as bicycling, golf, boating, hiking, river rafting and even skiing. There's even a few gimmicks, like panning for gold, but the real excitement of Sutter Creek is within walking distance from this lovely retreat.

Accommodations

The Hanford House Inn forgoes Gold Country kitsch, opting for classic appointments: four-poster beds and wicker chairs accented with flora and gingham prints. A few noteworthy rooms include the **Bellisimo**, a tasteful gold and cream chamber with a romantically draped bed, pair of wingback chairs and fireplace. The **Gallery** room is another excellent choice with expansive ceilings and an ample seating area with morning tray service provided. Guests of **The Gold Country Escape** can hole up in this very large and private suite complete with picture windows, a four-poster pewter and brass bed, a cozy fireplace and access to the rooftop deck.

With cable television, sound spas, CD players, crackling hearths and a slew of unexpected amenities, the rooms at The Hanford House really are the mother lode of accommodations.

Amenities

It's reassuring when you find all the usual suspects at a bed and breakfast; things you assume will accompany your stay like a gourmet breakfast and afternoon wine. The Hanford House even takes it a bit further with en-suite massage therapy, a guest pantry and complimentary transportation from the local airport to the inn. This is one of the only bed and breakfast inns to offer complete childbirth preparation classes. Hosted by **Silver Spoon Weekends**, experts in such matters, these Friday-Sunday classes are designed for expecting couples and include, besides lessons in how to breath, a dose of massage therapy. What a great getaway for parents to be, and an informative one at that.

At-A-Glance Features

9 Rooms
Children Welcome
Complimentary Breakfast
Complimentary Wine and Snacks
En-Suite Massage
Near Wineries and Attractions
Prepared Childbirth Classes
Transportation To and From Airport
Walk to Shops and Restaurants

Directions

From Sacramento, take Highway 50 east towards Lake Tahoe. Take the Bradshaw Road exit and head south to Highway 16. At Highway 16 turn left and head east to Highway 49. Travel south on Highway 49 to Sutter Creek. The inn is located in town on Highway 49.

Credit Cards Accepted

Visa, MasterCard, Discover.

TWAIN HARTE

Served by Sacramento International Airport (SMF).

McCAFFREY HOUSE BED & BREAKFAST INN

23251 Highway 108
Twain Harte, Tuolumne County
Tel. 888/586-0757 or 209/586-0757
Fax: 209/586-3689
Web Address: www.mccaffreyhouse.com
E-mail: innkeeper@mccaffreyhouse.com
Rates: $120-135
3pm check-in
Year Opened: 1996
Innkeepers: Michael and Stephanie McCaffrey

Profile

The McCaffrey House is a place you seek when you want to escape the rigors of everyday life. It's completely peaceful, unbelievably serene and very private.

Nestled in a quiet forest hollow surrounded by towering oaks, cedar and pine trees, the McCaffrey House was designed and built by its innkeepers Michael and Stephanie. The couple were first lured to the area some 30 years ago by the Gold Country's four-season climate and natural Sierra setting. Vacations were spent in the family's snug cottage, which was eventually replaced by the rambling inn. As the couple began to contemplate retirement, Twain Harte seemed like a natural choice.

The two decided to take on mid-life careers as innkeepers and, as a result, the McCaffrey House was born. Built with warmth and comfort in mind, the home is decidedly country with a flair for the fabulous. Its location, in the heart of California's Mother Lode, lends itself well to an abundance of year-round recreation.

Accommodations

Boasting a four-diamond rating from the Automobile Club, the timbered McCaffrey House offers a relaxing getaway.

Chambers, named for colors like **Sage** and **Evergreen**, are adorned with handmade quilts created by Amish hands. Each room is warmed by a cast-iron fire stove with queen-size beds, and televisions and VCRs are discreetly placed in pine armoires. Many rooms have balconies or private patios, offering Sherwood Forest-style views with pine scents to match. There are also telephones and modems available for those with a need to stay in touch.

Amenities

Though the inn doesn't have a trace of Spanish influence, the phrase "mi casa es su casa," *my house is your house*, seems to be the unofficial motto. The living room is often draped with relaxed guests who tend to gravitate to this inviting area. There is a reading area with an ample selection of literature, and late afternoon tea, cider, wine and cheese can be enjoyed while firmly grounded on a plush sofa or chair.

Breakfast is of the gourmet variety and whipped up by Stephanie each morning. The dining room is usually where this ritual takes place, but on cloudless days the spacious deck does double duty as both breakfast terrace and afternoon wine bar.

With a four-season climate, there are plenty of things to do year round. Winter offers downhill and cross-country skiing at nearby **Dodge Ridge** and **Bear Valley**. The warmer months are perfect for exploring the foothill wineries, trout fishing in nearby lakes and streams, or hiking through nearby meadows.

FROM COCHUMS TO B&BS

*Before this area was dotted with summer homes and pristine fairways, the region belonged to the Mi-Wuk Indians. The tribe called a lakeside camp home, and it was here where they built **oochums** or dwellings from tree limbs and bark. They also kept busy by weaving fine baskets from willows.*

With the Gold Rush frenzy of 1849, the surrounding area saw major changes. After the resources were exhausted, lumbermen and ranchers found ways to prosper by tapping into the area's abundant forests and grazing lands. The name Twain Harte, however, comes not from those who settled the land, but rather from a pair of famous authors, Mark Twain and Bret Harte.

At-A-Glance Features

7 Rooms
Children Welcome
Close to Ski Resorts

Complimentary Breakfast
Complimentary Wine, Cheese and Refreshments

Directions

From Sacramento, take Highway 99 towards Stockton. After passing the Stockton exit, look for signs leading to Highway 4/Farmington and follow the exit. Head towards Farmington, then turn right at the Copperopolis sign towards Highway 108/120. At the highway, turn left and go up the hill toward Sonora. You'll bypass Sonora and Twain Harte, but once you reach the 4,000 elevation marker slow down. The inn is 500 feet past the marker on a road located on your right.

Credit Cards Accepted

Visa, MasterCard, American Express.

5. WINE COUNTRY

ARRIVALS & DEPARTURES
FOR THE WINE COUNTRY

For all of the Wine Country entries in this chapter, which includes Sonoma and Napa counties, you can fly into either San Francisco International Airport (SFO) or Oakland International Airport (OAK).

CALISTOGA

COTTAGE GROVE INN

1711 Lincoln Avenue
Calistoga, Napa County
Tel. 800/799-2284 or 707/942-8400
Fax: 707/942-2653
Web Address: www.cottagegove.com
E-mail: innkeeper@cottagegrove.com
Rates: $235-295
4pm check-in
Year Opened: 1996
Innkeepers: Bob Beck, Monica Bootcheck and Tom Stimpert

Profile

It's hard to believe that before these cluster of roadside cottages were constructed, the land that the Cottage Grove Inn now occupies was a bona fide trailer park. In 1996, designer luggage and luxury vehicles replaced traversing clothes lines as the trailer park went by the wayside and the bungalows took its place.

The cottages, which line a narrow driveway on both sides, have a vintage quality about them with raised foundations, expansive porches, screen doors and pitched roofs. Simply motor up to your doorstep to unpack, and enjoy the convenience of walking to town. Calistoga, which was founded as a hot springs resort more than a century ago, is known for its healing spas. There are plenty of places in town to enjoy a mud or mineral bath and massage. Of course, you are in the Napa Valley, so wine tasting also tops the list of priorities.

Accommodations

Under a shadow of elm trees just at the edge of town is where you'll find this row of neatly lined cottages. From the outside, the small A-frame buildings look uniform with their shuttered windows, pillared porches and wicker rocking chairs. The interiors also share limited characteristics such as wet bars, deep two-person soaking tubs large, custom furniture, CD stereo systems, and wood-burning fireplaces. But beyond these handful of appointments, it's every room for itself.

Cottage names, such as **Provence**, **Music**, **Audubon** and **Vintners**, reflect each individual mood. The warm coral hues, slip covered chairs, and floral chintz fabrics belonging to the **Rose Floral Cottage** are reminiscent of a European parlor. The ruggedly refined **Fly Fishing Cottage** is flawless to a fault with a hand-carved wooden trout gracing the headboard, mosquito netting draped above the bed and lamps crafted from fishing creels. Be sure to closely examine your cottage's hardwood floors, as they're skillfully made from resurfaced old-growth fir obtained from a forgotten whiskey distillery.

Amenities

Each morning in the quaint guest lounge an expanded continental breakfast awaits, with a copy of the morning paper. Guests wander in and out nibbling on the morning treats and enjoying oversized cups of freshly roasted coffee. Come afternoon, a buffet table displays a selection of Napa Valley wines and special cheeses, which you can help yourself to. Pile high your plate, fill your glass and enjoy this afternoon ritual on the privacy of your porch while rocking in one of those wonderful wicker chairs. Should you wish to take advantage of the in-room fireplace, you'll find an ample supply of firewood left on your cottage porch.

At-A-Glance Features

16 Rooms
Complimentary Continental Breakfast
Complimentary Afternoon Wine & Cheese
Complimentary Bicycles
Near Wineries
Non-Smoking
Not Appropriate for Children Under 12
Within Walking Distance to Restaurants, Shops and Spas

Directions

Head north from San Francisco on Highway 101, exit towards Napa/Vallejo on Highway 37. Continue for about 10 miles before exiting left to Napa/Sonoma on Highway 121. Continue on this route for approximately 22 miles and turn left on Highway 29. Travel for about 25 miles up the west side of Napa Valley and turn left at Lincoln Avenue. Take Lincoln through downtown Calistoga, approximately six blocks, and turn left onto Wappo. The entrance to Cottage Grove Inn is on the right.

Credit Cards Accepted

Visa, MasterCard, American Express, Discover, Diners Club.

THE PINK MANSION

1415 Foothill Boulevard
Calistoga, Napa County
Tel. 800/238-7465 or 707/942-0558
Fax: 707/942-0558
Web Address: www.pinkmansion.com
E-mail: pink@napanet.net
Rates: $145-245
3pm check-in
Year Opened: 1982
Innkeeper: Toppa and Leslie Epps

Profile

The Pink Mansion is what it is – a pink mansion. The opulent house, with its grand turret and jutting angles, was built in 1875 by William F. Fisher. Fisher had a pioneering spirit and helped to establish Calistoga's first stage line linking the town with mining sites atop Mount St. Helena and points to the north. He was also a fabulous host, entertaining dignitaries and townspeople alike in his grand parlor underneath lavish chandeliers.

The inn was coated in its trademark pink sometime during the 1930s and has remained a Calistoga landmark ever since. Up until the early 1980s it was a private home until its last and longest resident, Alma Simic, passed on. Located just a quarter of a mile from town, The Pink Mansion is still a commanding presence more than a century later.

Accommodations

There are six intimate rooms, each eclectically outfitted with angelic cherubs and a smattering of Victorian and Oriental treasures.

The Master Suite and the Honeymoon Suite are certainly the most fetching of the half dozen chambers, as well as the most expensive. Spanning nearly 900 square feet, the **Master Suite** is without a doubt the inn's largest room. Hunker down in this 19th-century style chamber replete with a four-poster bed, wood-burning fireplace and two-person Jacuzzi tub. There is also a private sitting room with an extra bed, along with a welcoming redwood deck overlooking the landscape.

Though not quite as large at 800 square feet, the **Honeymoon Suite** is still larger than most apartments. Elegant and exotic, this neoclassical room is picture perfect, with gleaming hardwood floors, a canopied bed, wood-burning fireplace, private sitting room and observation deck with views of Mount St. Helena and the palisades.

The other rooms, though less grand, are equally enchanting. Notable features include claw- foot tubs, a spray of impressive antiques, crystal chandeliers, 12-foot ornamental ceilings and private entrances or decks.

Amenities

Opulence is evident within the inn's public rooms, from the Victorian parlor to the drawing room. Elegance gives way to extravagance in the form of a heated indoor swimming pool. While it may seem safe to assume that this convenient feature was added for the benefit of contemporary guests, the pool was actually installed during the 1930s. Feel free to take a dip whenever the mood strikes and, because there are so few rooms here, often you're the only one enjoying the heated waters.

A lavish breakfast is served each morning in the breakfast room and regional wines, some of the best in the country, are enjoyed in the late afternoon. Within walking distance is the town of **Calistoga** with its spa-lined streets and sampling of restaurants and shops. Even though you could easily go into town for a massage or facial, The Pink Mansion can arrange for a masseuse or esthetician to work their magic as you lay sequestered behind chamber doors.

At-A-Glance Features
6 Rooms
Children Welcome
Complimentary Breakfast
Complimentary Afternoon Wine Tasting
En-Suite Massage and Facials
Heated Indoor Swimming Pool and Jacuzzi
Near Wineries
Non-Smoking
Pet-Friendly
Within Walking Distance to Shops, Restaurants and Spas

Directions
From San Francisco, take Highway 101 north to Highway 37 East to Highway 29 north. Proceed on Highway 29 to the flashing light in Calistoga, and continue forward. The inn is located two blocks on the left-hand side.

Credit Cards Accepted
Visa, MasterCard, Discover.

CLOVERDALE

VINTAGE TOWERS
302 North Main Street
Cloverdale, Sonoma County
Tel. 888/886-9377 or 707/894-4535
Fax: 707/894-5827
Web Address: www.vintagetowers.com
E-mail: polly@vintagetowers.com
Rates: $85-165
3pm check in
Year Opened: 1982
Innkeeper: Polly Grant

Profile
The Vintage Towers is a lovely Queen Anne Victorian showpiece hailing from 1901. The trio of uniquely shaped towers – spherical, square and octagonal – were added in 1913 by then-owner Simon Pinchower, a wealthy merchant and mining executive. The unique design creates an unmistakable silhouette and sets the Vintage Towers apart from other period-style homes in this area. The inn also has the distinction of being listed on the National Register of Historic Places.

The inn is located where the redwoods meet the vineyards in Cloverdale, a town with an intimate population of about 4,000. Nearby are about three dozen wineries, groves of aged redwood trees and the picturesque waters of Lake Sonoma and the Russian River.

Accommodations
The Vintage Towers, with its 40-foot long verandah and classic porch swing, is a throwback to a gentler era. There are just seven rooms within its confines, each offering antiques, private baths and a cache of amenities. An old-fashioned claw-foot tub is a hallmark of the **Vintage Rose Room**, an oversized brass bed dominates **Alice's Room**, rose garden views are enjoyed in **Mary's Room**, and swatches of lace are draped about **Scarlet's Room**.

The best rooms are those located in the individual towers. The octagonal **Vintage Tower Suite** is the largest guest room with Eastlake Victorian furnishings, a dramatic sitting area complete with fainting couch and a private porch flanked with a telescope for high-powered star gazing. **Helen's Tower Suite**, another charming choice, is located in the square tower, while **Judith's Tower Suite** is set in the cylinder-shaped structure.

Amenities

Vintage Towers is an intimate and unpretentious property. Amenities are simple but thoughtful, with a full gourmet breakfast served each morning on either the wraparound verandah or on a collection of tables in the dining room. A hospitality center is stocked with a stash of hot and cold beverages along with cookies, cheese and crackers.

The inn is awaiting its wine license as of press time, but that doesn't prevent guests from bringing back their own finds after a day of visiting the nearby tasting rooms. Borrow a couple of glasses from the kitchen, and toast your good fortune from the porch swing. Though the rooms are void of televisions and VCRs, you can get your TV fix from the set in the parlor.

At-A-Glance Features

7 Rooms
Complimentary Breakfast
Complimentary Beverages and Snacks
Near Wineries
Not Appropriate for Children

Directions

From San Francisco, take Highway 101 north to Citrus Fair Drive. Go left on Citrus Fair Drive to Cloverdale Boulevard, and turn right. Proceed on Cloverdale Boulevard to 3rd Street, and turn right again. The inn is located on the corner of 3rd and Main.

Credit Cards Accepted

Visa, MasterCard, American Express, Discover.

GLEN ELLEN

GAIGE HOUSE INN

13540 Arnold Drive
Glen Ellen, Sonoma County
Tel. 800/935-0237 or 707/935-0237
Fax: 707/935-6411
Web Address: www.gaige.com
E-mail: gaige@sprynet.com
Rates: $150-395
3pm check-in
Year Opened: 1985
Innkeepers: Ken Burnet and Greg Nemrow

Profile

The Gaige House Inn is as un-Victorian as you'll find, yet the exterior of the original house looks every bit like a turn-of-the-century homestead. But beyond the doors of this 1890 Queen Anne-Italianate building, you'd be hard pressed to find a swatch of floral wallpaper or a cupboard containing a single chintz pattern. Instead, you'll discover a fusion of Asian and Indonesian influences creating a simple – if not Zen-like – place to nest.

As you wander about the grounds, which includes a 1.5 acre sprawl of creekside beauty, it's hard to believe that at one time, in another life, the building housed a butcher shop and rooming house before its present transformation. But just as the Gaige House Inn eschews its Victorian roots, it also shuns what many would define as the typical bed and breakfast experience. There is nary a resident cat or litter of stuffed teddy bears in sight and, instead of eating off an eclectic mix of antique china, you'll be served instead on new Asian art moderne tableware. Different? Definitely. Sophisticated? Absolutely.

Accommodations

The original house contains seven rooms and the additional eight are shared between the **Garden Annex**, which is attached to the home, or in the **separate pool house**. Decorated in subtle hues, handsome leathers, Chinese sea grass carpets and a mint of orchids, the rooms are sophisticated. All enjoy phones, fine linens, robes and European toiletries, with each room offering an unexpected appointment – whether it's a cozy fireplace, open-air deck or invigorating whirlpool.

All the rooms evoke a masculine similarity, but perhaps the best room to occupy is the **Creekside Suite**. A glass wall, so clear it appears as if the room is only partially sheltered, overlooks the Calabazas Creek. Spacious and spectacular, guests slumber in a king bed, slosh in a whirlpool tub, and get soaked in a tandem shower. There is also a fireplace, private deck and patio, plus wet bar to complete this indoor paradise. The **Woodside Suite**, the inn's other premier chamber, offers similar appointments with eight-foot windows, a two-person Japanese soaking tub and creekside coziness.

Amenities

Chef Charles Holmes presides over the daily two-course breakfast served in the sunroom. His visits to the local farmers' markets result in a decadent menu of zesty dishes, such as crisp yellow corn polenta rounds topped with fromage blanc, maple syrup, fresh figs and raspberries or lemon ricotta pancakes oozing with fresh blueberry sauce. A stash of homemade cookies, cold drinks and hot tea are available around the clock and, come late afternoon, the innkeepers invite guests to sample local wines. Enjoy a toast with other guests on the creekside patio, or pour yourself into an overstuffed garden chair.

After exploring the local wineries and gourmet markets, rejuvenate with a dip in the refreshing 40-foot swimming pool, heated May through October, or unwind in the all-season whirlpool spa. Several of the world's best spas are within driving distance, but why bother going in search of paradise when paradise has already been found? Enjoy en suite or poolside body treatments, from massage therapy to foot reflexology to seaweed algae wraps. Perhaps the most unusual treatment offered, if not the most relaxing, is the Watsu, a gentle form of water massage done in the pool while being cradled in the arms of a masseuse. Manicures and pedicures are also available, and treatments can be arranged with the concierge.

At-A-Glance Features

15 Rooms
Complimentary Afternoon Wine
Complimentary Breakfast
En-Suite Spa Treatments
Near Wineries
Non-Smoking
Not Appropriate for Children
Swimming Pool and Whirlpool Spa
24-Hour Snack Privileges

Directions

From San Francisco, travel north on Highway 101, taking Route 37 to Route 121 to Route 116. Exit onto Arnold Drive. The inn is at 13540 Arnold Drive.

Credit Cards Accepted

Visa, MasterCard.

SONOMA - FROM WINE TO OLIVE OIL!

*With its rolling vineyards and collection of Tuscan-style villas, Sonoma County seems more closely aligned with Italy than anything Californian. As if that's not enough, now locals are getting into the act of producing extra-virgin olive oil. The rich soil and temperate climate create ideal conditions for harvesting a variety of olives, resulting in a myriad of flavors. Local growers are pressing their own creations, as well as hauling bushels of ripe olives to the local presses for community crushing. Local oils are available for purchase directly from selected wineries or at specialty food stores scattered about the county. **The Olive Press**, 14301 Arnold Drive in Glen Ellen, Tel. 707/939-8900, sells its own extra-virgin olive oil and offers a selection of olive-related products at its gift shop in the form of ceramics, soaps and foods.*

GUERNEVILLE

APPLEWOOD INN & RESTAURANT
13555 Highway 116
Guerneville, Sonoma County
Tel. 800/555-8509 or 707/869-9093
Fax: 707/869-9170
Web Address: www.applewoodinn.com
E-mail: stay@applewoodinn.com
Rates: $135-325
3pm check-in
Year Opened:
Innkeepers: Jim Caron and Darryl Notter

Profile
Guerneville (pronounced "gurnville") hardly sounds like the setting for sophistication. But during the carefree 1920s, this patch of redwood-dotted land was home to more than 200 luxurious inns and a quartet of gracious ballrooms.

Fast forward to a new century. Guerneville, nestled in the Russian River Valley, is now a quaint town situated in the heart of Sonoma County's wine country. But it's not the bouquets of Chardonnay and Cabernets that have an intoxicating effect on its visitors, rather it's the chic Applewood Inn & Restaurant that casts a dizzying spell.

Located just 20 minutes from the coast and 90 minutes north of San Francisco, this refurbished 1920s estate resembles a Mediterranean villa. Guests are lured to the inviting courtyard by the sounds of trickling water spouting from an oversized fountain. It's here where new wine acquisitions are uncorked, good books are scoured, and lazy afternoons are spent.

Accommodations
The 16 rooms and suites are divided among the main house and a pair of zinfandel-colored buildings. In the main house are eight handsome and austere chambers offering everything from garden level entrances and cherry sleigh beds to soaring ceilings and shaded verandahs.

The **Piccola Casa** and **Gate House** are where a collection of sublime suites are stashed. Exceptional and secluded, romantics will fall in love with the bedside fireplaces, tandem showers and ample-sized whirlpool baths. Idyllic touches include Juliet-style balconies, window seats framing redwood vistas or fountain courtyards.

All rooms contain televisions and fireplaces, though I recommend disconnecting both as soon as you get settled.

Amenities

With six acres cradling the Applewood Inn & Restaurant, there are plenty of places to explore beyond the inn's entrance. Pour yourself a glass of wine or iced tea and accompany the chef through the kitchen garden where ripe fruit, vegetables and a cache of herbs will find their way onto the evening menu. In fact, guests are actually invited to take home some of the garden's harvest. On rainy days, and there are some, guests can enjoy the cozy surroundings of the solarium. Each morning a bountiful gourmet breakfast is served, and a wine hour rounds out the day. There's also a swimming pool, mini-vineyard and spa all loosely shrouded by redwoods.

Perhaps the inn's most gallant offering is its California-Provencal **restaurant**. Though an evening meal is not part of the nightly tariff, it's terribly convenient to have a recognized restaurant within easy reach. Under the culinary direction of Brian Gerritsen, a noted wine country chef whose most recent post was that of Chef de Cuisine at La Toque in nearby Rutherford, Chef Gerritsen also spent some time as sous chef at the renowned FENIX at the Argyle Hotel in Hollywood. The a la carte and six-course tasting menu is served in a spanking new French barn-style setting, beneath lofty beamed ceilings and warmed by a pair of river-rock fireplaces. Dine indoors near a bank of windows overlooking the redwoods or al fresco on the outdoor deck.

At-A-Glance Features

16 Rooms
Chef-led Garden Tours
Complimentary Breakfast
Complimentary Wine Hour
Concierge Service
Full-Service Restaurant
Outside Whirlpool Spa
Near Wineries
Non-Smoking
Not Appropriate for Children
Swimming Pool and Whirlpool Spa

Directions

From San Francisco, travel north on Highway 101 to Highway 116 at Cotati West. Travel 22 miles to the inn, which is located on Highway 116.

Credit Cards Accepted

Visa, MasterCard, American Express, Discover.

HEALDSBURG

HONOR MANSION

14891 Grove Street
Healdsburg, Sonoma County
Tel. 800/554-4667 or 707/433-4277
Fax: 707/431-7173
Web Address: www.honormansion.com
E-mail: concierge@honormansion.com
Rates: $140-300
3pm check-in
Year Opened: 1994
Innkeepers: Steve and Cathi Fowler

Profile

Once in a great while you stumble upon a place that's unforgettable. The Honor Mansion is such a place. However, when owners Cathi and Steve Fowler discovered it back in 1994, the Italianate Victorian home had seen better days. Together the duo set out to remodel the entire building, transforming a once dark and depressing relic into an elegant and engaging showpiece.

Built in 1883 for William S. Butcher, a wealthy cattleman and amateur botanist, the inn is **not named** for him but rather Dr. Herbert Honor, whose family and heirs owned the home for more than a century. A landmark magnolia and fleet of century-old trees, most likely planted by the original owner, softly frame the two-story structure.

Downtown Healdsburg, just a 10-minute stroll away, resembles small town America, Martha Stewart style. It offers an array of upscale antique shops, day spas and dining.

Accommodations

Behind the doors of the Honor Mansion are just a handful of accommodations – nine to be exact. Immaculate and artful, classic with a hint of whimsy, each offers an unforgettable escape.

The rooms highlight at least one outstanding amenity. The **Garden Suite** is an enticing choice with its outdoor garden spa tub; the two-room **Poolside Suite** offers private access to the inn's swimming pool; guests slumber in a hand-carved four-poster bed behind the doors of the **Magnolia Room**; and the sound of the koi pond's gentle waterfall resonates throughout the **Camellia Room**. A cobblestone path is the only thing connecting the **Squire's Cottage** with the original home. Mixing vintage pieces with contemporary touches, this lofty bungalow features a king-size canopy bed, a claw-foot soaking tub and separate tiled shower. Completing this comfort zone is a cozy sitting area, wet bar, television and VCR complete with a stash of video cassettes, CD player, fireplace, and a private deck with koi pond views.

Perhaps the inn's most prized chamber is the new two-room, two-level **Tower Suite**. In addition to a queen canopied bed, television and VCR, a library of video tapes, dual head shower for two (that's just the first floor) and a living room, wet bar and vineyard views above, the Tower Suite also boasts its own private outdoor garden spa tub with personal access to both the pool and sun deck.

All chambers are cloaked in European linens, down comforters and feather beds, and offer telephones with fax modems, his and her robes, and bouquets of fresh flowers.

Amenities

The Fowlers certainly know how to take care of their guests. Try waking up each morning to a multi-course breakfast served on antique china, silver and crystal. The settings, either in the dining room with the French doors swung open or outdoors on the redwood deck overlooking the koi pond, are just as appetizing as what appears on your plate. Prior to breakfast a selection of fresh juice, freshly-ground coffee, and an assortment of teas and cocoas are available as you skim over the morning paper.

Other filling perks include 24-hour espresso and cappuccino service, afternoon tea and refreshments, an evening wine and appetizer hour featuring a selection of local vintages paired with an array of hors d'oeuvres, late evening sherry, and an endless supply of cookies and tea biscuits. Temporary residents are also encouraged to help themselves to the soft drink-stocked refrigerator whenever they please.

Guests can plunge in the inn's swimming pool, raid the parlor for a stash of rainy day games or just lounge about in a wicker chair admiring the garden views.

At-A-Glance Features

9 Rooms
Complimentary Afternoon Wine & Cheese
Complimentary Breakfast
Complimentary Sherri and Soft Drinks
Complimentary 24-hour Cappuccino Service
Near Wineries

Non-Smoking
Not Appropriate for Children
Within Walking Distance to Restaurants, Shops & Spas

Directions

From San Francisco, take Highway 101 north and exit at Dry Creek. Turn right, and travel one block; turn right on Grove Street. The inn is the first white picket fence on the right.

Credit Cards Accepted

Visa, MasterCard, Discover.

THE HONOR MANSION'S BROILED
- YES, BROILED! - GRAPEFRUIT RECIPE

*The Honor Mansion is known for its gourmet breakfasts. Even if you're culinarily-challenged, **Cathi's Broiled Grapefruit** is nearly impossible to ruin.*

For each grapefruit use:
- *1 Tbs port wine*
- *1 Tbs brown sugar*
- *1 Tbs butter*

Cut grapefruit in half crosswise and section with serrated knife. Place in pan face up and top with one tablespoon each of the above. Broil in shallow pan for 10 minutes, and pour remaining mixture over grapefruit and serve.

MADRONA MANOR

1001 Westside Rd.
Healdsburg, Sonoma County
Tel. 800/258-4003 or 707/433-4231
Fax: 707/433-0703
Web Address: www.madronamanor.com
E-mail: madronaman@aol.com
Rates: $165-380
3pm check-in
Year Opened: 1982
Innkeepers: Maria and Joseph Hadley

Profile

This imposing structure, with its mansard roof and ominous hue, looks more like a haunted house than a bed and breakfast. And, while there have been hints that the estate may in fact be haunted, there are plenty of pleasant offerings to make your entire body tingle.

In 1879, the wealthy John Paxton purchased 240 acres for $10,500 as a future site for his home. A year later, at a cost of $12,000, an elegant mansion was erected across from the Dry Creek Bridge. Known to many as Madrona Knoll Rancho, the 17-room, 3 1/2-bath manor was the town's showpiece. John, along with his wife Hannah, employed a coachman, a footman, a groom and several maids. It is also believed that at least one indentured servant was part of the staff.

After the family sold the home in 1913, it experienced a number of owners but remained a private residence. In 1981, a new chapter began as the home was converted into a wine country inn and restaurant. Now listed on the National Register of Historic Places, Madrona Manor is one of Northern California's most celebrated inns.

Accommodations

Beyond the manor's expansive wraparound porch is where you'll find the collection of distinguished rooms. Spanning three floors, the original Victorian manor houses nine of the 21 rooms with five of the rooms displaying antiques belonging to the original owner. All of the rooms have king-size beds and fireplaces, and are some of the best the estate has to offer.

The original **Carriage House** has been converted into guest quarters with eight rooms and a suite, which boasts a Greek marble-cloaked bathroom, Jacuzzi tub and private deck. The **Meadow Wood Complex** is another annex believed to have been the original kitchen. Shunning Victorian themes, one of the two suites is decorated in an Asian motif and both offer private decks. The **Garden Cottage**, considered to be the manor's most secluded offering, features a sitting room and marble fireplace with a sheltered deck and hidden garden.

To decide what amenities are most important to you, Madrona Manor houses a total of 18 rooms with fireplaces, eight rooms with balconies or decks and five suites; some rooms provide one or more of these amenities. In keeping with the 19th-century era, the inn is completely void of television sets.

Amenities

The manor's **Music Room**, located in the original home, is very much the pulse of this wine country palace. Graced with many of the home's original furnishings, including a rosewood piano, guests seem to gravitate towards this room. There is a nook for reading, conversational enclaves for chatting and a selection of parlor games.

Breakfast is served in the lovely and highly acclaimed restaurant, a place you can return to in the evening for an award-winning meal prepared by Chef Jesse Mallgren. Elegant candlelight dinners, available at an additional cost, are served daily from 6pm-9pm in a trio of dining rooms. On Friday and Saturday evenings, usually during the warmer months, live music floats through the grounds.

The original 240-acre land parcel now consists of eight acres of meticulously landscaped gardens and woods. Among the greenery is a swimming pool, a great place to find yourself after a day of wine tasting.

At-A-Glance Features

21 Rooms
Children Welcome
Complimentary Breakfast
Near Wineries
Pet-Friendly
Swimming Pool
Near Shops and Restaurants
Non-Smoking

Directions

From San Francisco, head north on Highway 101, taking the Central Healdsburg exit. Make a sharp left onto Mill at the second stop light, and go under the freeway. The manor arches will be straight ahead.

Credit Cards Accepted

Visa, MasterCard.

KENWOOD

THE KENWOOD INN & SPA

10400 Sonoma Highway
Kenwood, Sonoma County
Tel. 800/353-6966 or 707/833-1293
Fax: 707/833-1247
Web Address: www.kenwoodinn.com
E-mail: none
Rates: $320-450
3pm check-in
Year Opened: 1989
Innkeepers: Terrence and Roseann Grimm

Profile

The rolling hills of Sonoma County are blanketed with acres of gangly vines that will eventually transform sun-ripened grapes into grappa. The region offers more than a hint of Tuscan flair, but nowhere is *la dolce vita* more aptly demonstrated than behind the ornate gates of The Kenwood Inn and Spa.

The owners of this luxe inn have done an incredible job of transforming what used to be an antique shop into a divine Tuscan-style retreat, where serenity prevails among the 2,000 acres of vine-shrouded slopes. Upon crossing the inn's threshold, guests are transported to another continent as classical music wafts through the intimate lobby. Tucked behind the reception area is a mustard-stucco courtyard flanked with Juliet-style balconies, blooming flora and a fleet of olive trees.

A series of cobblestone steps, which meander past prize-winning roses and a collection of cascading fountains, ascend to the various Italianate villas. If it weren't for the staff's flawless English, you might be fooled into thinking you were vacationing near Florence or Rome, rather than San Francisco.

Accommodations

The ivy-covered main building and dining room are joined by a trio of smaller two-story Tuscan-style buildings with pitched roofs, graceful colonnades and flower-filled terra cotta pots lining the arched windows. Behind each door is a capsule of luxury with European antiques, plush fabric treatments, cushy feather beds cloaked in down comforters, private baths and working fireplaces. The elegant and airy ambiance is further heightened by a pair of French doors leading to a private balcony, where it's tempting to toast your good fortune by uncorking a bottle of complimentary wine left chilling near the hearth.

Amenities

Just obtaining a room at this chic hideaway is a major coup, as this is one of Northern California's most sought-after establishments. Be sure to make reservations well in advance, in order to take advantage of all The Kenwood Inn & Spa has to offer. For starters, each stay includes a Mediterranean-style breakfast served in the guest-only restaurant or on the adjoining terrace. The inn's spacious kitchen is inviting with its collection of copper cookware and helpful staff, and guests are welcome to wander in throughout the day to refuel. Coffee, tea and wine are available whenever the urge may strike, and a prix fix lunch is offered at an additional cost.

One of the major draws of The Kenwood Inn & Spa is, of course, the **spa**. The menu of massages and facials hover around the $90 mark for 50 minutes of uninterrupted pleasure. Couples in search of togetherness will want to request the 90-minute Ti Amo in-room massage, administered in tandem by candlelight and accompanied by a bottle of chilled champagne. Other pleasures that await include a full-size outdoor swimming pool and Jacuzzi shaded by a thatch of grape arbors.

At-A-Glance Features

12 Rooms
All-Day Beverage Service
Complimentary Breakfast
Full-Service, Guest-Only Restaurant
Full-Service Spa
Near Wineries
Nightly Turndown Service
Non-Smoking
Not Appropriate for Children
Swimming Pool and Jacuzzi
A 15-minute Drive from Sonoma's Historic Plaza

Directions

From San Francisco, take Highway 101 to Santa Rosa and exit onto Highway 12 at the fairgrounds. Follow signs to Sonoma for about 17 miles. The Kenwood Inn & Spa is located on the right-hand side just before the Glen Ellen turnoff.

Credit Cards Accepted
Visa, MasterCard, American Express.

CELEBRITY GAZING AT
THE KENWOOD INN & SPA

If you enjoy star gazing, you're best bet is to lounge poolside in broad daylight. Rich and famous guests have included Goldie Hawn, Elizabeth Shue, supermodel Christy Turlington and Bruce Willis.

NAPA

BLUE VIOLET MANSION

443 Brown Street
Napa, Napa County
Tel. 800/959-2583 or 707/253-2583
Fax: 707/257-8205
Web Address: www.bluevioletmansion.com
E-mail: bviolet@napanet.net
Rates: $199-359
3:30pm check-in
Year Opened: 1991
Innkeeper: Bob and Kathy Morris

Profile

The Blue Violet Mansion is a graceful 1886 Queen Anne Victorian and an elegant refuge for wine tasting trotters. A recipient of many awards, including a preservation Award of Excellence, as well as a Gold Award winner for Best Bed and Breakfast in North America, the Blue Violet Mansion is a romantic find.

Thick pillars, jutting gables, an expansive balcony, and endless embellishments entice those with an appreciation for the past. Because of the on-site ministry, couples looking to elope often find themselves saying "I do" behind the inn's massive doors. Even if you're not looking to tie the knot, the Blue Violet Mansion is an ideal place to sneak away for a special occasion. The inn is within walking distance to Napa's fine shops and restaurants, and close to all the wineries that have made this region famous.

Accommodations

The Blue Violet Mansion provides the well-trodden with a gamut of accommodations. Aside from the typical antique-filled room, the inn also provides a set of upgraded accommodations located on the third tier and christened the **Camelot Floor**. This exclusive sun-filled retreat is a departure from the oridinary. The common sitting area resembles a castle courtyard, and residents of this floor are treated to a complimentary hot beverage bar with access to snacks, cold beverages, ice and wine service.

The four fairy tale-esque rooms are tucked away in the mansion's dormers, creating unique and fantasy-like hideaways. All are graced with hand-painted murals and stained glass, which creates a stunning prism effect. Appointments may vary to include coffered ceilings, gas-burning fireplaces, two-person whirlpool spas and so on.

The first floor also offers a trio of rooms that are classified as **Grand Rooms**. These tend to be roomier than the standard offerings with sitting areas, eight-foot laced windows and garden views. Those guests not staying on either The Camelot Floor or in the Grand Rooms are 'banished' to another set of flats located on both the first and second stories. Many of these less expensive rooms offer elegant appointments such as granite and hardwood floors, regal four-poster beds, tandem spas and sitting areas. The **Duchess' Parlor**, located on the ground floor, was originally the mansion's dining room, and both **Queen Victoria's Room** and **His Majesty's Room** have private access to the inn's 50-foot balcony.

Each room is equipped with such comforts as plush bathrobes, reading material, candles and filled candy dishes. Televisions and VCRs are available to rent, but with all the ambiance found here there's hardly a need.

Amenities

Mornings at the Blue Violet Mansion begin with a two-course gourmet meal, which may include a fluffy quiche or omelet, an extra-thick slice of French toast or a fritatta. These filling dishes are accompanied by fresh fruits and juices, morning breads and cakes, and fresh coffees and teas. If you prefer to dine a bit more lightly, an optional breakfast basket can be delivered to your doorstep; private in-room breakfast service is also available. Guests are welcome to enjoy afternoon tea in the grand salon, and a stash of sweets and cookies are available throughout the evening.

The inn also houses an elegant restaurant in its grand salon. **Violette's at the Mansion** is a work of art with its faux sky ceiling, dangling chandeliers, and French and European-inspired menu. Should you wish to dine in private, a five-course candlelight dinner can be arranged in the comfort of your room. The innkeepers can fill other in-room requests such as wine and champagne service.

While most people are out wine tasting, you can stay behind and enjoy the swimming pool or outdoor spa. The gardens, with its abundance of roses, features a gazebo and swing.

At-A-Glance Features

17 Rooms
Children Welcome
Complimentary Breakfast
Complimentary Afternoon Tea
Concierge Service
En-Suite Massage
Full-Service Restaurant

Near Wineries
Non-Smoking
On-Site Ministry for Impromptu Weddings
Swimming Pool and Outdoor Spa
Winemaker Dinners
Within Walking Distance to Shops & Restaurants

Directions

From San Francisco, take the Interstate 80 across the Bay Bridge. Veer left and follow the signs toward Sacramento and continue on Interstate 80. Exit at Highway 37, and drive two miles to Highway 29 (Sonoma Boulevard) where you'll make a sharp right turn. Travel Highway 29 and upon reaching the fork in the road, veer left toward Calistoga. Continue until you reach the 1st Street exit. Turn right at the intersection onto California, and go three blocks. Make a left onto Oak, and continue to Brown Street. Turn right onto Brown Street. The mansion will be the second structure on your right.

Credit Cards Accepted

Visa, MasterCard, American Express, Discover, Diners Club.

CHURCHILL MANOR

485 Brown Street
Napa, Napa County
Tel. 707/253-7733
Fax: none
Web Address: www.churchillmanor.com
E-mail: churchill@napanet.net
Rates: $125-235
3pm check-in
Year Opened: 1987
Innkeepers: Joanna Guidotti and Brian Jensen

Profile

Churchill Manor is an imposing and grand structure built in 1889 and situated on a plum one-acre parcel. Spanning three stories and 10,000 square feet, the manor was built in the Second Empire fashion with a grand Greek Revival-style, three-sided verandah added circa 1907. This spectacular feature, supported by 20 fluted columns of both ionic and doric styles, creates an eclectic melding of architectural characteristics.

Only the interiors can rival the outer opulence. Original ribbon-grained crown redwood moldings surround the four parlors, while fluted columns elegantly frame the grand staircase. There are a quartet of magnificent fireplace mantels and the solarium floors, originally part of an outdoor patio, retain more than 60,000 19th century mosaic marble tiles.

Listed on the National Register of Historic Places and located in the Napa Abajo National Historic District, Churchill Manor is one of Napa's most inviting landmarks.

Accommodations

If you ever wanted to know what it felt like to be a character in an F. Scott Fitzgerald novel, here is your chance. Those who stay here feel as if they're an elite guest at an elegant estate rather than merely a visitor passing through.

The collection of 10 rooms vary in their appointments. Expect antiques, claw-foot tubs, reading nooks, two-person showers, stained glass, Victorian wall coverings, bay windows, gas-burning fireplaces and other thoughtful appointments. For those who prefer roomy digs, the **Edward Churchill Room** is the largest chamber and features an assembly of ornate French furnishings, a giant pedestal bathtub and a two-person shower. Even the original 19th century fireplace still has its gold-leaf tiles intact.

Amenities

If there is one thing Churchill Manor can offer, it's privacy. The inn's extensive front lawns are shrouded by tall hedges and flowering crabapple trees, which mix nicely with the century-old cedars and redwoods. Aspiring botanists can keep busy trying to name the 55 varieties of tree roses and other foliage.

As for dining, the inn serves an enjoyable breakfast in the sunroom between the hours of 8:30am and 10am. The more crafty guests sneak out to the sun-soaked verandah for some added privacy, where there is a choice of intimate eating areas. Mornings begin with a medley of fresh-baked muffins and croissants along with gourmet coffee, fresh-squeezed orange juice, a display of fresh fruit, granola and cereal. In addition, more hearty fare, such as omelets and French toast, is prepared by the manor's chef.

There are four parlors to prowl about, an evening wine and cheese social, a endless plate of cookies and old-fashioned lawn games. There are even tandem bicycles available to guests, providing a great way to travel the wine trail.

At-A-Glance Features

10 Rooms
Children 12 and Older Welcome
Complimentary Breakfast
Complimentary Tandem Bikes
Complimentary Wine and Cheese
Lawn Games
Near Wineries
Tandem Bicycles
Within Walking Distance to Shops & Restaurants

Directions

From San Francisco, take Interstate 80 across the Bay Bridge. Veer left and follow the signs toward Sacramento and continue on Interstate 80. Exit at Highway 37. Drive two miles to Highway 29 (Sonoma Boulevard), where you'll make a sharp right turn. Travel Highway 29, and when you reach the fork in the road veer left toward Calistoga. Continue until you reach the 1st Street/Downtown Napa exit.

Follow the signs towards Downtown Napa and at Jefferson Street, the first traffic light you'll approach, turn right. Travel two blocks and turn left on Oak Street. Continue for seven blocks to the corner of Oak and Brown. Turn right onto Brown Street and pull into the first parking lot on the right-hand side.

Credit Cards Accepted

Visa, MasterCard, American Express, Discover.

LA BELLE EPOQUE

1386 Calistoga Avenue
Napa, Napa County
Tel. 800/238-8070 or 707/257-2161
Fax: 707/226-6314
Web Address: www.labelleepoque.com
E-mail: innkeeper@labelleepoque.com
Rates: $169-295
3pm check-in
Year Opened: 1981
Innkeeper: Georgia Jump

Profile

Luther M. Turton, an esteemed architect responsible for designing many of Napa's buildings between 1876 and 1925, also built La Belle Epoque. The 1893 home was created for Herman Schwartz, a successful hardware merchant and community leader, who presented it to his daughter Minnie as a wedding gift. Her marriage took place in the parlor, but sadly she died a few years later during child birth.

Following her death, the house remained vacant for several years before the 150-member Eagle Cycling Club took it over as their club-house. Their most noted accomplishment was the construction of one of California's first cycling paths, which ran from Napa to nearby Vallejo. After the club vacated the premises, the Silva family, owners of Napa Soda Springs Mineral Water, purchased the estate for their family home in 1903 and remained here for the next 40 years. The following decades saw a succession of owners until finally, in 1981, the stately home became one of the region's first bed and breakfast inns.

Thankfully, La Belle Epoque survived such ghastly trends as avocado linoleum floors and cottage cheese-textured ceilings to remain a fine example of 19th century Queen Anne architecture.

Accommodations

Each of the six rooms located beneath La Belle Epoque's roof are named for a particular wine. Like the wine itself, the **Zinfandel** is a light and airy room with an elevated canopied bed and a stained-glass dormer window. The other vintages – **Pinot Noir, Gamay, Merlot, Chardonnay, Cabernet** and **Champagne** – are all very romantic with antiques, fireplaces, sitting areas and Victorian light fixtures. Champagne is the largest chamber and, being on the ground floor, it has its own private entrance as well as the exclusive use of the wine tasting room after 8pm, where a fireplace, wet bar and entertainment center are located.

Recently the innkeeper incorporated **The Buckley House** into the compound. Located across the street, this 1885 Victorian charmer was acquired in 1998. The pair of corner suites, **Elizabeth** and **Caroline**, named for the two sisters who lived here most of their lives, are quite spectacular with bay windows, separate living areas, private porches, fireplaces and elegant touches that allow for more privacy than the average room. Although there are no public rooms, if guests find themselves feeling lonely, all they have to do is wander across the street to the main house.

Each room has a telephone with voice mail, data port, TV and VCR.

Amenities

Each stay includes a full gourmet breakfast served in the inn's formal dining room at 9am. Should the weather prove cooperative, and it often does, then guests can request to dine on the rose garden patio. Those slumbering at The Buckley House are served their morning meal en suite at 9:15 am. Expect to be full after noshing on a spread of poached pears, blueberry blintzes, crepes Florentine and Grand Marnier French toast. Low-fat and vegetarian breakfasts can be prepared upon request; just be sure to let the innkeeper know when making a reservation.

In addition, an evening **wine and hors d'oeuvres hour** takes place in the wine cellar each evening, and a hospitality bar is available 24 hours a day at the antique service bar located in the center foyer. If you're traveling the wine trail, bring a picnic lunch with you from the inn. Included for about $17 per person is a hamper full of gourmet sandwiches, salads, fresh fruit and treats along with linens, cutlery, dishes, wine glasses and opener. In-room massages can also be arranged, and the innkeeper has been known to provide guests with complimentary tasting passes to some great area wineries.

At-A-Glance Features

8 Rooms
Children Welcome
Complimentary Breakfast
Complimentary Wine and Cheese
En-Suite Massage
Near Wineries
Within Walking Distance to Shops & Restaurants

Directions

From San Francisco, take Interstate 80 across the Bay Bridge. Veer left and follow the signs toward Sacramento and continue on. Exit at

Highway 37, and drive two miles to Highway 29 (Sonoma Boulevard) where you'll make a sharp right turn. Travel Highway 29, and when you reach the fork in the road veer left toward Calistoga. Continue until you reach the 1st Street/Downtown Napa exit.

Follow the signs towards Downtown Napa and at Jefferson Street, the first traffic light you'll encounter, turn left. Travel four blocks to Calistoga Avenue and turn right. The inn is located on the left-hand side of the street at the corner of Calistoga Avenue and Seminary Street.

Credit Cards Accepted

Visa, MasterCard, American Express, Discover.

OCCIDENTAL

THE INN AT OCCIDENTAL

3657 Church Street
Occidental, Sonoma County
Tel. 800/522-6324 or 707/874-1047
Fax: 707/874-1078
Web Address: www.innatoccidental.com
E-mail: innkeeper@innatoccidental.com
Rates: $175-320
3pm check-in
Year Opened: 1994
Innkeeper: Jack Bullard

Profile

A perfect blend of comfort, charm and elegance, The Inn at Occidental is a clandestine retreat resting on a redwood-laden hillside just above the historic village of Occidental. A homestead hailing from the 1870s, the Victorian manor has the honor of being one of the town's first homes. Eventually it became the location of the Occidental Water Bottling Company and, in 1988, it was finally transformed into a bed and breakfast inn.

In 1993, Jack Bullard, a law firm administrator and aspiring innkeeper, purchased the Heart's Desire, as it was then known. He transformed the quaint inn into a lodging showpiece bringing with him a treasure trove of family heirlooms, antiques, Tiffany silver and other bits of fancy to fill his new place of employment.

You'll discover architectural details from a bygone era with fir floors, wainscoted hallways, and hand-carved mantles. Located just minutes from Northern California's rugged coast, The Inn at Occidental provides an ideal base for exploring the Wine Country or just enjoying the outdoor beauty along the banks of the Russian River.

Accommodations

You'll find eight rooms located in the original house with appellations reflecting the owner's penchant for collecting objects d'art. On display in the **Sugar Room** are an assembly of 19th century pattern glass designed to hold coarsely ground sugar. The **Quilt Room** offers a bit of whimsy with a pair of five-foot scissors and a dramatic coverlet. In the **Marbles Suite** you'll find scores of antique marbles, in the **Cut Glass Room** you'll discover antique English and Irish cut glass, and in the **Tiffany Room** you'll find yourself admiring the stash of trademark silver pieces.

A newly built annex, which forms an L-shape overlooking the courtyard garden, contains eight additional chambers. These too reflect the owner's love for the unique with such names as the **Kitchen Cupboard Room**, the **Wild West Room** and the **Folk Art Room.** Perhaps the most endearing chamber is the **Heritage Room** bedecked with personal family keepsakes belonging to the innkeeper. On display are decades-old family photographs, a 1908 friendship quilt, and even a black velvet ermine collar evening coat belonging to the owner's mum.

Aside from the innovative motifs found behind closed doors, many rooms offer such appointments as fireplaces, spa tubs, sitting areas, private decks, antiques, and a stash of Crabtree and Evelyn toiletries.

Amenities

Awake each morning to a cup of Jack's Blend, a full-bodied coffee created by the owner with the help of a local roaster. The Wine Cellar dining room is where breakfast is served; feel free to wander in anytime between 8am and 10am to sample a delicious gourmet spread of entrees infused with inn-harvested herbs and bowls of homemade granola. Come afternoon, relax in an oversized wicker chair along the verandah while enjoying Sonoma County wines and light hors d'oeuvres, or sneak away to the English cottage garden and unwind while listening to the sound of trickling water being dispersed by an ornate fountain. Coffee, tea and soft drinks are also available throughout the day.

The inn also hosts **Winemaker Dinners** six times a year. The food and wine pairing events feature a six-course dinner served on antique china accompanied by crystal goblets containing prized vintages from local wineries. These much-anticipated gatherings, held throughout the year, are limited to just 42 guests and are guaranteed sell-out events.

At-A-Glance Features

16 Rooms
Children 12 and Older Welcome
Complimentary Breakfast
Complimentary Afternoon Wine and Cheese
Concierge Service
Near Wineries
Within Walking Distance to Shops and Restaurants

Directions

Head north from San Francisco, take Highway 101 and exit 116 west at Rohner Park/Sebastopol. Pass under the freeway and travel 7.4 miles to Sebastopol. Turn left onto Highway 12, following signs to Bodega Bay. Travel about 6.4 miles to Freestone, and turn right on Bohemian Highway. Travel for 3.7 miles to the town of Occidental. At the stop sign turn right and proceed up the hill to the inn's private parking lot.

Credit Cards Accepted

Visa, MasterCard, American Express, Discover.

RELAX WITH AN ENZYME BATH & MASSAGE IN OCCIDENTAL

*If you're looking for an out-of-body experience, pay a visit to **Osmosis** (Tel. 707/823-8231, www.osmosis.com), specializing in the Japanese method of enzyme baths and massage. Located just a few miles from the Inn at Occidental, guests are treated to a soothing cup of enzyme tea amid the Japanese gardens. Next a fragrant enzyme bath is administered, which is believed to be especially beneficial for people suffering from tension, fatigue and stress.*

Following the bath, guests shower and relax in a 30-minute blanket wrap or opt for a 75-minute Swedish/Esalen massage administered in an outdoor pagoda. Rates range from $65 to $140 with discounts afforded to parties of two or more.

SANTA ROSA

THE GABLES INN

4257 Petaluma Hill Road
Santa Rosa, Sonoma County
Tel. 800/422-5376 or 707/585-7777
Fax: 707/584-5634
Web Address: www.thegablesinn.com
E-Mail: innkeeper@thegablesinn.com
Rates: $135-225
3pm check-in
Year Opened: 1989
Innkeepers: Mike and Judy Ogne

Profile

Santa Rosa is a sophisticated community with a touch of small town ambiance. There's a bustling downtown shopping district complete with sidewalk cafes, coffeehouses that brew robust java, and plenty of boutiques and shops. Centered in the heart of California's Wine Country, Santa Rosa also offers some idyllic accommodations. Among the best offerings is The Gables Inn.

Newlyweds William and Mary Jane Roberts settled on this land in 1852. As the years slipped away, their family, dairy and farmlands grew. Finally, in 1876, the couple began work on what would become their home, and a year later the structure, now known as The Gables Inn, was completed. A near perfect example of High Victorian Gothic Revival, elegance prevails throughout. There are graceful 12-foot ceilings, a trio of Italian marble fireplaces, and a striking mahogany spiral staircase that vanishes to the second floor. Of course, the assembly of 15 gables that crown the innovative keyhole-shaped windows provides The Gables Inn with its own architectural flair.

Just an hour drive from San Francisco, The Gables Inn is an ideal base in which to explore the scenic Wine Country.

Accommodations

Considering the scope of what The Gables Inn offers in terms of accommodations, it's one of the more reasonably priced establishments in Sonoma County. Bedrooms are spacious, tastefully furnished and quietly romantic.

Each room has its own distinct decor, from Edwardian splendor to country chic to rooms that resemble a gentleman's study. **William and**

Mary's Cottage, named for the original owners, is a separate creekside annex. Private and somewhat secluded, guests are swathed in luxury with a whirlpool tub for two, an in-room hospitality bar, a wood-burning stove, TV and VCR, a video library, and a queen-size bed hidden in the upstairs loft. Of course, this is the most expensive room, but at $225 per night, it's still a bargain – especially in Sonoma County.

Amenities

Mornings at the inn begin with a hearty and creative breakfast. A pot of gourmet coffee sits alongside a pitcher of fresh-squeezed orange juice. The fruit course, which usually consists of fresh tropical fruit topped with amaretto cream, is followed by a selection of just-baked pastries. The main course usually resembles a work of art, and frittatas are the house specialty.

The Gables Inn is located on 3 1/2 acres, and guests are welcome to wander freely. There's a 150-year-old barn that now belongs to a family of owls, and the sun deck is a great place to enjoy a glass of wine. And, speaking of wine, remember that 175 of the state's best wineries are just a cork-toss away.

At-A-Glance Features

8 rooms
Children 12 and Older Welcome
Close to Shops and Restaurants
Complimentary Breakfast
Non Smoking
Near Wineries

Directions

Head north from San Francisco; on Highway 101 and exit Rohner Park Expressway. Turn right from the offramp, and travel 2 1/2 miles to Petaluma Hill Road. Make a left. The inn is approximately four miles ahead.

Credit Cards Accepted

Visa, MasterCard, American Express, Discover, Diners Club.

SONOMA

INN AT CEDAR MANSION
531 Second Street East
Sonoma, Sonoma County
Tel. 800/409-5496 or 707/938-3206
Fax: 707/935-7721
Web Address: www.cedarmansion.com
E-Mail: inn@cedarmansion.com
Rates: $365-445
3:30pm check-in
Year Opened: 2000
Innkeeper: Robert Kowal

Profile
This opulent 1876 Italianate Victorian mansion is tucked away in a neighborhood just off Sonoma's Historic Plaza. The home was built by Johann Frederick E. William Clewe and his wife Marie Reinsch, German immigrants who were drawn to Sonoma by the fortunes of California's Gold Rush.

Typifying the later period of Italianate architecture – the inn has been lauded as a classic, remarkable example of this style – the original mansion features such design elements as low-pitched, hipped deck roofs, as well as classical one-story and chamfered columns. Until the mid-1990s, the Inn at Cedar Mansion was a private residence having only had four owners, including the Cleves. After undergoing a multimillion dollar renovation, the five-bedroom inn has become one of the most desirable bed and breakfast establishments in the wine region.

Accommodations
Looking like the fortress it is, the Inn at Cedar Mansion is set behind an ornate iron gate. There are three suites in the mansion, one located downstairs and two on the upper floor. The **Verandah Suite** opens onto a private terrace and comes complete with a wood-burning Italian marble fireplace, crystal chandelier and roomy queen-size bed. A dramatic spiral staircase leads to the pair of suites above, each offering 13-foot ceilings, cozy sitting areas and views of the gardens. The remaining two suites, which were recently added to complement the original structure, are located in separate cottages near the pool. Both offer the ultimate in privacy with separate entrances and private enclosed patios, and are decorated in an airy fashion.

All suites are furnished with entertainment armoires complete with TV, DVD and CD players, private baths coated in marble with either shower or tub/whirlpool and shower, and two-line telephones with data ports, plus complimentary newspapers, nightly turndown service and guest robes.

Amenities

Guests have full run of the house. The kitchen, a gourmand's nirvana, has an open-door policy allowing guests to grab a cold beverage or snack anytime during the day. A sit-down breakfast, which is lavishly prepared on fine china, is served each morning in the mansion's elegant dining room. However, if you're the type who prefers to lounge in your robe or dislikes idle chit-chat, take your morning meal in either the privacy of your suite or poolside. Come evening, complimentary wine and hors d'oeuvres are served in the parlor, and private dining or picnic lunches are available by advance request.

The mansion is surrounded by two acres of manicured lawns, tended gardens, fruit trees and a wisteria-covered porch with classical music piped throughout. There is also a swimming pool and tennis court on the premises, and with only a maximum of 10 guests you'll likely never encounter a problem grabbing a teak chaise or partaking in a friendly game of tennis. There are also a collection of Adirondack chairs scattered about the estate. Full-service luxury also includes **in-room spa services** such as massage, reflexology, body scrubs and wraps.

At-A-Glance Features

5 Rooms
Complimentary Breakfast
Complimentary Evening Wine and Hors d'oeuvres
Complimentary Newspaper
En-Suite Spa Services
Near Sonoma's Historic Plaza and Wineries
Not Appropriate for Children
Swimming Pool
Tennis Court

Directions

From San Francisco, take Highway 101 north to Highway 37 east to Highway 121 north to Highway 116. Highway 116 will become Arnold Drive. Take Arnold Drive to Watmaugh Road and go right. Take a left at Broadway, which is also Highway 12. As you enter the town of Sonoma, Highway 12 becomes Broadway. Continue until you reach Sonoma Plaza and City Hall. Turn right on East Napa Street, continue past the stop sign at 1st Street East to 2nd Street East. Turn right, and the Inn at Cedar Mansion is immediately on your right.

Credit Cards Accepted

Visa, MasterCard, American Express, Discover.

MACARTHUR PLACE

29 East MacArthur Street
Sonoma, Sonoma County
Tel. 800/722-1866 or 707/938-2929
Web Address: www.macarthurplace.com
E-Mail: info@macarthurplace.com
Rates: $150-375 – a two-night minimum is required on peak season weekends
4pm check-in
Year Opened: 1998
Innkeeper: Bill Blum

Profile

If you favor a B&B getaway and your traveling companion prefers the comforts of a full-service resort, then MacArthur Place is the ideal compromise. With an award-winning restaurant and deluxe spa located on the premises, MacArthur Place has the feel of a small inn rather than a typical bed and breakfast establishment.

Located on the former estate of David Burris, a prominent Missouri transplant and local farmer, the original 16-room house dates back to the 1850s and is reported to be one of the oldest Victorian homes in the area. One look around, and it's hard to tell where the old ends and the new begins.

Accommodations

Located behind a white picket fence near Nathanson Creek are the original house and a collection of newer cottages. Whether you choose to stay in the original structure or in a recently constructed annex, all boasting garden views, the present owners have been careful to preserve the architectural integrity. The interiors vary, but follow the same style with soothing color schemes, four-poster beds, sitting areas with apothecary-style coffee tables and plush chairs. Modern-day comforts, such as oversized showers, cable television, CD players and dual line telephones with data port and voice mail, blend tradition with convenience.

Guests are also invited to enjoy the grounds. Stroll through the rose gardens, lounge by the swimming pool or gather with fellow guests around the outdoor fireplace for a nightcap.

Amenities

A visit to the **spa** is highly recommended. Enjoy an array of ancient Indian rejuvenation treatments as well as more western techniques such as aromatherapy facials and body treatments. Tai Chi and Yoga classes are also available, as well as hiking and biking excursions.

The hotel's signature restaurant, **Saddles**, is housed in a century-old barn and features a carnivorous menu of corn-fed prime beef steaks, filets, ribs and chicken. This is also where a complimentary buffet breakfast is served each morning.

At-A-Glance Features

35 Rooms (64 after expansion)
Children Welcome
Complimentary Breakfast
Complimentary Afternoon Wine & Cheese
Concierge Service
Full-Service Restaurant
Full-Service Spa
Near Sonoma's Historic Plaza and Wineries
Nightly Turndown Service
Non-Smoking
Swimming Pool

Directions

From San Francisco, take Highway 101 north to Highway 37 east to Highway 121 north to Highway 116. Highway 116 will become Arnold Drive. Take Arnold Drive to Watmaugh Road and go right. Take a left at Broadway, which is also Highway 12. As you enter the town of Sonoma, turn right at the first stop-light, which is MacArthur Street. The inn is located one block down on the right.

Credit Cards Accepted

Visa, MasterCard, American Express, Discover.

RAMEKINS

430 W. Spain Street
Sonoma, Sonoma County
Tel. 707/933-0450
Fax: 707/933-0451
Web Address: www.ramekins.com
E-Mail: info@ramekins.com
Rates: $124-250
3:30pm check-in
Year Opened: 1998
Innkeeper: Suzanne Brangham

Profile

The red-tiled roof and peach-tinged stucco building housing Ramekins may not have much of a past, considering it was built just a few years ago, but what takes place inside is sure to make history.

Ramekins is both a bed and breakfast as well as a cooking school, allowing guests to dabble in the culinary arts if they choose. Located just a short distance from the town plaza, Ramekins is the only one if its kind in Sonoma Valley catering to the home chef. Renowned experts, authors and culinary pros from across the nation arrive throughout the year to inspire students. By offering such courses, Ramekins gives new meaning to the term "bed and breakfast."

Accommodations

Ramekins is both sophisticated and whimsical. The first floor is where the public is welcome to browse through the well-stocked **Kitchen Shop**, where a selection of cookbooks, chef's apparel, cutlery and kitchenware is on display and available for purchase. It is also on this floor where the test kitchens are located, as well as banquet facilities and an expansive courtyard. Beyond the doors is a working herb garden tended to by the plethora of visiting chefs.

Dividing the first floor from the half-dozen guest rooms that reside on the second floor is a balustrade designed to look like asparagus spears. Spacious in size, rooms offer either king- or queen-size beds with a single room offering twin beds for platonic travelers. Appointments vary to include expansive balconies overlooking a garden patio where 75-year-old olive trees thrive, beds cloaked in custom-made down comforters, a spray of antique pine furnishings, private oversized bathrooms with walk-in showers, cable television, air-conditioning and modem-ready telephones with voice mail. Chambers are also adorned with food-related artwork and strewn with a collection of culinary journals.

Amenities

Located on the same floor as the guest rooms is a cozy breakfast area where freshly-baked pastries, fresh-squeezed orange juice, and a medley of fruit are served along with tea and coffee.

Overnight guests can sign-up for an array of **cooking classes** at an additional charge. Recent classes have included Appetizers from the Grill, Bold Spa Cuisine, and Thai Curry Workshop. Thomas Keller of French Laundry fame stopped by recently to converse with guests and sign copies of his best-selling culinary epic, *The French Laundry Cookbook.*

At-A-Glance Features

6 Rooms
Children 12 and Older Welcome
Complimentary Breakfast
Cooking Classes
Near Sonoma's Historic Plaza and Wineries
On-Site Culinary Store

Directions

Take Highway 12 towards Sonoma. As you enter the town of Sonoma, Highway 12 becomes Broadway. Continue until you reach Sonoma Plaza where you'll turn left. Make an immediate right onto First Street West, and turn left at the stop sign onto West Spain Street. Ramekins is four blocks ahead on your right.

Credit Cards Accepted

Visa, MasterCard.

RAMEKINS' CULINARY ASSISTANT PROGRAM

If you want to participate in Ramekins highly-regarded culinary courses and save some money at the same time, you might consider becoming an instructor's assistant. Arranged by prior approval, chosen ones can save 50-75% off class fees. Call the inn for details, Tel. 707/933-0450.

ST. HELENA

CINNAMON BEAR BED & BREAKFAST

1407 Kearney Street
St. Helena, Napa County
Tel. 888/963-4600 or 707/963-4653
Fax: 707/963-0251
Web Address: none
E-mail: cinnamonbear@worldnet.att.net
Rates: $125-190
4pm check-in
Year Opened: 1980
Innkeeper: Cathye Ranieri

Profile

I have a special fondness for this particular bed and breakfast. It was here, on a rainy February evening, that my husband and I settled in for a few nights on our Northern California honeymoon. While it may not be the Wine Country's most elaborate inn, it certainly has all the hallmarks to create a memorable stay.

Tucked behind downtown St. Helena on a quiet residential street, the homey Cinnamon Bear Bed & Breakfast is housed in a two-story, shingled craftsman bungalow. Built in 1904 as a wedding gift for the bride of Walter Metzner, who eventually became mayor of the town, this is simplicity at its best.

While you may have to hop in your car to explore the plethora of wineries, when it comes to strolling about St. Helena, you are within walking distance to just about everything worthwhile.

Accommodations

With only three rooms, it's impossible to feel crowded here. The rooms are located on the second floor, and each offers an eclectic mix of antiques with cast-iron beds, simple armoires, free-standing mirrors, and claw-foot tubs. Handmade quilts and an army of vintage teddy bears stand guard throughout.

The center room, the inn's most spacious, provides gazing views of the Napa Valley through a single dormer window and a king-size bed. The other two rooms are equipped with queen-size beds and are equal opportunity charmers.

Amenities

Ascending the steep steps to the Cinnamon Bear Bed & Breakfast is a bit of a déjà vu. Not that you've ever been here before, but there is definitely an air of familiarity. Perhaps it brings back childhood memories of trips to grandma's, or maybe a favorite aunt had a home as inviting.

Gleaming hardwood floors, coupled with original arts and crafts appointments, create an unpretentious setting. The main floor is tidy with an inviting sitting room warmed by a fireplace, and a pair of formal dining rooms with the original redwood wainscoting still intact. It's here that a hearty breakfast is served by the chef-cum-innkeeper who whips up filling fare with items like Panettone French Toast, an Italian brioche dipped in cinnamon-almond egg batter, griddled and served with fresh pear butter or a crop of seasonal berries. When the weather is cooperative, the wraparound front porch, in all its wicker glory, offers some of the best seats in the house for a morning meal.

Afternoon refreshments include cloud-like chocolate chip cookies and other edibles, plus there are sherry and sweets displayed each evening alongside non-alcoholic beverages. On warm summer nights, bring home a bottle of wine from one of the local vintners and drink in the evening calm from the terrace.

At-A-Glance Features

3 Rooms
Children 10 and Older Welcome
Complimentary Breakfast
Complimentary Sherri and Snacks
Near Wineries
Non-Smoking
Within Walking Distance to Shops and Restaurants

Directions

Head north on Highway 101 from San Francisco. Take Highway 37 east to Highway 121 to Highway 29 north (the main artery through Napa Valley). At Adams turn left and proceed two blocks. Turn right on Kearney. The inn will be on your left-hand side at the corner of Kearney and Adams.

Credit Cards Accepted

Visa, MasterCard, American Express.

THE INK HOUSE

1575 St. Helena Highway
St. Helena, Napa County
Tel. 707/963-3890
Fax: 707/968-0739
Web Address: http://inkhouse.com
E-mail: inkhousebb@aol.com
Rates: $100-205
3pm check-in
Year Opened: 1980
Innkeeper: Diane DeFilipi

Profile

The Ink House, named for its original owner Theron H. Ink, has been a fixture in Napa Valley since 1884. Listed on the National Register of Historic Places, this Italianate Victorian manor was where Ink, along with his wife, raised their children while involving himself with many hometown ventures.

Perhaps the inn's most notable architectural element is the glass-enclosed cupola jutting from the rooftop. From here, guests have a 360-degree view of the rolling vineyards and sloping hillsides. Scottish stained-glass windows create magical prisms in the snug 12 x 20 room, and guests often choose to spend some reflective time in this hidden nook.

Nearby is a surfeit of attractions: museums, gourmet grocers, wineries and tasting rooms, not to mention a cache of excellent restaurants. Another ideal way to enjoy the scenery is aboard the Wine Train, a slow-moving link of rail cars connecting Napa's small hamlets, which chugs past the vineyards as passengers nosh on gourmet foods and sample local vintages.

Accommodations

With its elegant architecture, national landmark status and envious address, The Ink House manages to avoid any pretense. The emphasis is on enjoying the home and its surroundings to the fullest, so guests are encouraged to relax and feel as comfortable here as they would in their own abode.

Each of the five guest rooms are situated on the second floor and are flanked with heirloom antiques and curious collectibles. Though the rooms vary with amenities, each offers a queen-size bed, private bath and an eclectic mix of styles including French, English, American, Georgian, Eastlake and Italian. A small common parlor is also located on this floor.

Amenities

Mornings are bountiful with a full gourmet breakfast of baked pears topped with cream, fresh-baked breads, hot entrees and a helping of the innkeeper's signature Bella Torta. In the late afternoon, wine and appetizers are served along with a selection of brandy and ports. Throughout the year the innkeeper spontaneously invites winemakers to pour for guests, sharing with them their knowledge of the industry.

Lounge on the wraparound verandah, in the glass-enclosed observatory or on the garden swing. If you're in the mood for some music, pay a visit to the first floor parlors where a concert grand piano and 1870-era pump organ reside. There is also a pool table located in the stone cellar, bicycles for exploring the wineries, and a video library.

At-A-Glance Features

5 Rooms
Complimentary Bicycles
Complimentary Breakfast
Complimentary Wine and Appetizers
Near Wineries
Non-Smoking
Not Appropriate for Children
Picnic Area

Directions

Head north on Highway 101 from San Francisco. Take Highway 37 east to Highway 121 to Highway 29 north (the main artery through Napa Valley). At Whitehall make a left. The inn is located on Highway 29 at Whitehall.

Credit Cards Accepted

Visa, MasterCard.

6. THE BAY AREA

HALF MOON BAY

CYPRESS INN

407 Mirada Road
Half Moon Bay, San Mateo County
Tel. 800/832-3224 or 650/726-2249
Fax: 650/712-0380
Web Address: www.cypressinn.com
E-mail: lodging@cypressinn.com
Rates: $215-365
3pm check-in
Year Opened: 1989
Innkeeper: Dan Floyd and Suzie Lankes

Profile

The Ritz-Carlton is staking its claim in Half Moon Bay, but it'll face some stiff competition from Cypress Inn. Never mind that there are only a dozen rooms – that's part of the allure – but it's the amenities and breathtaking views that will likely give the tony Ritz a run for its money.

The emphasis at Cypress Inn is on solitude, seaside living and sublime surroundings. The contemporary design features jutting balconies, a pitched roof, expansive windows, skylights and maximum views. As for noise, the inn has its share of distractions, like the sound of gently rolling waves crashing onto the shore.

Accommodations

The general consensus at Cypress Inn, at least when it comes to decor, is to invite the outside indoors with a palette of muted colors borrowed from the sea, sky and earth. A menagerie of hand-carved wooden animals and Mexican folk art, along with natural pine and wicker accents, further create a fuss-free environment.

Rooms are housed in two buildings, the **Main Building** and the **Beach House Building**. The former contains eight of the units named for natural elements, while the latter offers just four. All rooms are capsules of luxury, but if you're going to stay here go ahead and pay a little extra for a balcony overlooking the ocean. Your best bets are the second and third floor accommodations in the Main Building (**El Cielo**, **El Viento**, **La Lluvia**, and **Las Nubes**). **Dunes Beach** in the Beach House Building is another fine choice. All rooms are equipped with soaking tubs, color televisions, fireplaces, VCRs and terra cotta heated floors.

Amenities

The emphasis at Cypress Inn is privacy, which is why so many Bay Area locals and dot-commers from Silicon Valley are frequent visitors. Breakfast is served in the dining area, but the staff is more than willing to deliver a hot morning meal to your room upon request. Afternoon tea, wine and cheese are also part of the package.

The inn employs a **resident masseuse**, who works from her studio atop the third floor. She offers everything from foot reflexology to traditional body treatments to lessons in the art of massage for interested couples.

At-A-Glance Features

12 Rooms
Complimentary Breakfast
Complimentary Afternoon Tea, Wine and Cheese
Non-Smoking
Not Appropriate for Children
Within Walking Distance to Shops, Restaurants and Beach

Directions

From San Francisco, head south on Highway 101 and take Highway 92 westbound to Half Moon Bay. Turn right onto Cabrillo Highway/Highway 1 north. At Mirada Road turn left.

Credit Cards Accepted
Visa, MasterCard, American Express, Discover.

MILL ROSE INN
615 Mill Street
Half Moon Bay, San Mateo County
Tel. 800/900-7673 or 650/726-8750
Fax: 650/726-3031
Web Address: www.millroseinn.com
E-mail: info@millroseinn.com
Rates: $230-360
3pm check-in
Year Opened: 1982
Innkeepers: Terry and Eve Baldwin

Profile
It takes the right mix to not only open a bed and breakfast, but to create a magical retreat for unsuspecting guests. The owners of the Mill Rose Inn definitely have what it takes to be innovators as well as innkeepers. Eve's expertise in interior and floral design, coupled with Terry's skills as a landscape contractor, have resulted in a wondrous seaside retreat.

The duo spent a good chunk of the 1970s restoring this turn-of-the-century cottage, and their sweat equity has certainly paid off. The home is now a four-diamond inn and one of the most sought-after escapes to grace the Bay Area. Together the Baldwins have turned this once shabby shack into their own thriving 'cottage' industry.

Accommodations
The half-dozen rooms at the Mill Rose Inn are bona fide boudoirs, bordering on decadent. Oversized beds, claw-foot tubs designed for two, and deep burgundy accents are just some of the appointments you'll encounter. Each room features sprays of fresh flowers, private entrances, European antiques, hand-painted tiles framing the fireplaces and sinks, and claw-foot tubs. There's a few bells and whistles, things like cable television and VCRs, stereos, video libraries, phones, well-stocked refrigerators and Japanese dressing robes for lounging.

Roses are an underlying theme, and the room's names say it all: the **Burgundy Rose**, the **Briar Rose**, the **Bordeaux Rose Suite**, the **Renaissance Rose Suite**, the **Baroque Rose**, and the **Botticellie Rose**. Each is uniquely opulent and ultimately romantic. It's the type of place you'd hope to be stranded on a rainy afternoon.

Amenities

If morning mingling isn't your idea of a vacation, you'll be glad to know that breakfast is delivered to your room each morning along with a copy of the *San Francisco Chronicle*. Socializing occurs during the afternoon wine and cheese hour, but you can fill a plate and glass and enjoy this from your room as well. There is also a fantastic dessert table to which you'll want to give careful consideration.

Guests can also use the enclosed garden Jacuzzi spa at their leisure with robes, towels and spa slippers provided. Picnic baskets and beach towels are also provided, just ask. And, come bedtime, evening turndown service includes more flowers and chocolate.

At-A-Glance Features

6 Rooms
Complimentary Breakfast
Complimentary Afternoon Wine, Cheese and Dessert
Complimentary Newspaper
Evening Turndown Service
Not Appropriate for Children
Outdoor Jacuzzi
Within Walking Distance to Shops, Restaurants and Beach

Directions

From San Francisco head south on Highway 101, and take Highway 92 westbound to Half Moon Bay. Turn left at Main Street, this will be the first signal, and then right onto Mill Street. The inn is at the end of the block on the right-hand side.

Credit Cards Accepted

Visa, MasterCard, American Express, Discover, Diners Club.

OLD THYME INN

779 Main Street
Half Moon Bay, San Mateo County
Tel. 800/720-4277 or 650/726-1616
Fax: 650/726-6394
Web Address: www.oldthymeinn.com
E-mail: innkeeper@oldthymeinn.com
Rates: $140-290
3pm check-in
Year Opened: 1988
Innkeepers: Rick and Kathy Ellis

Profile

At the turn of the century, 1898 to be exact, local druggist George Gilcrest built this home for his family. The manor is a fine example of "spindle post," a folk-style Victorian blend sometimes referred to as Princess Anne. The Gilcrests were a respected and prominent family, and remained in the area until the 1950s. The local drug store, which continued to operate under the Gilcrest name, closed its doors for good some 20 years later.

The home was a private residence for many years, as well as the headquarters for the school board and various other enterprises. In 1987 the residence, which sits behind a white picket fence, was transformed into a bed and breakfast inn, and its present owners have completely redecorated it from top to bottom, revamping the gardens, menus and overall amenities to create an impressive Bay Area destination.

Accommodations

There are seven rooms at the inn whose names are taken from the well-tended garden just beyond the front door: **Garden**, **Thyme**, **Rosemary**, **Mint**, **Lavender**, **Chamomile** and **Oregano**. The collection is thoughtfully decorated with antiques, original art and bouquets of fresh flowers. Each contains a fireplace and/or whirlpool tub à deux plus television and VCR, data port and a stash of spa amenities.

There is no wrong choice when selecting a room at the Old Thyme Inn. Two rooms are located on the ground floor, while the remainder are located on the second level. With the turn of a crystal doorknob, you'll discover a comfortable and inviting chamber to call home, at least for the time being. The **Garden Room** is the most expensive of the lot, but worth every penny just to have the pleasure of spending the night in the handsome, carved wood four-poster bed and be waited on at sunrise with breakfast served en suite. On the other end of the spectrum, the least expensive room is just as enchanting only on a smaller scale. Those rooms

sandwiched in between run the gamut from masculine to bold to delicate
– take your pick.

Amenities

Before breakfast, sink into one of the parlor's overstuffed sofas to mull
over the day's events and enjoy a cup of coffee. Breakfast, served from 8-
9:30am in the dining room, is filling with extraordinary offerings such as
lemon-cheese pancakes, zucchini soufflé and basil featherbed eggs.

Evenings are typically cool, so it's not uncommon to find the patio's
chiminea fireplace at full blaze while guests unwind over glass of wine.
Those homesick for their pets will find Jenny, the resident Kerry Blue
Terrier, an adequate substitute. And, while the inn doesn't offer spa
services, you can book a treatment at **Primrose Country Day Spa**, *Tel.
650/726-1244*, located just two blocks away.

At-A-Glance Features

7 Rooms
Complimentary Breakfast
Complimentary Wine and Cheese
Not Appropriate for Children
Within Walking Distance to Shops, Restaurants and Beach

Directions

From San Francisco, head south on Highway 101 and take Highway 92
westbound to Half Moon Bay. Turn left at Main Street (this will be the first
signal) and continue for six blocks. The inn will be on your left-hand side.

Credit Cards Accepted

Visa, MasterCard, American Express, Discover.

WINE, HORSES, GOLF & RELAXATION IN HALF MOON BAY

*There's not a lot to do in Half Moon Bay, and frankly that's the whole
reason for coming. There's wine tasting at **Obester Winery** on San Mateo
Road, Tel. 650/726-9463, beachfront horseback riding, shopping along
historical Main Street, or golfing at **Half Moon Bay Golf Links**, Tel. 650/
726-4438. For area activities and attractions, contact the **Half Moon Bay
Chamber of Commerce and Visitors' Bureau** at 650/726-8380 or
www.halfmoonbaychamber.org. For the relaxation-challenged, San Francisco is just an hour away.*

IVERNESS

BLACKTHORNE INN
266 Vallejo Avenue
Iverness, Marin County
Tel. 415/663-8621
Fax: 415/663-8635
Web Address: www.blackthorneinn.com
E-mail: susan@blackthorneinn.com
Rates: $175-300
4pm check-in
Year Opened: 1982
Innkeeper: Susan and Bill Wigert

Profile
If you were one of those kids who longed for a tree house to call your own, then welcome to the Blackthorne Inn.

Located on Point Reyes Peninsula, about an hour's drive north of San Francisco, the inn is a playhouse for adults. What started out as a modest weekend retreat for its owners somehow evolved into a modern-day Swiss Family Robinson habitat. Some of the beams were acquired from the San Francisco Pier and hearthstones were collected from Donners Pass. As for the spiral staircase, sky bridge, fireman's pole and ladders, we'll chalk that up to creative licensing on both the part of the owners and the builders.

Though it's unlikely you'll depart with skinned knees, the whimsical architecture creates an urge to act like a kid again...a very well-behaved kid.

Accommodations
Crafted from redwood, cedar and Douglas fir, the four-level inn is lavishly rustic with just five rooms and outrageously unique appointments. The **Forest View Suite**, a first-level hideaway, is the most spacious of the lot with a glass wall opening onto a secluded redwood deck complete with private entrance and separate sitting room. The **Overlook**, a lofty chamber with stained-glass windows and a pair of small balconies, offers views of both the landscape and the main living room.

Without a doubt the **Eagle's Nest** is the most fetching with an octagonally shaped, glass-enclosed cupola offering 360-degree views. Situated in a tower-like setting, though not quite as dramatic as Rapunzel's digs but pretty close, it takes a little finesse to reach the bathroom, located in an annex just on the other side of the catwalk-style sky bridge. After

10pm, the communal hot tub is strictly off limits to all guests except those residing in this treetop chamber.

Amenities

If you think the rooms are spectacular, wait until you get a look at the public offerings. The main level, surrounded by a 3,500-square-foot deck, is a retreat in itself. Luxurious and sprawling, guests can stake claim to any number of tables and chairs shaded by tall, leafy trees. On cooler days, stay warm inside the confines of the glass solarium, whose doors were salvaged from the old San Francisco railroad depot. The adjoining living room, in all its A-frame glory, is another place to unwind with the latest magazine in hand. A great stone hearth and wet bar area create added comfort.

Coffee and juice are available for early birds, and a breakfast buffet is served each morning at 9:30am. With advanced notice, a take-away breakfast can also be arranged and enjoyed in your room, and afternoon refreshments are also included. The hot tub is also for everyone's use and remains available until 10pm.

Point Reyes National Seashore, a collection of jagged cliffs, craggy coastline, avis sanctuaries and other treasures left by mother nature, is ideal for exploring. **Tomales Bay** is caked with die-hard kayakers, and for those who want to glimpse the mighty gray whales as they make their annual migration south to Mexico, just follow the trailing steps, about 300 of them, down to the **Point Reyes Lighthouse**.

At-A-Glance Features

5 Rooms
Close to Beaches and Wildlife
Complimentary Breakfast
Complimentary Afternoon Refreshments
Non-Smoking
Not Appropriate for Children
Outdoor Hot Tub

Directions

From San Francisco, follow Highway 101 north across the Golden Gate Bridge. Take the Sir Francis Drake Boulevard/San Anselmo Exit. Travel west on Sir Francis Drake Boulevard, through the redwoods of Samuel P. Taylor Park and to the village of Olema. Turn right onto Route One/Shoreline Highway and proceed for approximately two miles. Turn left just before the green bridge, and continue for another mile, keeping your eyes peeled for a green city sign that says Iverness Park. Just beyond the bend, take a left onto Vallejo Avenue (a bakery and grocer are located on the corner). The Blackthorne Inn is almost at the end of the road on the right-hand side.

Credit Cards Accepted
Visa, MasterCard, American Express.

MUSIC & DANCING NEAR IVERNESS

Huey Lewis fans (remember him?) take note: Bob Brown, owner of **Rancho Nicasio** *in nearby Nicasio, Tel. 415/662-2219, about a 15-minute drive from Iverness, is also the manager of this 1980s lead singer and co-star of the recent film* **Duets** *with Gwenyth Paltrow. An extensive menu is flavored with live music and dancing on weekends. Call for directions.*

SANDY COVE INN
12990 Sir Francis Drake Boulevard
Iverness, Marin County
Tel. 800/759-2683 or 415/669-2683
Fax: 415/669-7511
Web Address: www.sandycove.com
E-mail: innkeeper@sandycove.com
Rates: $185-275
4pm check-in
Year Opened: 1979
Innkeeper: Kathy and Gerry Coles

Profile
Except for maybe diamonds, bigger doesn't necessarily mean better. Case in point is the Sandy Cove Inn. This gem of a hideaway contains only three rooms, but they are among the best you'll find in the Bay Area.

The inn, in all its shingled glory, looks as if it were plucked from the shores of Cape Cod. Located on a plum four-acre beachfront sprawl overlooking Tomales Bay, Sandy Cove Inn puts an emphasis on privacy, not pomp. Yes, you may become friendly with fellow nesters but only by mutual choice. And, if you start to miss city life, San Francisco is just an hour's drive to the south, making for a convenient day trip. But most people who come to Iverness, especially those staying at Sandy Cove Inn, are trying to flee the big city, not the other way around.

Accommodations

Sandy Cove Inn doesn't aspire to be the region's biggest inn, just the best. So far it's doing an outstanding job.

With only three secluded rooms, that means only six guests at any given time, life at the inn is peaceful. This is the type of place you'd want to hole up in if you were a writer or poet – just you, your imagination and the breathtaking scenery right outside your door. The triad of rooms, each with private entrances and fireplaces, are graced with antique pine and wicker furnishings with special attention paid to detail. Uncluttered and refreshingly simple with Turkish Kilim rugs and original artwork, it's sometimes hard to convince yourself that there is more to admire than those things that lie between the four walls. All you have to do is step onto your private sun deck to discover some unexpected pleasures.

Rooms come equipped with small refrigerators, coffee makers, cassette players and a selection of tapes, oversized bath towels, telephones, plush robes and candles for a little added ambiance – not that this place needs any help.

Amenities

Even though this stretch of coast is often chilly, don't bother over-packing. Layered clothes are recommended, but anything else you may need has already been taken care of, including robes and slippers, binoculars and backpacks, even walking sticks. At some point during the day be sure to arrange for **an en-suite therapeutic massage** administered fireside.

Breakfast, a feast seasoned with herbs and organic produce from the inn's garden, is served in either the Solarium, complete with bay views, or in the privacy of your suite. Menus vary and include fresh fruit, pumpkin pecan pancakes and other innovative fare unlikely to surface again in your lifetime.

An added attraction are the horses, deer and sheep that graze in the shadow of the inn. Simply sway back and forth in one of the garden hammocks and enjoy the show. Surrounded by the **Point Reyes National Seashore**, there is plenty to do, including doing nothing at all.

At-A-Glance Features

3 Rooms
Close to Beaches and Wildlife
Complimentary Breakfast

En-Suite Massage
Non-Smoking
Not Appropriate for Children

Directions

From San Francisco, follow Highway 101 north across the Golden Gate Bridge. Take the Central San Rafael exit, and turn left at the second traffic light. Continue west on 3rd Street/Sir Francis Drake Boulevard for about a half hour until you reach the town of Olema. At Highway 1 turn right, then make a left at Bear Valley Road. Continue three miles to the stop sign, and turn left onto Sir Francis Drake Boulevard. Continue for approximately four miles to the village of Iverness and continue for another mile.

After Barnaby's Restaurant, which will be on your right, look for an orange school bus sign just before the inn's entrance. The inn will be on your right, just past the restaurant, on Tomales Bay. If you hit Camino Del Mar, you've gone too far.

Credit Cards Accepted

Visa, MasterCard, American Express, Discover, Diners Club.

MUIR BEACH

PELICAN INN
Highway 1
Muir Beach, Marin County
Tel. 415/383-6000
Fax: 415/383-3424
Web Address: www.pelicaninn.com
E-mail: innkeeper@pelicaninn.com
Rates: $158-190
3pm check-in
Year Opened: 1978
Innkeeper: Katrinka McKay

Profile

Pelican Inn is a magnet for Anglophiles and transplanted Brits homesick for the taste of bangers and warm beer. Created by a fourth generation English publican, the Inn looks more like it belongs on the shores of Devon instead of the less formal California coast.

Fashioned after a 16th century Tudor-style inn, the fleet of leaded windows, inglenook fireplace, used bricks and chunky beams lend a sense of authenticity. The inn's restaurant is a study in the British culinary arts and the adjoining pub, in all its English glory, would have put Winston Churchill at ease.

The inn's location is another plus. Situated just 20 minutes north of the Golden Gate Bridge, guests can travel from Fisherman's Wharf to merry old England in record time.

Accommodations

A narrow stairway leads from the main level to the second floor where the guest rooms, numbered one through seven, are located. English formality is slightly evident behind each door with heavily draped canopy beds and leaded glass windows casting light on the spray of English antiques, fresh-cut flowers, and sherry-filled decanters. Though Agatha Christie would not have been inspired (there's just not enough old dusty things), the editors of *Architectural Digest* may be impressed with the inn's overall elegance. In keeping with the 16th century theme, phones and televisions simply don't exist.

Amenities

Culinary history has never been kind to the British. Or is it the other way around? Never mind, you'll be pleased with the choices offered at breakfast. Aside from bacon and eggs, bangers, grilled tomatoes, toast, tea and coffee, the inn also provides cereal and oatmeal for the light eater.

The inn's restaurant offers a hearty blend of English country fare for lunch and dinner with such typical dishes as prime rib, Yorkshire pudding and cottage pie alongside some more contemporary offerings like chicken breast sautéed in garlic, rack of lamb, and linguini served with a medley of fresh vegetables. The pub is a lesson in British tradition with a list of fine ales, draft beers, lagers and stouts as well as wines, sherries and ports representing various parts of the globe. Adjoining the bar is what is known as a "snug," a semiprivate sitting room where, in less modern times, the publican would entertain special guests and people staying at the inn. In keeping with tradition, this annex is strictly for the use of overnight guests.

The inn's location unleashes the nature lover within, offering a menagerie of nearby hiking and equestrian trails, beaches and a stunning grove of redwoods at **Muir Woods**. And, for a littled added revelry, plan to motor up for Mary, Queen of Scot's Birthday Bash or Bobbie Burns Night. If you miss those, there's always Maypole Dancing and Celtic singing to look forward to.

CHEW THE FAT AT THE PELICAN INN

If you ever wandered where the phrase "chew the fat" comes from, The Pelican Inn holds the answer. The inn houses a unique inglenook fireplace replete with a "priest hole," a feature once used for members of the clergy to make a quick getaway in the days when Catholics and Protestants were at odds. Another unique feature is the fireplace's smoke chamber designed for cooking hams. It's been said that those who would cut a slice of the rind from the ham during conversation were said to "chew the fat." Hence, they would gather around and engage in local gossip.

At-A-Glance Features

7 Rooms
Closed December 24 and 25
Complimentary Breakfast
Non-Smoking

Not Suitable for Children
Restaurant and Pub On-Site
Within Walking Distance to Beaches

Directions

From San Francisco, head north on Highway 101 crossing the Golden Gate Bridge. Take the Stinson Beach Highway 1 exit and follow Highway 1 north to Muir Beach. The inn is the only business in town.

Credit Cards Accepted

Visa, MasterCard.

POINT RICHMOND

EAST BROTHER LIGHT STATION

117 Park Place
Point Richmond, Contra Costa County
Tel. 510/233-2385
Fax: 510/291-2243
Web Address: www.ebls.org
E-Mail: info@ebls.org
Rates: $290-390 – open Thursday-Sunday evenings year round
4pm check-in
Date Opened: 1980
Innkeepers: Ann Sclover and Gary Herdlicker

Profile

The deep, throaty fog horn that resonates across the San Francisco Bay is, at times, the only reminder that the East Brother Light Station exists. The fog-shrouded island on which the inn rests is one of a pair of tiny land parcels located on the east side of San Pablo Strait, a passage spanning a width of two miles linking the bays of San Francisco and San Pablo. Covering just three quarters of an acre, the island neighbors the smaller uninhabited West Brother isle.

The rectangular wooden beacon was constructed in the late 1870s and was one of about a dozen such structures built by the federal government on greater San Francisco Bay. Its primary purpose was to provide nighttime navigation assistance, which was later enhanced with the installment of the bellowing diaphone fog signal in 1934. Other changes took place through the years as electricity replaced kerosene, keeper's duties were delegated to rotating Coast Guard crews and, finally, 1960s technology helped to automate the entire operation with a rotating beacon. Eventually the six-room lighthouse was earmarked for demolition, and offered in its place was a proposed light placed on a steel or concrete tower.

In 1971 a group of preservationists rallied to have the lighthouse placed on the National Register of Historic Places. While this stopped any further thoughts of leveling the structure, it did nothing to restore it. For the next decade the only guests to visit the island were flocks of birds and an occasional Coast Guardsman assigned to ensure the light and electric fog signal were operating. In the meantime, the natural elements and years of neglect slowly took their toll on the lighthouse as the paint peeled, the iron eroded and the wood slowly rotted.

In 1979, a non-profit citizens' group calling themselves the East Brother Light Station, Inc., set out to restore this coastal landmark. With the Coast Guard's support, the group successfully applied for a Maritime Preservation Matching Grant from the U.S. Department of the Interior. Armed with a slew of private donations and the dedication from a roster of volunteers, the lighthouse and its island structures were painstakingly restored.

Today the island's upkeep is financially supported by day use fees, bed and breakfast tariffs, and volunteer efforts.

Accommodations

The 10-minute boat ride from the mainland to the island of East Brother is one of seafaring nostalgia. As you forge ahead to your destination, choppy waters are seen lapping against forgotten sardine canneries and the West Coast's last whaling station. Suddenly, as wisps of fog begin to part, maritime history comes full circle with the first glimpse of East Brother Light Station.

In order to reach this secluded bed and breakfast, passengers must scale a 12-foot steel ladder to the dock unless, of course, the tide is high and then it takes only half the length. Most overnight guests have no complaints as they are ushered inside the butter-colored Victorian structure. There are a quartet of chambers located inside the historic lighthouse, which once sheltered the keepers and their families. Each is named for its stunning view – **Marin, San Francisco, Two Sister** and **West Brother** – and the **Fog Signal**, the inn's fifth room, is located in its namesake building and was also used in a previous life as keepers' quarters. Normally I don't recommend shared-bath inns, but East Brother's is such a magnificent experience, this is one convenience worth sacrificing. The other is the short supply of water. For the record, the 70,000-gallon cistern is the only source of H20, which explains why guests who spend a single night on the island are denied shower privileges.

Amenities

Those who have a passion for history, lighthouses and solitude will find solace at East Brother. The inn accommodates a maximum of eight guests, and day trippers who visit the island are ferried back to the mainland prior to your arrival. The nightly tariff includes roundtrip boat transportation, hors d'oeuvres and beverages upon arrival, a multi-course dinner with wine, and a full breakfast.

One of the inn's greatest assets is its unique location. Shaded by trees and a vibrant blanket of poppies, roses and other colorful flora, East Brother Light Station is brimming with plenty of reading material, wildlife and fishing opportunities. Picnicking, losing yourself in a good book or scouring the inn's historical files about past lighthouse keepers and shipwrecks are other ways to spend time on the island. There are also tours of the island detailing the history and restoration efforts, as well as demonstrations of the old diaphone fog horns. Perhaps the most rewarding place to find yourself is at the end of the narrow spiral staircase that leads to the light deck, where the most breathtaking bay and city views are enjoyed.

The island covers about 3/4 of an acre. The main attraction is the converted lighthouse, but those arriving for the day can picnic and/or fish.

At-A-Glance Features
5 Rooms, 2 with Private Bath
Complimentary Continental Breakfast
Complimentary Evening Wine and Snacks
Complimentary Multi-Course Dinner
Complimentary Roundtrip Boat Service
Island Tours Available
Non-Smoking
Not Appropriate for Children
Shower Privileges to those Guests Spending 2 or More Nights

Directions
From Interstate 80, take the San Rafael exit to Interstate 580 west towards the Richmond-San Rafael Bridge. Just before the toll plaza, exit at Point Molate and follow the signs to Point San Pablo Yacht Harbor. Meet the Lighthouse Keeper in front of The Galley Cafe. Pick up time is 4pm, return time to the mainland is 11am.

Credit Cards Accepted
Visa, MasterCard, American Express.

VISIT THE LIGHTHOUSE AS A DAY TRIPPER
If for some reason it's not possible to spend a night at East Brother Light Station, you can still enjoy its beauty by day. Guests can come for the afternoon to enjoy the wildlife and take a tour of the island. Be sure to dress appropriately year round, as wind-driven swells will shower you with ocean sprays. It's recommended that passengers wear sturdy shoes, not sandals, and dress casually in appropriate outdoor clothing. Day reservations can be made by calling 510/812-1207.

SAN FRANCISCO

THE ARCHBISHOP'S MANSION

1000 Fulton Street
San Francisco, San Francisco County
Tel. 800/543-5820 or 415/563-7872
Fax: 415/885-3193
Web Address: www.archbishopsmansion.com
E-mail: abm@jdvhospitality.com
Rates: $165-425
3pm check-in
Year Opened: 1983
Innkeeper: Rachel Huestis

Profile

I'm sure we'd all be willing to take an oath of celibacy if we could live in a place as opulent as The Archbishop's Mansion. Built in 1904 in the Belle Epoque style, the estate was the home of San Francisco's Archbishop, Patrick Riordan. After surviving the Great Fire of Chicago in 1871, he insisted that the interior be made of stucco and that it be located in Alamo Square, San Francisco's most fashionable district at the time.

Archbishop Riordan played a pivotal role in the city's history as he set about building churches, schools and hospitals, transforming this city by the bay from a Gold Rush boomtown to one of America's most thriving cities. Two other archbishops resided in the home before the Archdiocese moved the residence to Pacific Heights. The Catholic Church maintained the mansion as a working boys' home, functioning as both an orphanage and an alternative to juvenile hall. The church finally let go of the estate in 1972, and it was acquired by a medical center, transforming it into a residential drug rehabilitation clinic.

The present owners purchased the building in 1980 and spent two and a half years renovating the property. Today the Archbishop's Mansion, located just a few blocks from Haight-Ashbury between the Civic Center and Golden Gate Park, is one of San Francisco's premier bed and breakfast inns.

Accommodations

With three stories, 15 bedrooms, a collection of formal public rooms and several stairways, it's surprising the archbishop didn't get lost in his own home. A grand staircase leads to most of the bedrooms, which are located off long, wide corridors. There are five categories of rooms, each distinct and more impressive than the last with operatic names such as the **Daughter of the Regiment, Italian Girl in Algiers,** and **La Boheme.** The **Intimate Charmers** are the least expensive, offering partial-canopied beds and French antiques, while the **Intimate Fireplace** chambers come equipped with hearths.

The **Romantic Fireplace** rooms are spacious with sitting areas, as are the **Romantic Jacuzzi** rooms that boast large bathrooms and tandem whirlpools. The **Grand Suites** are large and lavish, featuring cozy sitting areas, claw-foot tubs, four-poster beds, multi-head showers and scenic parkside views.

Amenities

The public rooms offer more than a hint of formality with their expansive ceilings and dangling chandeliers. Guests have no need to make a mad dash for the dining room at the break of dawn as a filling continental breakfast is delivered to your doorstep. However, if you're the type who likes to swap stories with fellow travelers, there's plenty of time for mingling in the formal parlor over a glass of wine. The staff can also create a personalized tour itinerary to the hidden sights, sounds and tastes of San Francisco.

The inn offers **complimentary parking** to its guests, something almost unheard of in the city. If you arrive in San Francisco without a car, there's no need to fret. The city has a great transportation system, BART (Bay Area Rapid Transit), with buses stopping near the inn every few minutes.

At-A-Glance Features

15 Rooms
Complimentary Continental Breakfast
Complete Concierge Service
Complimentary Evening Wine and Cheese
Complimentary Newspaper
Elevator Access
En-Suite Massage
Limited Off-Street Parking
Non-Smoking
Not Appropriate for Children
Personalized Tour Itineraries

Directions

Head north on Highway 101, take the Central Skyway and merge onto Fell Street. Turn right onto Fillmore Street and left onto Fulton. The mansion will be on your right-hand side.

Credit Cards Accepted
Visa, MasterCard, American Express.

GRAND ACCOUTREMENTS AT THE ARCHBISHOP'S MANSION

Except for the chandelier dangling in the foyer, the mansion's original furnishings have long since vanished. With a keen sense for the spectacular, the owners have managed to acquire some rather unusual pieces during their travels. Notice the gold-leafed mirror that graces the Great Hall; it comes from the home of Mary Todd Lincoln. The 1904 Bechstein baby grand piano belonged to none other than Noel Coward, and the chandelier that illuminates the regal parlor is from the set of 'Gone With The Wind.'

JACKSON COURT
2198 Jackson Street
San Francisco, San Francisco County
Tel. 800/738-7477 or 415/929-7670
Fax: 415/929-1405
Web Address: www.jdvhospitality.com
E-mail: jc@jdvhospitality.com
Rates: $150-215
2pm check-in
Year Opened: 1983
Innkeeper: Evelyn Bing

Profile
Pacific Heights is a hilly district flanked with Victorian rowhouses and impressive mansions. Among the prized relics is Jackson Court. Housed in a stately turn-of-the-century brownstone, the home was built by the daughter of the Callahans, a prominent and wealthy shipping industry family. The home next door, which shares a common courtyard and garage with the inn, was built for the Callahan's son.

While the son's home has remained a private single-family residence, Jackson Court eventually became an all women's guest house and, much later, a timeshare rental. Today, it is an elegant bed and breakfast inn located in one of San Francisco's most esteemed neighborhoods.

Accommodations

As the morning fog hangs heavy over the city streets, catch a couple of extra winks behind the doors of Jackson Court. Behind the arched entrance and jumble of flora are 10 delightful rooms. Though each chamber is individually decorated, incorporating a melange of antique and contemporary treasures, all feature sitting areas, sprays of fresh flowers, televisions and telephones, with many rooms offering fireplaces.

Though all rooms are exceptional and tastefully adorned, there are a couple that particularly stand out. The **Executive Room**, the largest of the collection, features an Italian marble fireplace, built-in bookcases and a roomy king-size bed. The **Buchanan Room**, graced with floral walls, features an intimate foyer. The **Garden Court** is the former dining room with many of the original appointments, such as the hand-crafted paneling, cabinets and fireplace, still intact. The **Library**, which at one time served as the study, is another stunning chamber.

Amenities

This is one of those places where you want to utter "they just don't build 'em like they use to," and, quite honestly, they don't. An extended continental breakfast is served each morning in the second floor kitchen. If you prefer to take this meal in your room, simply fix yourself a tray and retreat to your chamber. The wood-paneled parlor is where afternoon tea is served, and if you take a closer look at the stone fireplace, brought over from Europe by the family, you'll notice a ghostly carving of Mr. and Mrs. Callahan.

The inn is located in one of San Francisco's finest residential neighborhoods and is surrounded by vivid Victorian mansions, and boasts some of the city's most breathtaking views. Nearby is Union Street, not to be confused with Union Square. This bustling avenue is lined with Victorian rowhouses that have been converted into upscale boutiques and bistros, and offers a less touristy shopping experience. Public transportation is also nearby.

Make note that Jackson Court offers limited off-street parking. It's best to snag a spot if you can, then see the city on foot using public transportation whenever possible.

At-A-Glance Features

10 Rooms
Children Welcome
Complimentary Continental Breakfast
Complimentary Afternoon Tea
Complete Concierge Service

Limited Off-Street Parking
Non-Smoking

Directions
Approaching the city south of San Francisco, take 101 North to the Fell Street exit. Turn right at Fillmore, then right on Jackson Street. Proceed two blocks to Buchanan. Jackson Court is located on the northeast corner of Jackson and Buchanan.

Credit Cards Accepted
Visa, MasterCard, American Express.

"PERSONALITY HOTELS ON UNION SQUARE"

San Francisco is a popular destination, and for good reason. It's romantic and eclectic with great shopping, dining and attractions. Because of this, you might find that the smaller inns are typically booked to capacity, but don't despair.

Personality Hotels on Union Square offers an enchanting collection of boutique properties at some of San Francisco's best addresses near Union Square. They include the Kensington Park Hotel, Hotel Union Square, Hotel Diva, Hotel Metropolis and the Steinhart Hotel. Though the rooms number 50-plus, special touches often found at more intimate establishments are given priorty. Complimentary continental breakfast and afternoon wine reception are standard, with fresh-brewed coffee and tea available throughout the day. And, like the name says, each has its own personality and plenty of it, from funky to functional, extraordinary to ornate. For reservations, call 800/553-1900 or take a virtual visit at www.personalityhotels.com.

PETITE AUBERGE

863 Bush Street
San Francisco, San Francisco County
Tel. 800/365-3004 or 415/928-6000
Fax: 415/673-7214
Web Address: www.foursisters.com
E-mail: info@foursisters.com
Rates: $120-145 – parking additional
3pm check-in
Year Opened: 1983
Innkeeper: Christie Stembel

Profile

Petite Auberge, translated to mean "small inn," is reminiscent of a Parisian hotel. If it weren't for the clang-clang of the nearby Powell Street cable car, you might be convinced you're in Paris instead of one of America's most romantic cities.

Built during the early part of the 20th century, the five-story Petite Auberge is located in a typical San Francisco row building. The inn's marble steps are strewn with teddy bears, and an original caged elevator whisks guests to the upper levels. As for the inn's location, you can't do much better. Petite Auberge is within strolling distance to Union Square and Chinatown, near landmark cable cars that chug through the city streets towards garlic-scented North Beach and the bustling planks of Fisherman's Wharf.

Accommodationa

From the outside, Petite Auberge looks just like any other San Francisco inn built at the turn-of-the-century: quaint, a tad worn and hard to distinguish from the next. But once inside, it's easy to see that the owners have taken great strides to create an unforgettable retreat.

Provincial enchantment and European élan are the buzz words that aptly describe the interiors. Though it would have been much simpler to standardize the 26 rooms, each boasts its own unique personality and flair. Floral wallpaper, canopied beds, carved armoires and crackling fireplaces are just some of the appointments offered behind chamber doors. If you're coming to the city to celebrate, consider reserving the **Petite Suite**, with French doors opening onto a private deck, plus a hand-painted king bed and ample spa tub.

Amenities

Though you may feel as if you're in Paris, save the yearning for croissants, the Eiffel Tower and lattes for your next trip abroad. Instead, savor traditional San Francisco sourdough bread, peek-a-boo views of the Golden Gate Bridge, and hot Ghiradelli cocoa.

Breakfast is served in the lower level dining room against a mural depicting a realistic French market scene. Croissants and quiche are morning staples, but there are also loaves of signature sourdough bread and hot chocolate. Guests travel through the buffet line plucking fresh fruit and omelets to fill their plates, while mugs contain robust coffee and pools of real cream.

After a full day exploring the shops at Union Square, guests return to the inn's parlor for a serving of wine and hors d'oeuvres. The crackling fire and lively conversation creates an inviting atmosphere, and guests have been known to linger long after the last bottle has been uncorked.

At-A-Glance Features

26 Rooms
Complimentary Breakfast
Complimentary Evening Wine and Hors d'oeuvres
Complimentary Morning Newspaper
Evening Turndown Service
Within Walking Distance to Union Square and Chinatown

Directions

Head west on Interstate 80 and exit at Fremont Street, which eventually becomes Front Street. Turn left onto Pine Street and travel to Jones Street. Take a left onto Jones Street and another left onto Bush Street. Petite Auberge will be on your left-hand side.

Credit Cards Accepted

Visa, MasterCard, American Express.

WHITE SWAN INN

845 Bush Street
San Francisco, San Francisco County
Tel. 800/999-9570 or 415/775-1755
Fax: 415/77-5717
Web Address: www.foursisters.com
E-mail: info@foursisters.com
Rates: $165-250 - parking additional
3pm check-in
Year Opened: 1986
Innkeeper: Christie Stembel

Profile

If the White Swan Inn looks hauntingly familiar, with its barrage of teddy bears and inviting entrance, perhaps that's because it resides just a few doors down from its sister property, Petite Auberge. Though the two are owned and operated by Four Sisters Inns and were built at around the same time, the similarities end there.

British overtones create a London townhouse feel behind the doors of this early 20th century inn. Located just below Nob Hill, or "Snob Hill" as its more commonly known, guests simply have to walk a half-block to reach the Powell Line cable car. Union Square and Chinatown are within walking distance, as are an array of fabulous restaurants and cafes.

Accommodations

White Swan Inn has an almost clubby feel to it, like an exclusive London's gentlemen club. Each of the 26 spacious rooms is cloaked in shades of British racing green and deep burgundy with a splash of floral for good measure. The four-poster beds, wingback chairs and entertainment armoires were designed to emulate the Edwardian period, while Laura Ashley florals and glowing fireplaces add a touch of warmth.

All rooms feature sitting areas, wet bars stocked with complimentary soft drinks and bottled water, coffee makers, data ports, concealed televisions and phones.

Amenities

If there's one thing you can count on when staying at any of the Four Sisters Inns, it's that you'll never go hungry. The White Swan's feast of morning favorites is served in the quaint breakfast cellar, where scattered tables and an oversized hearth create a warm environment. On mild days, you can watch the fog lift from beyond the French doors at a quiet table for two. Return in the afternoon for an hour of tea, snacks and oversized cookies.

At-A-Glance Features
26 Rooms
Complimentary Breakfast
Complimentary Evening Tea and Cookies
Complimentary Morning Newspaper
Evening Turndown Service
Within Walking Distance to Union Square and Chinatown

Directions
Head west on Interstate 80 and exit at Fremont Street, which eventually becomes Front Street. Turn left onto Pine Street and travel to Jones Street. Take a left onto Jones Street and another left onto Bush Street. The White Swan Inn will be on your left-hand side.

Credit Cards Accepted
Visa, MasterCard, American Express.

SAN RAFAEL

GERSTLE PARK INN

34 Grove Street
San Rafael, Marin County
Tel. 800/726-7611 or 415/721-7611
Fax: 415/721-7600
Web Address: www.gerstleparkinn.com
E-mail: innkeeper @gerstleparkinn.com
Rates: $189-275
3pm check-in
Year Opened: 1995
Innkeepers: Jim and Judy Dowling

Profile

There was a time when Gerstle Park Inn was part of two larger estates, the four and a half acres of Sloss Estate and the four acres of Gerstle Estate. The two prominent families were friends and, not only did they hold the deed to San Rafael's most elaborate homes, together they hosted the most lavish parities.

More than a century later, elegance has been transferred to the former servants' quarters, a 7,000 square-foot traditional Craftsman home. The one and a half acre sprawl also includes an 1880 Carriage House and blooming gardens. Its location, just north of the Golden Gate Bridge and folded into the Marin foothills, makes for an ideal base in which to explore the Bay Area and its environs. Both San Francisco and the Napa Valley are within easy driving distance, and neighborhood restaurants and shops are a short stroll away.

Accommodations

With its limited number of rooms and attentive service provided to guests, Gerstle Park Inn has all the trappings of an elegant inn with the added intimacy of a bed and breakfast.

Fronting the shingle-covered abode is an expansive and inviting verandah flanked with wicker rocking chairs and a tea cart filled with refreshments. Inside are eight suites, each uniquely decorated in classic styles with a hint of Asian and European influences, while the **Carriage House** and **pair of cottages** are located adjacent to the inn. Several chambers offer private decks or balconies overlooking either the gardens or foothills, and an eclectic spray of antiques creates a balance somewhere between classic and comfortable.

A few noteworthy chambers are the **Sloss Suite** offering soaring ceilings, a bank of French windows, rose and mint accents, and private balcony. For platonic travelers, the second-floor **San Rafael Suite**, with its slated ceiling and roomy deck, boasts a pair of ornate Victorian twin beds. The **Sunrise and Sunset Suites**, located on the top floor of the adjacent carriage house, are the ultimate hideaways. Both have kitchens, living rooms, dining areas and patios.

All rooms are equipped with modems, telephones with private voice mail, cable television and VCRs, CD players and an extensive library of recently released videos.

Amenities

Unlike most bed and breakfasts, where a set morning menu is designed to feed the masses, the innkeepers here prefer to create individual breakfasts in order to satisfy the palate of each guest. An early light breakfast is served before 7am, and a full gourmet breakfast is served on either the glass-enclosed sunporch, outside on the terrace, or behind the doors of your suite. In the evening a selection of regional wines and homemade snacks are taken either in front of the fireplace or on the ample verandah. And, should hunger strike at an odd hour, no worries, as guests have free range of the kitchen day and night.

The inviting grounds, shrouded by mature cedars, oaks, fruit trees and some of Marin County's oldest redwoods, creates an inviting backdrop for croquet. Sometimes guests find themselves competing with grazing deer, who are often spotted on the property and in nearby **Gerstle Park**.

At-A-Glance Features

12 Rooms
Children Welcome
Complimentary Continental Breakfast
Complimentary Evening Wine and Snacks
Complimentary Newspaper
Non-Smoking

Directions

From San Francisco, take the Golden Gate Bridge north and onto Highway 101. Continue to travel north until you reach the Central San Rafael exit. Turn left on 4th Street, make another left onto D Street. Proceed on D Street to San Rafael Avenue and turn right. Continue on

San Rafael Avenue until you come to Grove Street, and turn left. The inn's parking lot is on the upper right side.

Credit Cards Accepted

Visa, MasterCard American Express.

SAUSALITO

THE GABLES INN

62 Princess Street
Sausalito, Marin County
Tel. 800/966-1554 or 415/289-1100
Fax: 415/339-0536
Web Address: www.gablesinnsausalito.com
E-mail: gablesinn@aol.com
Rates: $185-325
3pm check-in
Year Opened: 1998
Innkeeper: Meredith Asch

Profile

The Gables Inn, sculptured into a magnificent hillside, reigns high above town on a street aptly named Princess. Built in 1869, this was Sausalito's first full-service hotel catering mostly to drifters and shipyard workers.

The three-story inn, now listed on the National Register of Historic Places, has evolved into a cozy nine-story hideaway replete with breathtaking views and seaside sophistication. Located just a short stroll from Sausalito's pleasures – shops, restaurants and galleries – the inn is a great base for exploring the Bay Area. San Francisco is just a ferry ride away, and California's famed Wine Country is less than an hour's drive.

Accommodations

After a multimillion-dollar renovation, The Gables Inn, which opened its doors in 1998, is among Sausalito's most intimate offerings. The collection of guest rooms have been meticulously combed over to ensure a comfortable and luxurious stay. Behind the nine portals are queen- or king-size beds, vaulted ceilings, duo tubs and fireplaces with brick accents. There are also televisions and VCRs to entertain, but with a setting this spectacular they're hardly needed.

The best rooms are undoubtedly the suites, the **Skyline** and **Honeymoon**, both serving up stunning views from Juliet-style balconies. The pair of **Bay View Suites** also deliver postcard vistas with French doors leading to garden patios. Once the fog parts, images of Angel Island, Alcatraz and the San Francisco skyline quickly come into view.

Amenities

If you're staying in a room with a balcony, my advice is to get as much mileage from this feature as possible. A simple continental breakfast can be enjoyed in the dining area or upstairs in privacy. In the evening, guests congregate around the hearth in the Terrace Lounge to sample local wines and cheeses. The inn also maintains a full selection of award-winning wines from the vineyards of nearby Sonoma and Napa valleys.

Take an early morning stroll past some neighboring homes and landmarks. Publishing tycoon William Randolph Hearst had a nearby pied-à-terre he called Sea Point, and a once unknown seaman by the name of Jack London is said to have written his novel *Sea Wolf* while residing at an old rooming house and beer garden just down the road.

At-A-Glance Features

9 Rooms
Children Welcome
Complimentary Continental Breakfast
Complimentary Evening Wine and Cheese
Morning Newspaper
Non-Smoking

Directions

From San Francisco, cross the Golden Gate Bridge and exit on Alexander Avenue. Proceed for a mile. Alexander becomes Bridgeway; continue into Sausalito. Turn left onto Princess Street, and travel up the hill. The inn will be on your right.

Credit Cards Accepted

Visa, MasterCard, American Express, Discover, Diners Club.

INN ABOVE TIDE

30 El Portal
Sausalito, Marin County
Tel. 800/893-8433 or 415/332-9535
Fax: 415/332-6714
Web Address: www.innabovetide.citysearch.com
E-Mail: inntide@ix.netcom.com
Rates: $215-540 - parking additional
3pm check-in
Year Opened: 1995
Innkeeper: Mark D. Flaherty

Profile

If I have any regrets about my stay at the Inn Above Tide, it's that I didn't make arrangements to have a massage on my bayside balcony. Thankfully, for me, there will be a next time.

The Inn Above Tide isn't your typical bed and breakfast. There are no Victorian touches, salvaged antiques or resident cats, just a haven of contemporary luxury. Literally built over the waters of the San Francisco Bay, the inn's structure almost resembles a piece of driftwood that has found its way to the shoreline. If the outside appears a bit worn, it's only an illusion. The intimate lobby is cloaked in cool marble, and open-air corridors segue to the collection of tiered, streamline rooms.

Located in the heart of Sausalito, guests can leave their car keys with the valet for the remainder of their stay as everything is within walking or ferry distance. The Mediterranean-style village is flanked with boutiques, galleries, restaurants and sidewalk cafes. Just beyond the hotel's doors is the ferry landing, where boats arrive frequently to whisk visitors across the bay to San Francisco.

Accommodations

With 30 rooms and suites, the inn is better classified as a boutique hotel. All rooms jut out over the bay; most boast roomy balconies where guests can watch the seaside show unfold as kayaks glide quietly by, varied watercraft dart back and forth, and colorful ferries chug along the choppy waters.

The decor of the rooms blend harmoniously with the watery vistas with walls and fabrics cloaked in soft hues of tidal blues, seafoam greens and shell whites. Beds are thoughtfully placed to make the most of the views, so guests not only awake to postcard seascapes but are also lulled to sleep by the sound of lapping waves. Most rooms come equipped with fireplaces, and a pair of binoculars allows you to get a closer look at Alcatraz, the San Francisco skyline, and whatever else might be taking place above the water's surface.

Amenities

Each morning a spread of fresh fruit, cereal, muffins, croissants, pastries, coffee, tea and juice are displayed in the first floor **Drawing Room**. You can nibble here or, as I highly recommend, request the night before that a tray be delivered to your room. Then, enjoy the spread al fresco on the privacy of your balcony. May I suggest you do the same for the evening wine and cheese buffet? Although room service is not an option for this, simply fix your own plate and pour yourself a glass of wine, then scurry back to your room in time to watch the sunset.

At-A-Glance Features

30 Rooms
Complimentary Continental Breakfast
Complimentary Evening Wine and Cheese
Complimentary Newspaper
Complimentary Shoeshine
En-Suite Massage Available
Evening Turndown Service

Directions

From San Francisco, cross the Golden Gate Bridge and exit on Alexander Avenue. Proceed for a mile; Alexander becomes Bridgeway, and continue into Sausalito. Turn right on El Portal, and the hotel will be just to your right. A valet will come out to assist you.

Credit Cards Accepted

Visa, MasterCard, American Express, Diners Club.

TAKE THE SAUSALITO-TO-SAN FRANCISCO FERRY

Want to see San Francisco, but aren't in the mood to tackle its sloping avenues and fog-laden streets? Take a morning ferry boat to either the city's Financial District near the Embarcadero or sail to the docks of Fisherman's Wharf. There are two ferry companies that offer service between San Francisco and Sausalito, with fares averaging about $6 per person for a one-way ride. You'll see the Golden Gate Bridge in the distance, and cruise right past "The Rock," better known as Alcatraz. Once you get to the other side, explore the city on foot, via taxi or aboard a landmark cable car. Ferries returning from the city run as late as 8:30pm.

7. THE CENTRAL COAST

CAMBRIA

Served by Los Angeles International Airport (LAX) or San Jose International Airport (SJC).

J. PATRICK HOUSE

2990 Burton Drive
Cambria, San Luis Obispo County
Tel. 800/341-5258 or 805/927-3812
Fax: 805/927-6759
Web Address: www.jpatrickhouse.com
E-mail: jph@jpatrickhouse.com
3pm check-in
Year Opened: 1984
Innkeepers: Ann O'Connor and John Arnett

Profile

When you think of log cabins maybe your first thoughts are of Abraham Lincoln. After all, didn't our history lessons tell the story of a modest man who built his home out of logs? Oh my, what would Abe think today if he got a peek at the J. Patrick House?

Rustically elegant and constructed entirely out of chunky logs, the inn is anything but modest. The timbered setting and towering forest of Monterey pines gives the illusion that this is a mountain retreat, but in reality the glistening California coast is just minutes away. Nearby are an abundance of attractions, including the quaint village of Cambria with its collection of shops, restaurants and galleries. To the north is the opulent Hearst Castle and the pounding shores of Big Sur, plus you'll find a number of local wineries whose tasting rooms are open to the public.

Accommodations

I have fond memories of the J. Patrick House. This was where my husband and I spent our wedding night on a brisk February evening back in 1993. Not too much has changed in the last eight years, except for maybe the owners.

Only one room is located in the main log cabin and is the one that can accommodate couples with children. The remaining chambers are hidden in the rear carriage house framed by a vine-covered arch. The rooms are inspired by the regions of Ireland with names like **Limerick, Donegal** and **Kilkenny,** and are furnished with lovely antiques along with woodburning fireplaces, window seats and cozy appointments. Oversized afghans and plump pillows add to the overall comfort.

Amenities

Each morning guests gather inside the main log cabin's kitchen nook for an abundant breakfast. The big picture window seems more like an observation room for witnessing flitting hummingbirds in search of the perfect nectar. The revolving menu offers everything from apple pie bread pudding with creme fraiche to a vegetable strata drizzled with homemade salsa.

In the evening, the living room's fireplace is lit and a selection of hors d'oeuvres are passed while guests sample local wines. The conversation tends to be lively as everyone recounts their afternoon jaunts. Before bedtime you'll find a stash of chocolate chip cookies waiting for you along with a pitcher of ice-cold milk. And, if that's not enough, you can also arrange to have a **massage** administered in the privacy of your room. Wine, chocolate and massage therapy – what more do you need?

At-A-Glance Features

8 Rooms
Children Welcome
Close to Hearst Castle and Big Sur
Complimentary Breakfast
Complimentary Evening Wine and Hors d'oeuvres
En-Room Massage
Near Shops, Restaurants and Beach
Non-Smoking
Wineries Nearby

Directions

From Los Angeles, travel north on Highway 101 to San Luis Obispo and exit at the Hearst Castle/Highway 1 exit. Follow Highway 1 north for about 40 miles, passing Morro Bay and Cayucos. At the Burton Drive signal, turn right and continue for approximately a half-mile. The J. Patrick House will be on the right side.

Credit Cards Accepted
Visa, MasterCard, American Express, Discover.

TOUR HEARST CASTLE WHEN IN CAMBRIA

*Cambria is an ideal place to stay if you're planning to visit **Hearst Castle**, the once opulent home of newspaper publisher William Randolph Hearst. The compound, once known as La Cuesta Encantada – The Enchanted Hill – features 127 acres of gardens, terraces, pools and guest houses. Rumor (or is it legend?) says that after having the castle up on the auction block, with no takers in sight, Hearst finally donated his creation to the state and simply accepted the write-off.*

Hearst Castle, a State Historical Monument, is open daily for tours except on major holidays. There are four daytime tours which begin at 8:20am and a single evening tour offered at various times. Prices range from $14-25 for adults, $8-13 for children. For tickets and information, call 800/444-4445 or 805/927-2020.

CAPITOLA

Served by San Jose International Airport (SJC).

INN AT DEPOT HILL

250 Monterey Avenue
Capitola-by-the-Sea, Santa Cruz County
Tel. 800/572-2632 or 831/462-3376
Fax: 831/462-3697
Web Address: www.innatdepothill.com
E-mail: lodging@innatdepothill.com
Rates: $225-295
3pm check-in
Year Opened: 1990
Innkeepers: Suzie Lankes and Dan Floyd

Profile

The parlor area belonging to this upscale bed and breakfast inn was constructed in 1901 and used as a railroad depot, hence the inn's name. By the time the innkeepers acquired the building in the late 1980s, it was on the fast track to destruction. After several months of painstakingly restoring the property and, at the same time, trying to convince the city council that a bed and breakfast inn was exactly what the town needed, the Inn at Depot Hill made its long awaited debut.

Overlooking the quaint seaside village of Capitola-by-the-Sea, the inn offers the perfect romantic hideaway. Just a short stroll from a cluster of shops, eateries and stretch of shoreline, the Inn at Capitola provides an ideal base for exploring the Monterey Bay area and nearby Silicon Valley.

Accommodations

Travel from Paris to the Côte d'Azure and beyond behind the doors of 12 thematic rooms and suites, with many evoking a feel of European élan. Each chamber has a distinctive ambiance, whether it's **The Railroad Baron's** regal use of red and gold hues or the Far East design elements found in the **Kyoto** room. A handful of rooms are located just off the parlor, but my favorites happen to be the freestanding variety.

I highly recommend staying in the **Valencia Suite** with its intimate verandah offering ocean peeks and an elevated soaking tub that plunges so deep it could easily double as a wading pool. Wherever you happen to rest your head, all accommodations offer private entrances, televisions with VCRs, stereo systems, desks, phones with fax/modem connections, and fireplaces.

Amenities

Guests are treated to a full gourmet breakfast each morning in the elegant dining room, which was transformed from a bank of ticket windows into its present state. The room, with its large dining table and bay window, also offers a smaller table for the well-trodden, with a trompe l'oeil seaside painting and a stack of vintage luggage with dangling tags completing the first-class rail experience.

If weather permits, guests can also dine amid the garden courtyard complete with blooming flora, reflecting pool and cascading fountain. Or, if you prefer, you can wrap your body up in one of the prize fighter-style lounging robes found hanging in your closet and request that breakfast be brought to your room. In the evening a spread of imported cheeses, crackers, fruits and local wines are also served in these settings.

At-A-Glance Features

12 Rooms
Book and Video Library
Complimentary Breakfast
Complimentary Evening Wine and Hors d'oeuvres
Near Town Center and Beach
Not Appropriate for Children

Directions

From the San Jose area, take Highway 101 to Highway 17 and exit Highway 1 south. Take the Park Avenue exit and head towards the ocean for about one mile. Take a left onto Monterey Avenue and an immediate left into the inn's driveway

Credit Cards Accepted

Visa, MasterCard, American Express, Discover.

FINE DINING AT SHADOWBROOK

If you were to ask anyone where's the best place to dine in the Santa Cruz area, they'll likely tell you **Shadowbrook***. The restaurant, which opened in 1947, was originally a 1920s log cabin retreat built along the banks of the Soquel Creek. Cascading down a steep embankment, guests are ferried to the reception area via cable car.*

The three-star restaurant caters to couples as well as families, and we witnessed a marriage proposal from our table. The menu features mostly steak, seafood and chops with a limited selection of vegetarian dishes. There's also a kids menu, and an extensive wine list. Call 831/475-1151 or go to www.shadowbrook-capitola.com.

CARMEL

Served by San Jose International Airport (SJC).

CYPRESS INN
Lincoln & 7th Street
Carmel, Monterey County
Tel. 800/443-7443 or 831/624-3871
Fax: 831/624-8216
Web Address: www.cypress-inn.com
E-mail: info@cypress-inn.com
Rates: $125-275
3pm check-in
Date Opened: 1929
Innkeeper: Hollace Thompson

Profile
Staking claim on a quiet corner in the heart of Carmel's village is the delightful Cypress Inn. Though the photos and movie posters featuring Doris Day may seem a bit out of place amid the classic Spanish architecture, there's a logical explanation. This landmark inn is owned by the famous singer-actress, along with her son Terry Melcher and business partner Dennis LeVett.

Moorish accents, such as white stucco, a red-tiled roof, intimate courtyard and exposed beam ceilings, are refreshing among Carmel's mostly Comstock facades. When residents claim the hotel has gone to the dogs, they mean it in the kindest fashion. Day is an animal rights activist and, when she purchased the property in 1985, she opened the hotel to four-legged travelers. It's not the least bit unusual to see purebreds and mutts enjoying the same pleasures as their human counterparts.

With its cozy living room lobby, postage stamp-size cocktail lounge, and menagerie of dogs and cats, Cypress Inn makes guests feel truly at home.

Accommodations
A word to the wise: If you're not traveling with a pet, you at least better like animals if you're going to stay at the Cypress Inn. Not only are they free to roam about with their owners, but it's rather likely that a dog or cat recently occupied your room. So if you're allergic to animals or simply don't embrace the hotel's philosophy, stay elsewhere.

However, if you're like me, a sucker for a wag and a pant, then you can't help but fall in love with the Cypress Inn. The rooms are delightfully simple and surprisingly large, with no two exactly alike. You may find yourself slumbering in an oversized iron bed, relaxing in a snug sitting area, pushing back French doors that lead to a private balcony, or feeling diminutive beneath an expansive ceiling. All rooms are equipped with telephones, televisions, a complimentary decanter of sherry and the delivery of the morning paper to your doorstep.

Perhaps the most unique accommodation to grace this three-story building is the **Tower Room**. This two-level hideaway features a living room with a spiral staircase ascending to the bedroom loft, which is actually located within the hotel's main tower. With plenty of natural rays beaming in from the skylights, the lofty Tower Room offers book nooks, original tile work and village views.

Amenities

Each morning a continental breakfast is served in either the small lounge or, weather permitting, amid the bougainvillea-draped courtyard. The lobby living room, with its collection of plump sofas and chairs, is comforable if not underused. Under a veil of rafters with a pair of French doors opening onto the courtyard, you may find you're the only one enjoying the crackling fire and chubby sofas.

Just down the tiled corridor is the **Library Bar,** where afternoon tea is served from 2-4pm. Complete Tea Service is offered at $12 per person or you can order from the a la carte menu consisting of homemade scones, tea sandwiches and cookies. Come evening, the bantam bar gets quite lively as guests drop by for drinks with their pets in tow.

Furry friends are greeted upon arrival with dog biscuits and a special bed has been readied for their arrival. Since it is forbidden to leave dogs or cats alone in the rooms, pet sitters are available at an additional charge. Keep in mind, however, that Carmel residents and shopkeepers are rather tolerant of pets, so don't feel shy about parading yours around town.

At-A-Glance Features

34 Rooms
Children 12 and Over Welcome
Complimentary Continental Breakfast
Complimentary Afternoon Tea
Complimentary Newspaper
Full Bar

Near Shops, Restaurants and Beach
Non-Smoking
Pet-Friendly

Directions
From San Francisco, take Highway 1 south to Ocean Avenue. Turn left on Lincoln. The inn is on the left-hand side at the corner of Seventh Street.

Credit Cards Accepted
Visa, MasterCard, American Express, Discover.

HAPPY LANDING INN
Monte Verde, Between 5th & 6th Streets
Carmel, Monterey County
Tel. 831/624-7917
Fax: none
Web Address: none
E-mail: none
Rates: $90-180
2pm check-in
Date Opened: 1975
Innkeeper: Dick Stewart

Profile
The Happy Landing Inn is just that, a happy place to land. At least that's what my husband and I felt when we stumbled upon this fairy tale enclave on our honeymoon.

Built in 1926 as a retreat for two families, the three Comstock-designed cottages could easily double as the homes of Hansel and Gretel. In 1948, the compound was sold to Thelma Craig, an eccentric woman who would rent rooms on occasion to weary tourists. If a young couple arrived, they were asked to produce a certificate of marriage before being shown to their room – if they were shown at all.

Sometime during the 1970s, Thelma sold the inn to Dr. Thorngate and his wife. Together the two created a bona fide retreat for travelers, converting the main house into a cozy lobby and letting the collection of cottage rooms. The present owner, Dick Stewart, was a frequent guest at the Happy Landing Inn during this time. With each arrival he would half-jokingly ask the Thorngates if they were interested in selling the place. After several persuasive attempts, Stewart became the new proprietor in 1981.

Accommodations

Happy Landing Inn offers a real storybook setting. An arched trellis, leading to the petite gardens, provides the gateway to each of the seven cottages framed by wisps of flowers and ivy.

Behind each curved portal is an enchanting chamber with stenciled walls, cathedral ceilings, laced curtains, arched breezeways and a swarm of antiques – some even offer fireplaces. There are two master suites and five bedrooms overlooking the gardens, and a few boast their own garden entrance and stained-glass windows, which sheds ample light in the small bathrooms.

Just a few blocks away is the beach and the bustling village. Once you arrive at the Happy Landing Inn, simply park your car and explore on foot.

Amenities

When it comes to serving breakfast, the innkeeper has a unique delivery method. Like something from a fairy tale, guests simply raise their shade to signal that breakfast shall be served. Within minutes, a tray of airy quiche, fruit and coffee cake arrive, and these treats can be enjoyed within the confines of your room or in the garden.

Come afternoon, relax with a cup of steaming tea or glass of sherry by the reflecting pond or under the flower-laden gazebo.

At-A-Glance Features

7 Rooms
Children 12 and Over Welcome
Complimentary Expanded Continental Breakfast
Complimentary Afternoon Tea and Sherry
Within Walking Distance to Shops, Restaurants and Beach

Directions

From San Francisco, go south on Highway 1 to Ocean Avenue, and turn left on Monte Verde (towards the end of town). The inn is on the right-hand side between 5th & 6th Streets.

Credit Cards Accepted

Visa, MasterCard.

MAKE HIS DAY –
STAY AT CLINT EASTWOOD'S MISSION RANCH

*Clint Eastwood, the same tough guy who coined the phrase "make my day," is also an innkeeper. But don't expect to see him running around clad in an apron and catering to the whims of guests; instead, he prefers to stay close to his ranch in nearby Carmel Valley. During his tenure as Carmel's mayor he purchased the **Mission Ranch**, a former ranch that was eventually transformed into a restaurant, bar and dance barn. When he learned it was destined to be bulldozed during the 1980s, he came to its rescue.*

It seems that the Academy Award-winning actor/director had a soft spot for the old ranch, a fondness that began during the 1950s when he was a frequent guest while stationed at nearby Fort Ord. After the acquisition, Eastwood donated 11 adjoining acres to the town as a nature preserve and transformed the original 1850s farmhouse and bunkhouse into accommodations. Eventually he added a collection of newer buildings, which also house overnight guests. Mission Ranch is located at 26270 Delores Street in Carmel behind the Mission Basilica, Tel. 831/624-6436. Rates start at $85 per night.

VAGABOND'S HOUSE INN

4th and Dolores Streets
Carmel, Monterey County
Tel. 800/262-1262 or 831/624-7738
Fax: 831/626-1243
Web Address: www.vagabondshouseinn.com
E-mail: innkeeper@vagabondshouseinn.com
Rates: $115-175
2:30pm check-in
Date Opened: 1929
Innkeeper: Dawn Dull

Profile

The brick and half-timbered Vagabond's House Inn was originally built during the late 1930s as officers' quarters to accommodate the overflow from nearby Fort Ord. The inn is named for Don Blanding's *Vagabond House*, which was written when the poet, author, artist, actor and original vagabond stayed here many years ago.

A collection of cobalt blue doors, concealing the interiors of the 11 guest rooms, are clustered around an ivy-draped courtyard. A verdant ancient oak tree and cascading waterfall dominate the cobblestone swatch surrounded by a tapestry of flora – camellias, rhododendrons, dangling flower pots and ferns – all illuminated by strings of twinkle lights.

Nestled on an elevated plot of land on a quiet lane, Vagabond's House Inn is a short walk to Carmel's shops, restaurants and beach.

Accommodations

Even if you never stepped foot inside one of the inn's rooms, the striking blue doors would have you wondering what you might have missed. The rooms, which face the courtyard and have private entrances, offer a touch of country elegance.

Once the threshold is crossed, you'll discover each individually appointed room is a capsule of comfort with roomy beds, floral coverings, beamed ceilings and simple but elegant furniture.

Amenities

Rise each morning to an expanded continental breakfast, served either in the sun-drenched courtyard or in the confines of your guest room. After a day of prowling about town, return home to a traditional afternoon tea served in the guest parlor.

The inn also displays a unique collection of original British lead soldiers, Big Little Books, and toys hailing from the '20s, '30s and '40s. Pets are also welcome at this inn, and many guests come here specifically for that reason. If you don't embrace the motto 'Love Me, Love My Dog,' then perhaps this inn is not for you.

At-A-Glance Features

11 Rooms
Complimentary Continental Breakfast
Complimentary Afternoon Tea
Pet-Friendly
Within Walking Distance to Shops, Restaurants and Beach

Directions

From San Francisco, head south on Highway 1 to Ocean Avenue and turn right on Dolores. The inn is on the right-hand side near 4th Street.

Credit Cards Accepted

Visa, MasterCard, American Express.

CARMEL VALLEY

Served by San Jose International Airport (SJC).

STONEPINE, AN ESTATE RESORT

150 East Carmel Valley Road
Carmel Valley, Monterey County
Tel. 831/659-2245
Fax: 831/659-5160
Web Address: www.stonepinecalifornia.com
E-mail: director@stonepinecalifornia.com
Rates: $295-1250
3pm check-in
Date Opened: 1987
Innkeepers: Gordon and Noel Hentschel

Profile

Stonepine is a place for people with extravagant tastes and weighty wallets.

In 1929, Henry Potter Russell and his wife, the former Helen Crocker of San Francisco banking fame, longed for a quiet hideaway in which to breed thoroughbred horses and raise their family. They discovered a prime piece of property adjoining the Los Padres National Forest, and together they built the Double H Ranch, a moniker romantically linking their initials.

The European-style chateau earned a reputation as being the foremost breeding farm for thoroughbreds west of the Mississippi. More than 200 champion horses called Double H Ranch home, including Kentucky Derby winner Majestic Prince. In 1937, as para-mutual betting was becoming established at such infant racetracks as Santa Anita Park and Del Mar, Henry Russell founded the renowned California Breeders' Association.

In the lower fields, on the banks of the picturesque Carmel River, Helen played hostess at the couple's polo field. Invitational battles with the Pebble Beach and Santa Barbara clubs were held on a regular basis, and the Russells hosted society's creme de la creme on these grounds, which were later transformed into the present-day Equestrian Center. The Russells' son, Charles, was as passionate about the Sport of Kings and polo as his parents. When Henry died in 1943, the torch was passed to Charles, who oversaw the ranch and its stable of thoroughbreds. When

Charles passed away in 1981, his heirs did not share the same enthusiasm for the family business and decided to put the estate on the market.

In 1987, for the first time in its esteemed history, the estate was open to the public as a first-class retreat for celebrity and non-celebrity guests. In fact, the estate was the backdrop for Brooke Shields and Andre Agassi's 1997 post-nuptial celebration, and other celebrity guests have included Dennis Franz, Harry Hamlin and Demi Moore.

Accommodations

Situated on 330 acres, the country-like setting of Stonepine resembles more of a Tuscan estate rather than something you'd find along California's Central Coast. Only the towering oak trees and the effulgent Santa Lucia mountains beyond are reminders that this is in fact the Golden State. Stonepine offers four separate structures, from country quaint to Euro elegance. Slip behind doors leading to **Chateau Noel**, the **Briar Rose**, the **Gate House**, the **Paddock House** and the **Hermes House**.

Chateau Noel, the main house, is reminiscent of an Italian villa, and features eight distinctively appointed suites. Two suites are housed on the lower floor, and six are found at the top of the circular stairway, segueing off a central, arched hallway. Each suite includes a private library, ample closet pace, a Jacuzzi tub, his and her robes plus bouquets of flowers that are freshened daily.

The secluded **Briar Rose** is a country cottage with its own porch and rose garden, and often delights its occupants with glimpses of deer feeding nearby. This ultimate hideaway features a dining room, kitchen, master bedroom, second bedroom and rustic fireplace. The **Gate House** is a mini Spanish-style estate complete with separate guest house, heated swimming pool and tennis court. The **Paddock House** contains a quartet of rooms and an overall feeling of being stranded on a luxurious horse farm. Each room offers country charm plus the convenience of being a horseshoe-toss away from the Equestrian Center. The 5,000 square-foot **Hermes House**, located at the end of a sycamore-lined lane, is incredibly luxurious. It offers more room than you could ever need with a grand entry foyer, a formal dining room overlooking the four-furlough race-track and thoroughbred barn, a state-of-the-art kitchen and a collection of oversized fireplaces.

By the end of 2001, **The Stonehouse**, a newly constructed manor containing a pair of luxury rooms, will make its debut.

Amenities

While most bed and breakfast inns are serving up a hearty morning meal, guests of Stonepine are preparing for a full day. Without ever stepping foot off this glorious property, you can take a plunge in the swimming pool, give archery your best shot, play a friendly game of croquet, pedal about on a bike, pump iron in the weight room, serve up a game of tennis, or take an enjoyable nature walk. For an additional fee, but worth every penny, the **Equestrian Center** offers an array of lessons including Western trail rides, English/Western riding lessons and carriage driving lessons, as well as less skilled activities such as Victorian carriage rides and group hayrides.

The estate also serves a pleasant afternoon tea and an **evening champagne reception** inside the elegant confines of Chateau Noel's living room. Around the corner is the regal dining room where tables are dressed in Limoges china and Waterford stemware, and a savory multicourse dinner (not included in the fare) is served nightly.

And, in keeping with the spirit of the bed and breakfast concept, this splendid estate also services a complimentary European-style continental breakfast each morning in either the dining room or on the loggia with views of the gardens, lake, golf course and soaring Santa Lucia mountains.

If you arrive at Monterey Airport, located 25 minutes from the estate, you can arrange to be picked up in the estate's own Phantom V Rolls Royce.

At-A-Glance Features

16 Rooms (18 when The Stonehouse opens at the end of 2001)
Car Service from Local Airport
Children Welcome
Complimentary Continental Breakfast
Complimentary Afternoon Tea and Evening Champagne
Equestrian Center
Full-Service Dining Room
Swimming Pool
Tennis Courts
Equestrian Center

STONEPINE'S RECENT HOLLYWOOD FORAY

Stonepine has the distinction of being the first establishment in the world to host a pregnant man. Strange, but true in a Hollywood sort of way. The estate served as the setting for the film **Junior,** *starring Emma Thompson and the very pregnant Arnold Schwarzenegger.*

Directions

From San Francisco, take Highway 101 south to the Monterey Peninsula exit. At South Sanborn Road, turn right and make a slight right onto East Blanco Road. At South Main Street turn left; South Main becomes Monterey Road. Follow Monterey Road to Los Laureles Grade, which becomes Los Laureles Grade Road, and continue to Carmel Valley Road. Turn left onto Carmel Valley Road and continue to the inn.

Credit Cards Accepted

Visa, MasterCard, American Express.

MONTEREY

Served by San Jose International Airport (SJC).

OLD MONTEREY INN

500 Martin Street
Monterey, Monterey County
Tel. 800/350-2344 or 831/375-8284
Fax: 831/375-6730
Web Address: www.oldmontereyinn.com
E-mail: omi@oldmontereyinn.com
Rates: $$200-350
3pm check-in
Year Opened: 1978
Innkeepers: Gene and Ann Swett

Profile

You almost have to wonder why Gene and Ann Swett would open the doors of their stunning three-story manor to overnight guests. It would seem logical to hoard this historic beauty for themselves. But, as they came to realize, something as magnificent as the Old Monterey Inn, where the couple raised their six children, deserves to be shared.

The home was built by Carmel Martin Sr., elected the first mayor of Monterey and a member of one of the area's founding families. In 1929 he and his new bride Lydia built their dream home. The three-story English Tudor estate, situated in the midst of more than an acre of sculptured gardens dotted with some 100 trees, English hedges and old stonework, reflects Mrs. Martin's taste for elegance. Beyond the threshold you'll find such details as hand-carved newel posts, window frames and balustrades complementing hand-plastered Gothic archways, bullnose corners and hand-painted ceiling panels created in two designs.

Carmel Martin was a crusader for preservation and, as a result, such Monterey landmarks as California's First Theater, the Custom House, the Brown-Underwood Adobe, House of the Four Winds, and the Gutierrez Home were spared demolition and opened for the public's enjoyment. The street the Old Monterey Inn sits on, Martin Street, is named in his honor.

The Swetts are only the second owners of this home, having bought the house after Carmel Martin's passing in 1965.

Accommodations

In a town where everything is distinctly of Spanish influence, the ivy-covered Old Monterey Inn breaks the mold with its English presence. But in an effort to pay homage to the city's heritage, there is a wonderful Mexican plaza-style fountain where the trickle of water can be heard falling from its every tier. The offering of rooms and suites include such appointments as wood-burning fireplaces, stained-glass windows that allow the sun to filter through, skylights, plush featherbeds and down duvets, oversized towels, a stash of current magazines, CD players and mood-enhancing candles.

For those in search of seclusion, the **Garden Cottage** should be at the top of your list. Aside from having its own private entrance, you'll also find a separate bedroom with a king-size canopy bed and a window seat overlooking the garden. The **Serengeti Room**, also with its own entrance, creates an adventurous setting with a safari motif enhanced with vintage travel mementos and an oversized bed draped in mosquito netting. The remaining rooms are a mix of floral splendor, beamed ceilings and classic antiques, each elegantly appointed.

Amenities

Monterey has the ideal climate for creating picture-perfect flower gardens. Nowhere is this better illustrated than at the Old Monterey Inn. Stone paths ramble through the grounds under a veil of towering oak trees and flowering pots.

Take advantage of the surroundings by eating breakfast amid the gardens or, if you prefer, join the other guests at the long communal oak table in the dining room. If you can't seem to get moving come morning, the innkeepers will have a tray brought to your room. Return in the afternoon, and again in the evening, for refreshments and beverages.

Something that may appeal to the gentleman traveler is the inn's **"car care" service**. After motoring along the region's famed 17-mile Drive, you can give your vehicle a complete roadster cleaning as the inn provides all the necessities to make your automobile shine. For those who are foot bound, you'll find such attractions as the **wharf** and world-class **aquarium** within walking distance.

At-A-Glance Features

10 Rooms
Car Care Service
Complimentary Breakfast
Complimentary Afternoon and Evening Hors d'oeuvres

Complimentary Passes to Local Fitness Center
Near Shops, Restaurants and Attractions
Non-Smoking
Not Appropriate for Children

Directions

From San Francisco, take Highway 1 south and exit Soledad/Munras. Cross Munras Avenue, turn right on Pacific Street, and go about a half mile. Martin Street will be on your left.

Credit Cards Accepted

Visa, MasterCard.

THE MONTEREY BAY AQUARIUM

In 1984, the fish returned to Monterey's Cannery Row for the first time in decades. Their future was more promising this time around, considering they serve as the centerpiece for the Monterey Bay Aquarium (rather than being served for dinner).

Located along historic Cannery Row on the fringes of Pacific Grove, the non-profit attraction offers more than 100 galleries and exhibits devoted to the diverse habitats of Monterey Bay. The largest exhibits are the one-million gallon Outer Bay, the Kelp Forest, the Monterey Bay Habitats and the Sea Otters frolicking along the Rocky Coast. The aquarium is also home to the largest jellyfish gallery, as well as the largest living deep-sea exhibits. You'll come face-to-fish with more than 300,000 animals and plants representing 571 species of invertebrates, mammals, reptiles, birds and plants indigenous to the Monterey Bay. There's also interactive displays geared towards children, plus feeding shows throughout the day. Be sure to pay a visit to the waterfront decks drenched with telescopes and postcard views.

The Monterey Bay Aquarium is open daily from 10am to 6pm. For ticket prices and information, call 831/648-4888.

PACIFIC GROVE

Served by San Jose International Airport (SJC).

GRAND VIEW INN

557 Oceanview Boulevard
Pacific Grove, Monterey County
Tel. 831/372-4341
Fax: none
Web Address: www.7-gables-grandview.com
E-mail: none
Rates: $165-285
2:30pm check-in
Date Opened: 1995
Innkeepers: The Flatley Family

Profile

The owners of the Grand View Inn didn't have far to venture when they decided to purchase this 1910 Victorian home. As the owners of the Seven Gables Inn, they simply had to walk next door.

Noted biologist Dr. Julia Platt chose this stunning location, overlooking Lover's Point Beach, in which to build her home. As the first woman mayor of Pacific Grove, she was instrumental in preserving the beach and park for future generations to enjoy. Ironically, no one bothered to preserve her house in the years prior to the Flatley's acquisition. It had been long abandoned and, having seen better days, it would take more than 18 months to restore it to its original splendor.

Little of the home is original, but only a true expert would know otherwise. The wood flooring, plastering and winding staircase are all new, and the addition of a new wing blends effortlessly with the original structure. Though the Seven Gables Inn and the Grand View Inn operate separately, the two are connected by a narrow pathway and trickling stream.

Accommodations

Ornate and opulent, the Grand View Inn looks illustrious as it faces the sometimes fierce Monterey Bay. The public rooms are dressed in formal furnishings with gilded embellishments and crystal-laden chandeliers, although the regal theme becomes a bit more relaxed behind chamber doors.

There are three rooms located on the first floor with the remainder situated on the upper level – only the **Rocky Shores** chamber has the good fortune of being isolated on the third landing. Just like its sister inn, each room at the Grand View Inn offers unparalleled views of the rugged Pacific Ocean and mimic the Edwardian period in which the inn was built. No matter where you rest your head, you simply can't go wrong. Each offers queen-size beds with plump down comforters and welcome baskets.

Amenities

Overlooking the pounding surf is the parlor, where a gourmet breakfast is served each morning with tea follwing in the late afternoon. Pacific Grove has a number of fine restaurants, and the innkeeper is pleased to offer suggestions and make any needed reservations. Since you are a guest of the Grand View Inn, don't miss your opportunity to take a tour of the Seven Gables Inn next door.

At-A-Glance Features

10 Rooms
Complimentary Afternoon Tea
Complimentary Breakfast
Non-Smoking
Not Appropriate for Children
Within Walking Distance to Town and Attractions

Directions

From San Francisco, take Highway 1 south to the Pacific Grove/Pebble Beach exit. Follow the signs to Pacific Grove, and once in town the road becomes Forest Avenue. Follow Forest Avenue to Oceanview Boulevard. Turn right, and proceed two blocks to the Grand View Inn.

Credit Cards Accepted

Visa, MasterCard.

GREEN GABLES INN

104 5th Street
Pacific Grove, Monterey County
Tel. 800/722-1774 or 831/375-2095
Fax: 831/375-5437
Web Address: www.foursisters.com
E-mail: info@foursisters.com
Rates: $120-240
3pm check-in
Date Opened: 1975
Innkeeper: Lucia Root

Profile

When I discovered that the Green Gables Inn was once the family home of the Posts, the owners of several West Coast bed and breakfasts including this one, I nearly gasped. How could anyone be so generous as to abandoned this gorgeous Victorian manor – ocean views and all – in order to open it up for the sake of other's enjoyment? If this home were mine, I would have kept it all to myself. Thankfully the Posts, who operate Four Sisters Inns, are more altruistic than I.

Built in 1888 for Englishman William Lacy, most likely as a summer retreat, Lacy never lived at Green Gables. Instead, the first resident was his divorced friend Emma Murdoch. She, along with her infant daughter and housekeeper, were the occupants of this grand estate. On occasion, Mr. Lacy, who lived in Los Angeles, would sail his yacht to Monterey bringing with him gifts and toys for Emma and her daughter. On one such trip in 1899 his vessel capsized near the Monterey Bay, and he died days later of pneumonia. As a result, the house was sold and Emma and her daughter settled in Southern California.

After several subsequent owners, Mrs. Ethel Wright purchased the home in 1954 and rented rooms for the first time in its history. It was later bought by the Flatly family, owners of the neighboring Seven Gables Inn, who renovated the house and rented rooms first to students then to travelers. Then, in 1971, Roger and Sally Post purchased the home raising their four daughters on the edge of the coast. During the summer months, they'd transform the home once again into an inn, and the Posts would reshuffle their living quarters in order to rent out the prime waterview chambers to eager tourists.

Finally, in 1983, they turned their seasonal hobby into a full-time business. Today Four Sisters Inns is a family collaboration featuring a dozen inns located throughout Southern California, Washington and Colorado.

Accommodations

As you walk through the pair of stained-glass doors that lead to the main parlor, you're in for an unforgettable stay. Constructed from a grove of redwoods with a blanket of solid maple floors, brass and copper doors and window fixtures, exposed dark wood interior trim and an enormous wooden mantelpiece, the overall appearance of Green Gables was originally much darker than its present airy self. The Queen Anne Victorian home retains its original windows, fixtures and woodwork, while the rear postwar, five-room annex complements the original architecture.

There is one room on the first floor with five delightful rooms located off a central hallway upstairs. While all the rooms are inviting, it's the Balcony, Gable and Chapel Rooms that offer the most breathtaking views of the bay. The **Balcony Room** is a cozy retreat and ideal for traveling trios as it has an extra single bed in the room's snug solarium. The **Gable Room** features a ladder leading to an attic loft in one of the home's protruding gables, and the **Chapel Room**, concealed behind a pair of expansive mahogany pocket doors, is filled with a tapestry of antiques.

The two-story **annex**, located behind the home, features five rooms opening up onto a common breezeway. The structure is complementary to the original home as are the spacious interiors, collection of antiques, private baths and partial ocean views.

Amenities

I happened to visit Green Gables Inn on a chilly autumn afternoon. How I wish I could have spent the rest of my day lounging in the parlor just gazing out at the million-dollar views. It's here, against the rugged and pounding surf, where afternoon tea is served in the front parlor as passersby below appear to be just a tad envious.

In the morning, the dining room, which also offers its share of seascape vistas, is where a bountiful breakfast is enjoyed. Borrow one of the inn's bicycles for a short ride to the **Monterey Bay Aquarium** (the innkeepers can assist in obtaining tickets), or challenge a fellow guest to a board game.

At-A-Glance Features

11 Rooms
Bicycles Available
Children Welcome
Complimentary Breakfast
Complimentary Afternoon Tea
Non-Smoking
Within Walking Distance to Town and Attractions

Directions

From San Francisco, take Highway 1 south to the Pacific Grove/ Pebble Beach exit. Follow the signs to Pacific Grove, and once in town the road becomes Forest Avenue. Follow Forest Avenue to Oceanview Boulevard. Turn right, and proceed to Green Gables Inn at the corner of 5th and Oceanview.

Credit Cards Accepted

Visa, MasterCard, American Express.

THE MARTINE INN

255 Oceanview Boulevard
Pacific Grove, Monterey County
Tel. 800/852-5588 or 831/373-3388
Fax: 831/373-3896
Web Address: www.martineinn.com
E-mail: none
Rates: $165-300
3pm check-in
Year Opened: 1984
Innkeeper: Don Martine

Profile

The gracious Martine Inn is coated in a pleasing shade of zinfandel with views of the pounding coastline below. The home was built in 1899 and purchased two years later by Laura and James Parke of Parke Davis Pharmaceuticals. The family's 55-room compound consisted of the original main house, a carriage house and a pair of buildings situated on a 2 1/2 block site.

Originally the home was the epitome of Victorian elegance replete with a cupola, dormers and grape arbors, but perpetual remodeling helped transform this turn-of-the-century manor into a Mediterranean-style villa. The dormers were removed, the cupola dismantled, and the exterior eventually coated with stucco. Any trace of Victorian charm has long since vanished.

During World War II, the Parkes, now in frail health, were able to spot submarines skimming the bay from within the confines of their home. They decided it was time to sell the home, and together relocated into a nearby hotel where they lived out the rest of their days. Decades later,

1972 to be exact, Don Martine purchased the home with the help of his parents and began the painstaking task of returning the estate back to its pre-war splendor.

At present, The Martine Inn is a museum of sorts with furnishings acquired from the Malaren Estates Mahogany Suite exhibited at the 1893 Chicago World's Fair; bedroom furniture from the estate of costume designer Edith Head; and an 1860s signed Chippendale Revival four-poster bed complete with canopy and side curtains. The inn's owner also has a fascination for old MG cars, and pieces from his collection are on display to the rear of the carriage house.

Accommodations

Only Oceanview Boulevard down below divides The Martine Inn from the sea, so if you're going to stay here it only makes sense to have a room with an ocean view. Framing the pounding waves are windows located in the **Suite, Parke, Maries, Eastlake, Victoriana, Malarin,** and **Cottage** rooms. Other chambers either overlook the rooftops or court-yard, and all offer unique antiques and private bathrooms with such unexpected appointments as claw-foot tubs and fireplaces.

Rooms to reckon with include the **Parke** chamber with its outstanding panoramic views, sitting area, corner Victorian fireplace and 19th century Chippendale bedroom set; the **Garden** chamber complete with mahogany corner fireplace, four-poster bed and courtyard views; and the **Art Deco** room, a name that speaks for itself.

Amenities

The Martine Inn creates a casually elegant ambiance in its public rooms. There's a formal library, an enclosed fountain courtyard for sunbathing, and a delightful parlor in which to watch the whales and sea otters at play. There's also a **whirlpool spa** on the premises; just pack your swimsuit as towels and robes are provided.

Each morning between 8am and 10am a full breakfast is served tableside in the parlor, and a buffet of hot and chilled hors d'oeuvres, paired with local wines, is served from 6-8pm. Your thirst for beer, wine and cider can be quenched daily till 10pm in the privacy of your room as the staff delivers the requested beverage on a silver tray. Bottled water and soft drinks are also available throughout the day.

At-A-Glance Features

23 Rooms
Complimentary Breakfast
Complimentary Wine and Hors d'oeuvres

Game Room
Not Appropriate for Children
Whirlpool Spa
Within Walking Distance to Town and Attractions

Directions

From San Francisco, take Highway 1 south to the Pacific Grove/ Pebble Beach exit. Follow the signs to Pacific Grove, and once in town the road becomes Forest Avenue. Follow Forest Avenue to Oceanview Boulevard. Turn right, and proceed to The Martine Inn.

Credit Cards Accepted

Visa, MasterCard, American Express.

SEVEN GABLES INN

555 Oceanview Boulevard
Pacific Grove, Monterey County
Tel. 831/372-4341
Fax: none
Web Address: www.7-gables-grandview.com
E-mail: none
Rates: $165-475
2:30pm check-in
Date Opened: 1982
Innkeepers: The Flatley Family

Profile

The butter-colored Seven Gables Inn, built in 1886, was part of a cavalcade of large, showpiece Victorian homes scattered along the Monterey Peninsula's waterfront. This particular location is the envy of the block as it boasts unobstructed bay views at every turn.

Lucie Chase, a well-to-do widow, was one of the more colorful owners of the estate and a civic-minded leader. Her contributions to the home are the magnificent sun porches and fleet of gables, which protrude from the exterior. More than two decades ago the Flatley family purchased the home, and in 1982 they transformed their dwelling into one of the region's most talked about inns.

Accommodations

The Seven Gables Inn is regal and stately, with its gilded antiques, intricate chandeliers, and delicate figurines and ornaments covering nearly every flat service. What sets this inn apart from its neighbors along Oceanfront Boulevard is that every room and cottage boasts unbelievable ocean vistas. Accommodations are housed in the three-story **Main House**; the **Cottages** (the single level served as the original carriage house while the two-story building was used as maids quarters); the **1946 Guest House**, which looks every bit as vintage as the original structures; and the two-story **Jewell Cottage**, a freestanding 1884 Victorian cottage that is larger than most homes.

Two noteworthy rooms are the Gable and the Carriage House. The **Gable**, the only room tucked away on the third floor of the Main House, was the home's big play attic. A fleet of steps leads to this charming hideaway, which is set amongst five of the seven gables. The angled ceiling offers up a cozy retreat, and with windows on all four sides the views are simply unbelievable. The **Carriage House** is one of the **Cottage** accommodations and is more streamlined than the rooms found in the Main House. The bay window provides the framing for some incredible views of the gardens and surf, and the gas-burning fireplace provides some added warmth. Other rooms to consider are the **Arbor** and **Garden** chambers, which are also located in the Cottage.

For couples traveling together or those in town for business, the **Jewell Cottage** is like a home away from home. It features two bedrooms, a living room with ocean views, a gas-burning fireplace, television, VCR, breakfast room, refrigerator, microwave, telephone and modem hookup.

Amenities

Sharing a common manmade brook and cobblestone path with the Seven Gables Inn is the Grand View Inn, also owned by the Flatleys. The compact gardens, tucked behind the Main House, offer a tiny nest of flora between meandering pathways leading to the various annexes.

A generous sit-down breakfast is served every morning in the **Grand Dining Room**, and at 4pm an English-style high tea gets underway. With the exception of the Jewell Cottage, rooms do not have telephones and televisions; these modern-day distractions can be found in the parlor.

At-A-Glance Features

14 Rooms
Complimentary Breakfast
Complimentary Afternoon Tea
Near Shops, Restaurants and Attractions

Nightly Turndown Service
Non-Smoking
Not Appropriate for Children

Directions

From San Francisco, take Highway 1 south to the Pacific Grove/ Pebble Beach exit. Follow the signs to Pacific Grove, and once in town the road becomes Forest Avenue. Follow Forest Avenue to Oceanview Boulevard. Turn right, and proceed two blocks to the Seven Gables Inn.

Credit Cards Accepted

Visa, MasterCard.

SAN LUIS OBISPO

Served by Los Angeles International Airport (LAX) or San Jose International Airport (SJC).

GARDEN STREET INN

1212 Garden Street
San Luis Obispo, San Luis Obispo County
Tel. 800/488-2045 or 805/545-9802
Fax: 506/545-9403
Web Address: www.gardenstreetinn.com
E-mail: innkeeper@gardenstreetinn.com
Rates: $110-180
3pm check-in
Date Opened: 1990
Innkeeper: Lynn Clements

Profile

Located in the heart of downtown San Luis Obispo, a college town half-way between Los Angeles and San Francisco, the Garden Street Inn is a charming find.

Built in 1887 as a single story residence for local merchants Morris and Helen Goldtree, this Italianate/Queen Anne home grew to two stories when local brewery owners Patrick and Elizabeth McCaffrey acquired it in 1898. They then divided the residence into four flats and, 25 years later, a subsequent owner by the name of Dollie McKeen divided it once again into eight units. Dollie lived here until her death in 1965, and it wasn't until 1989 that Dan and Kathy Smith purchased the property and began the painstaking task of restoring it.

Looking at the home today, it would be hard to guess that at one time the Garden Street Inn was an apartment building. The transformation to elegant bed and breakfast inn is nearly flawless.

Accommodations

The Garden Street Inn offers a collection of 13 guest rooms and suites with individual embellishments and a hint of whimsy. The steep staircase leading to the second floor is the passageway to most of the rooms and from this level guests have access to a common rear balcony.

Stately antiques and vintage fabrics are hallmarks of the Garden Street Inn. Whether you're staying in the least expensive room or the most costly, there is something special about each. The names of the rooms and suites reflect the mood: **Edelweiss, Field of Dreams, Amadeus** and **Concours d'Elegance**, just to name a few. The **Emerald Isle** reflects its namesake with a shamrock motif and offers a private deck, while the **Close to Home** suite, named for the Pulitzer Prize-winning author Ellen Goodman, offers more roomy surroundings with a sitting area and bedroom separated by imposing pocket doors. Other touches concealed by the fleet of vintage doors include Victorian fireplaces, claw-foot tubs, cast-iron stoves and stained-glass windows.

Amenities

The **Goldtree Library**, named for the original owners, is a welcoming parlor filled with shelves of books, plush sofas and chairs, a glowing fireplace and plenty of conversation. Each evening guests gather to sample local wines that are paired with a tray of hors d'oeuvres. The **McCaffrey Morning Room**, with its original stained glass, lace curtains and soaring ceiling, is where a bountiful breakfast is served.

The Garden Street Inn is close to everything the San Luis Obispo area has to offer. The 1772 historic **Mission and Plaza** are within walking distance, **Pismo Beach** is just a short drive, the **vineyards of Edna Valley** are within tasting distance and, if you like strolling through the grounds of universities, a visit to **Cal Poly San Luis Obispo** is a must. If you prefer to stay nearby, the town center is at your doorstep. There's plenty of shops, restaurants and pubs to keep you content, along with the usual suspects like Starbucks and the mega bookstores. But, for the most part, at least for the time being, San Luis Obispo is devoid of any major commercialism.

At-A-Glance Features

13 Rooms
Children 16 Years and Older Welcome
Complimentary Breakfast
Complimentary Wine and Hors d'oeuvres
Non-Smoking
Within Walking Distance to Town and Attractions

Directions

Head north or south on Highway 101 and exit on Marsh Street. You'll be heading on a one-way street for about five or six blocks before turning right on Garden Street. The inn will be on the left-hand side.

Credit Cards Accepted

Visa, MasterCard American Express.

SANTA CRUZ

Served by San Jose International Airport (SJC).

BABBLING BROOK INN

1025 Laurel Street
Santa Cruz, Santa Cruz County
Tel. 800/866-1131 or 831/427-2437
Fax: 831/427-2457
Web Address: www.babblingbrookinn.com
E-Mail: lodging@babblingbrookinn.com
Rates: $160-220
3pm check-in
Date Opened: 1981
Innkeepers: Suzie Lankes and Dan Floyd

Profile

The Babbling Brook Inn rests on a knoll and is set back from a busy thoroughfare. Once behind the inn's gates the only sounds that permeate are cascading waterfalls and a meandering brook.

The inn's grounds are somewhat sacred, having once belonged to an Indian fishing village more than 2000 years ago. The foundation also housed an 18th century grist mill and a tannery before Mr. and Mrs. Charles Place built their log cabin home here, which is now the lobby. The Places were actors, and in 1911 the silent movie *Danites* was filmed at the log cabin. In the following years, many stars of the era, including Jack Hoxie, Marian Sikes and Hopalong Cassidy, summered here. During the next few decades, the home changed hands several times and eventually housed several restaurants.

Today, The Babbling Brook Inn is a collection of shingled chalets and lush gardens located just a short distance from the town's famed seaside boardwalk, bustling wharf, and revitalized downtown area.

Accommodations

A web of bridges, footpaths and stairways lead to an ensemble of two-story shingled buildings, creating an unusual layered design. Each of the 13 rooms are capsules of coziness with fireplaces, individual decks and terraces, and outside entrances. Many of the rooms are named for famous artists – **van Gogh, Monet, Renoir** – and offer various appointments, from 10-foot wrought-iron beds to expansive French doors.

Two of my favorite rooms are the secluded **Artist's Retreat**, which rests just below the waterwheel and has its own hidden Jacuzzi deck and generous floor plan. The other is the **FMRS Garden**, whose initials pay homage to a past owner responsible for the gardens' design during the property's reign as a French bistro. One of the more intimate rooms, it features hardwood floors and a picture window overlooking the gardens, gazebo and flowing brook.

Amenities

A sumptuous breakfast is served buffet-style each morning, and guests are greeted in the afternoon by a display of local wines and cheeses. These culinary gatherings can be enjoyed in either the parlor by a roaring fire or under an umbrella-shaded table on the outside terrace. If you're not a morning person, simply fix a plate, pour yourself a cup of coffee, and head back to your private deck. Not to be missed are the plate of moist cookies left each evening on the lobby tea cart.

At-A-Glance Features

13 Rooms
Complimentary Breakfast
Complimentary Evening Wine and Hors d'oeuvres
Near Beach, Boardwalk and Downtown Shopping
Non-Smoking
Not Appropriate for Children

Directions

Head north or south on Highway 101, and take exit Highway 17 towards Santa Cruz. Merge north onto Highway 1, which is also Mission Street, and continue to Laurel Street. The inn will be located 1 1/2 blocks down the hill on your right.

Credit Cards Accepted

Visa, MasterCard, American Express, Discover.

SOQUEL

Served by San Jose International Airport (SJC).

BLUE SPRUCE INN

2815 Main Street
Soquel, Santa Cruz County
Tel. 800/559-1137 or 831/464-1137
Fax: 831/475-0608
Web Address: www.bluespruce.com
E-Mail: ytjecha@bluespruce.com
Rates: $85-175
3pm check-in
Year Opened: 1989
Innkeepers: Victoria and Thomas Jechart

Profile

Soquel is one of those California towns few people know about. Located just four miles from Santa Cruz, this sleepy hamlet has the good fortune of being close to many of the area's attractions.

The town became a homestead for lumberjacks hired to log the redwoods in the nearby Santa Cruz mountains. These hardworking men built small farms for their families, and to help supplement their income, they sold food and produce to local residents. The Blue Spruce Inn, a two-structured hideaway, is part of one of the original lumberjack farmhouses. A renovation revealed stall doors and striking redwood slabs, making it easy to conclude that at one time the home was one of the original barns.

Both of the inn's structures, built in 1873, are a part of the Historic Inventory of Santa Cruz County.

Accommodations

The farmhouse ambiance lends itself well to the quiet existence of Soquel. You might hear the sputter of engines as a car motors past the inn, but it's more likely you'll encounter chirping birds and little else.

The emphasis at the Blue Spruce Inn is on simple comforts. The two buildings, the Main House and Carriage House, each feature three rooms. Hunker down in a room in the **Main House** with its eclectic blend of early American appointments, nautical touches and plantation heirlooms. The **Carriage House**, where the wagons and farm carts were once stored, has been converted into a lovely retreat and has its own private entrance, patio and spa tub for two. Two smaller rooms are located here as well. Terry robes and televisions with VCR are standard offerings, and some rooms are equipped with whirlpool tubs.

Amenities

Simple morning grub, like granola and fresh fruit, are enhanced with a dash of decadence. You may awake to find crepes stuffed with fresh peaches or a potato frittata browning in the oven. Morning meals can be enjoyed at the communal dining table or at the more intimate two-person window seat. If the weather is agreeable, move off to a spot in the garden or enjoy the first meal of the day on your private patio. During the afternoon, special treats are laid out for everyone's enjoyment.

Though the inn doesn't offer spa services on site, they do have arrangements with a local pamper parlor, and the innkeepers can set up a treatment for you at the facility. Pets are also welcome.

At-A-Glance Features

6 Rooms
Close to Wineries
Complimentary Breakfast and Snacks
Concierge Service Available
Not Appropriate for Children
Pet-Friendly
Walk to Antique Shops

Directions

From the San Jose area, take Highway 101 to Highway 17 and exit Highway 1 south. Travel through Santa Cruz and exit Capitola/Soquel at Bay Avenue and Porter Street (there's one exit for both streets). Turn left from the exit going under the freeway pass and turn right at the second signal, which is Main Street. The inn will be up the road on your left.

Credit Cards Accepted

Visa, MasterCard, American Express, Discover.

8. SOUTHERN CALIFORNIA

BALLARD

Served by Los Angeles International Airport (LAX).

THE BALLARD INN

2436 Baseline Avenue
Ballard, Santa Barbara County
Tel. 800/638-2466 or 805/688-7770
Fax: 805/688-9560
Web Address: www.ballardinn.com
E-mail: innkeeper@ballardinn.com
Rates: $195-275
3pm check-in
Year Opened: 1985
Innkeeper: Kelly Robinson

Profile

The Ballard Inn may look the part of historic hideaway, but the 15-room retreat was only built during the 1980s. Surrounded by vineyards and the aroma of freshly stomped grapes, The Ballard Inn is an idyllic choice for a weekend in California's *other* wine country. With its gabled accents, expansive porch and classic picket fence, it looks every bit like a Victorian showpiece surrounded by manicured lawns, potted plants and blooming flowers.

Though the mood is decidedly casual in these parts – think sundresses and sandals – money flows as freely as an uncorked bottle of the latest vintage. Many of Hollywood's heavyweights, such as the gloved-one Michael Jackson, have homes in the Santa Ynez Valley. The towns of Los Olivos and Solvang are nearby, and only a mountain pass divides this area from Santa Barbara proper.

Accommodations

Behind the clapboard facade are 15 delightful rooms. Though the inn is best described as vineyard country, don't look for any lace doilies or dried flowers tied together with raffia. Instead, embrace the simple elegance of oversized quilts, wood-burning fireplaces, elegant antiques and wine-related artwork. As for televisions, telephones or modems, they don't exist.

Among my favorite rooms are the unexpected **Jarado**, a boldly colored Santa Fe-style chamber with hardwood floors and Native American touches. Traditional picks include the **Vineyard Room**, one of the larger chambers replete with an inviting circular bay window, paying homage to the great winemakers of Santa Barbara County. **Cynthia's Room**, with its angled fireplace, is popular for wedding nights and anniversary celebrations. The innkeeper leaves the doors to unoccupied rooms open, so don't be shy about browsing around and taking mental notes of where you'd like to slumber on your next visit.

Amenities

The oak and Italian marble fireplace in the foyer creates an inviting entrance for arriving guests, whether just checking in or awaking for the morning meal. A full breakfast, cooked to order, is served in the dining room along with such offerings as cinnamon rolls, oatmeal and freshly roasted coffee. The afternoon takes on a different mood as guests wander back home, drunk from happiness (and perhaps some local vino), ready to settle down for the night. Local vintages from nearby wineries are poured and hors d'oeuvres are laid out for all to enjoy. Nightly turndown service yields a stash of plump homemade cookies. The inn also offers bikes for rent, and in-room massages can be arranged.

There are few dining choices in the area, so the inn's **Cafe Chardonnay** is an obvious choice for dinner. The setting is relaxed and refined with a menu of wine country cuisine and a list of vintages to go along with it. Main courses include fresh salmon or ahi tuna, vegetarian pasta, or grilled chicken breast served on a warm spinach salad topped with pancetta, tomato and curry dressing. The wine list is intoxicating with an emphasis on local vintages from the vineyards of Firestone, Sunstone, Fess Parker and Zaca Mesa, places you're likely to visit while staying at The Ballard Inn. Even the limited selection of beer includes mostly local ales, with an Amstel Light thrown in for good measure.

At-A-Glance Features

15 Rooms
Children 12 and Older Welcome

Close to Wineries
Complimentary Breakfast
Complimentary Evening Wine and Hors d'oeuvres
En-Suite Massage
Evening Turndown Service
Full-Service Restaurant
Near Shops, Restaurants and Attractions
Non-Smoking

Directions

From Los Angeles, take Highway 101 north to Highway 154. Continue on Highway 154 for about 30-35 miles. You'll exit left at the Edison-Baseline turnoff. Turn right at the stop sign directly on Baseline Avenue, and follow the road for about two miles. The inn will be on your left.

Credit Cards Accepted

Visa, MasterCard, American Express.

SANTA BARBARA WINE TASTING

Many of the Santa Barbara County wineries have tasting rooms, offer picnic areas, house gift shops and host guided vineyard tours. Most of the tastings and tours are complimentary, but some do charge a minimum sampling fee.

*If you prefer to take a guided tour of the wine country, there are two excellent companies that host worry-free escapes. The **Blue Sky Bus**, Tel. 805/564-1811 or 800/977-1123, is based in Santa Barbara and will take you on a fun and informative trip through the county's various wineries. The Pismo Beach-based **Breakaway Tours**, Tel. 805/783-2929 or 800/799-7657, takes you to both the well-known and the hidden favorites for half-day, full-day or weekend excursions.*

*If you're visiting the area during the months of April or October, the Vintners' Association hosts two annual festivals during the spring and fall seasons. The **Vintners' Festival** is held each April in a beautiful outdoor setting, usually at one of the wineries, and features food from local restaurants, wine tastings, music, entertainment and a silent auction. During the month of October, the organization hosts **A Celebration of Harvest** commemorating the grape harvest and featuring wine, gourmet foods, music, demonstrations and other afternoon fun. Both events are casual affairs. Tickets are limited and can be purchased by calling Tel. 800/218-0881.*

BORREGO SPRINGS

Served by San Diego International Airport (SAN).

BORREGO VALLEY INN
405 Palm Canyon Drive
Borrego Springs, San Diego County
Tel. 800/333-5810 or 760/767-0311
Fax: 760/767-0900
Web Address: www.borregovalleyinn.com
E-mail: info@borregovalleyinn.com
Rates: $95-155
3pm check-in
Year Opened: 1998
Innkeepers: Mary and Don Robidoux

Profile
As you make your way across the flat dusty road that winds its way through the Anza-Borrego Desert, the red-tiled roof crowning the Borrego Valley Inn could easily be mistaken for a mirage. This Taos-style retreat is situated among the tumbleweeds and barren landscape in, of all places, San Diego County.

Far removed from San Diego's glistening beaches and barrage of surfboards, the Borrego Valley Inn is located smack in the middle of the arid **Anza-Borrego State Desert Park**. The park was established in 1933 in part to preserve the habitat of the bighorn sheep. Although the majestic animal is slowly headed for extinction, owing to illness and changes in their habitat, it's quite possible you might spot one in the distance while lounging by the inn's pool.

Accommodations
Quenching guests' thirst for luxury and desert chic are a collection of 14 pueblo-style rooms. From the outside, the pair of long adobe buildings look rather ordinary with their sloping red-tiled roofs, thick pillars and earthy hues, but behind each portal is a stylish southwestern chamber. Cool tiles cloak the floors, queen-size beds are angled, rear doors lead to private patios, and windows provide the framing for peaceful views. Some rooms turn the comfort factor up a notch with such amenities as fireplaces, kitchenettes and whirlpool tubs.

Of the 600,000 acres that encompass the Anza-Borrego State Desert Park, the Borrego Valley Inn rests on a 10-acre parcel of land. Looking diminutive against the majestic mountain ranges, this seems an ideal place for a serious author or painter to hole up for months on end, and the inn hosts its share of visiting artists throughout the year.

Amenities

Days at Borrego Valley Inn can be as leisurely or active as you choose. As the sun begins to rise, wander into the lobby area for a buffet feast of fresh fruit, croissants, local citrus and other favorites. Then take your plate and fresh-brewed coffee, and grab a table on the covered patio.

Spend the afternoon reclining by the **swimming pool** and **spa**, or head to one of the **local golf courses** to improve your handicap. One of the most delightful times to be a desert dweller is from dusk till dawn, when a galaxy of stars illuminates the ebony sky. For guests who wish to take advantage of the region's nighttime beauty, the inn provides a high-powered telescope. End the day with an **en-suite massage**.

At-A-Glance Features

14 Rooms
Closed During the Months of July and August
Complimentary Continental Breakfast
Complimentary Newspaper
En Suite Massage Available
Non-Smoking
Not Appropriate for Children
Swimming Pool and Spa

Directions

From Downtown San Diego, take Interstate 5 north to Interstate 8 east. Then follow Highway 163 north until it crosses with Interstate 5, and head north on Interstate 5 to the Scripps/Poway Parkway north. At Highway 67, turn left into the town of Ramona; here it will change to Highway 78, which continues on. Stay on Highway 78, turn left onto Highway 79 and travel for approximately 12 miles.

At Intersection S2, go right and travel for another five miles until reaching S22. Follow S22 down the mountain for about 17 miles. At the bottom of the hill turn right and follow the road for about half a mile. The inn will be on your right.

Credit Cards Accepted

Visa, MasterCard, American Express, Discover, Diners Club.

DON'T MISS ANZA-BORREGO PARK

The **Anza-Borrego State Desert Park** is a natural wonder. The expansive visitors center, located at the west end of Palm Canyon Drive, Tel. 760/767-4205, is open October through May and on weekends only from June through September. The center hosts such gatherings as naturalist talks and guided nature walks, including one that leads from the desert canyon to one of North America's only natural palm groves in a span of less than two miles.

Another great way to see the park's highlights is with **Desert Jeep Tours**, Tel. 888/295-3377 or www.desertjeeptours.com, a company that conducts guided four-wheel outings starting at around $59 per person.

CATALINA ISLAND

Served by Los Angeles International Airport (LAX) or John Wayne/
Orange County International Airport (SNA).

THE INN AT MT. ADA

398 Wrigley Road, P.O. Box 2560
Avalon, Catalina Island, Los Angeles County
Tel. 800/608-7669 or 310/510-2030
Fax: 310/510-2237
Web Address: www.catalina.com/mtada
E-mail: none
Rates: $280-620
2pm check-in
Date Opened: 1985
Innkeeper: Susie Griffin and Marlene McAdam

Profile

This fabulous home, now Catalina Island's premier bed and breakfast
inn, was built by chewing gum magnate William Wrigley. In 1919, Wrigley
purchased the entire island and brought his baseball team, the Chicago
Cubs, to the remote area for spring training.

Soon after his land acquisition, Wrigley chose the most magnificent
hillside in which to nest. The whitewashed Georgian Colonial revival
mansion was said to be his wife Ada's summer dream house, and the
trademark green shutters were her contribution to the design. Covering
7,000 square feet of space with prime ocean views, the home was the most
elaborate the islanders had seen. The main floor included arched door-
ways leading to the den, sun room, living room, drawing room, dining
rooms and butler's pantry; a curved staircase disappeared to the second
floor where six additional bedrooms could be found.

The Wrigleys occupied their summer home for the next 30 years, and
after they passed away, the estate was donated to the University of
Southern California. USC leased the property to the Institute of Marine
Coastal Studies as a quasi-campus for cultural and academic studies. In
1985, two local residents signed a 30-year lease investing more than a
million dollars to restore the estate to its original splendor.

Accommodations

A stay at the Inn At Mt. Ada is probably equivalent to some of the spectacular gatherings found between the pages of *The Great Gatsby*. The setting is superb, the service impeccable and the surroundings remote.

After arriving at the Catalina ferry terminal or island airport, just tell any car for hire that you're headed to the inn. Not only will they quickly transport you to this grand estate, but the fare is included in your stay. A tiny circular driveway, skirted with colorful flowers, leads to the column entryway of the mansion. Once inside the compound, you're made to feel as if you're the only guest that matters as the innkeeper ushers you about, introducing you to other guests, and showing you where a stash of cookies are kept in the pantry.

There are four bedrooms and two suites, all with spectacular ocean views, located on the second floor. Each room features period-style antiques, a private bath plus his and her terry robes; some offer separate dressing areas, sitting rooms, fireplaces and private balconies. Even the most inexpensive room and one of my favorites, the **Garden Porch**, is more elegant than many other inn's most touted suites. Although there are no televisions or phones in the guest rooms, the main parlor provides a television for those who simply can't do without, and a phone is located at the top of the stairs.

Amenities

The dining room, with its hardwood floors, large picture window and breathtaking ocean views, is where guests gather for juice and coffee prior to feasting on a hearty country-style breakfast. When weather permits, and it most always does, a deli lunch is served on the verandah, and chilled wine, beer and hors d'oeuvres greet guests after a day of island exploring. In between, a supply of soft drinks and snacks are available in the butler's pantry, so help yourself. Guests may lounge in any of the public rooms, including the club room stocked with board games, the formal library/ parlor with its grand piano awaiting a player, the wicker-filled sun porch with a cart full of fresh coffee and baked goods, or the expansive verandah overlooking the ocean. Or wander over to the telescope and just admire the beauty from where you are standing.

Avalon, the island's quaint town fronting the ocean, entices guests from far below. You could hike to town, but why bother when a complimentary golf cart is at your disposal. Use it for puttering up and down the hill instead of walking. However, be warned: once you check in it's unlikely that you'll want to leave the premises at all.

At-A-Glance Features

6 Rooms
Complimentary Breakfast
Complimentary Deli Lunch
Complimentary Golf Carts
Complimentary Snacks, Beer, Wine, Champagne and Soft Drinks
Not Suitable for Children Under 14

Directions

Catalina Island is located 26 miles from Los Angeles Harbor, yet feels a world apart. There are only two ways to reach the island – by boat or helicopter, so take your pick. The cheaper way to go is by boat from San Pedro or Long Beach. The trip takes about an hour with **Catalina Express'** fleet of boats, *Tel. 800/429-4601* or *310/519-1212*. **Island Express Helicopter Service**, *Tel. 310/510-2525*, also departs from San Pedro and Long Beach and takes only about 15 minutes. Once you arrive at either terminal, just tell a taxi driver your staying at the Inn at Mt. Ada; the innkeeper will pay your fare.

Credit Cards Accepted

Visa, MasterCard.

WRIGLEY'S ISLAND PARADISE

When William Wrigley resided here during the early part of the 20th century, he owned 99% of the island. He chose this palisade location, which teeters 350 feet above the town and harbor, because it received the first sunlight in the morning and the final rays at sunset. As the owner of the Chicago Cubs, he invited the team to hold their spring training on the island and, from his vantage point high above, kept a watchful eye on their progress. During his time on Catalina, he and his wife entertained Presidents Calvin Coolidge and Warren Harding, and the Prince of Wales.

DANA POINT

Served by Los Angeles International Airport (LAX) or John Wayne/
Orange County International Airport (SNA).

BLUE LANTERN INN

34343 Street of the Blue Lantern
Dana Point, Orange County
Tel. 800/950-1236 or 949/661-1304
Fax: 949/496-1483
Web Address: www.foursisters.com
E-mail: none
Rates: $150-500
3pm Check-in
Year Opened: 1990
Innkeeper: Patty Olsen

Profile

Performing a balancing act on one of the most scenic bluffs to skirt
the coastline, the Blue Lantern Inn was designed to resemble the
traditional Cape Cod-style lodges found along the craggy New England
shores. Built a little more than a decade ago, the architectural elements,
such as the gabled roof, expansive porch and even choice of a slate-blue
hue, are deceivingly vintage.

Even the bluffside location, which offers commanding harbor views
along with echoes of the pounding surf, resembles an East Coast fishing
village. Never mind that the boat slips are tethered to luxury yachts rather
than weathered vessels, this is just another gentle reminder to let you
know you're still in Southern California.

Dana Point, sandwiched between Laguna Beach and San Clemente,
is a quiet outpost consisting mostly of antique shops, casual eateries, an
impressive yacht harbor and the beach. From the Blue Lantern Inn, you
can basically walk to most everything, though the harbor and beach areas
require a bit of a hike.

Accommodations

Managed like an efficient hotel, yet with all the personal touches of
a family-run business, the Blue Lantern Inn is a heavenly place to be
stranded.

Spanning three floors, with most of the rooms located on the top two
levels, only four rooms are without ocean views. Behind each threshold

you'll find a cozy fireplace, sitting area, expansive bathroom complete with whirlpool tub and separate shower, plus a mini-fridge stocked with complimentary soft drinks. Many of the rooms also offer ample balconies outfitted with tables and chairs to enjoy your morning coffee, which is promptly delivered to your room upon request. You'll also find plenty of reading material and plush terry robes for lounging.

If you're looking to splurge, request the **Tower Suite**, a stunning hideaway complete with vaulted ceiling, a four-poster king bed and 180-degree views of the Pacific Ocean.

Amenities

I could spend as much time in the airy library as I could in my room. It's an inviting setting where guests spend idle hours sifting through the countless magazine and books lining the hearth.

On the other side of the room, nearest the cliffside, is the quaint dining area and adjoining porch where a satisfying display of wine, tea and hors d'oeuvres are served each afternoon. If you're planning on sampling one of the nearby restaurants at dinnertime, be sure to stack your plate lightly as this is no cheese and crackers display. This cozy area, with its antique furnishings, doubles as the breakfast room where a magnificent buffet of bagels, fresh fruit, homemade breads, a daily main course and rich coffee are served until 10am. If weather permits, try to claim one of the outdoor tables just beyond the French doors.

The inn, which rests at the end of a narrow road, sits adjacent to a lovely cliffside gazebo. Come weekends, a turnstile of brides and grooms pose for wedding photos beneath the lattice structure. But, if you time it right, you can spend a blissful morning scouring the newspaper in total peace.

At-A-Glance Features

29 Rooms
Bicycles Available
Children Welcome
Complimentary Breakfast
Complimentary Newspaper
Complimentary Wine and Hors d'oeuvres
Exercise Room
In-Room Refrigerators With Complimentary Soft Drinks
Nightly Turndown Service
Within Walking Distance to Shops and Restaurants

Directions

From Los Angeles, take the 405 Freeway south to Interstate 5 (this merges in Orange County near Irvine). Travel south on Interstate 5 exiting at Pacific Coast Highway/Camino Las Ramblas. At the fork in the ramp, stay to your right heading north on the Pacific Coast Highway. Turn left onto Blue Lantern; the inn is at the end of the road on your right.

Credit Cards Accepted

Visa, MasterCard, American Express.

JULIAN

Served by San Diego International Airport (SAN).

THE JULIAN GOLD RUSH HOTEL
2032 Main Street
Julian, San Diego County
Tel. 800/734-5854 or 760/765-0201
Fax: 760/765-0327
Web Address: www.julianhotel.com
E-mail: bnb@julianhotel.com
Rates: $92-185
3pm check-in
Year Opened: 1897
Innkeepers: Steve and Gig Ballinger

Profile
Walk through the doors of Julian's only historic landmark, and you'll feel as if you're in a time warp. The Julian Gold Rush Hotel doesn't just bill itself as a Victorian inn, it *is* a Victorian inn and reportedly the oldest, continuously operating hotel in Southern California.

The hotel was built by Albert Robinson, a freed slave from Missouri, and his wife Margaret who was often noted for being the wife of the "first colored man ever summoned as a juror in San Diego County." After the two were married in the early 1880s, they started a restaurant and bakery on the hotel's premises. In the late 1890s, construction began on the hotel, and the aged cedar and locust trees encircling the hotel were planted and tended to by Albert himself. Many senators and congressmen stayed at the Hotel Robinson on their stops through San Diego County, and after Albert's death in 1915 Margaret continued to run the inn until 1921.

For the next 47 years the Jacobs family were the proprietors, and the inn became known simply as the Julian Hotel. Now listed on the National Register of Historic Places, this peerless inn managed to retain its 19th century charm despite such fleeting trends as Formica and shag carpeting.

Accommodations
The rooms, like the Victorian era, have a genteel quality; perhaps all that is missing are some smelling salts and fainting couches. The two-story main building features 13 rooms offering verandah views, cast-iron beds, vintage quilts and other bygone comforts.

A short cobblestone pathway segues from the main building to the pair of cottages out back. The **Patio Cottage** is the most secluded and offers a fireplace, a patio made from native stones and a snug verandah. The neighboring **Honeymoon House** looks like a mini-fortress behind a white picket fence and features a Franklin-style fireplace, a bridal canopied bed and an oversized claw-foot tub. The private entrance, just off a sloping side street, creates a sense of seclusion.

As in Victorian times, rooms are sans televisions, radios and any other modern-day distractions.

Amenities

Possessing an almost museum-like quality, those who register at the Julian Gold Rush Hotel are offered a rare glimpse at Victorian life. The historic dining room features groups of antique-laced tables where guests are treated to a proper breakfast served on fine china. Return later in the day for the ritual of afternoon tea and all the fanfare that goes along with it.

The inn's location, right along Main Street, puts you in the middle of everything Julian has to offer. While away the afternoon on the inn's porch, and watch the town unfold before you.

At-A-Glance Features

15 Rooms
Children Welcome
Complimentary Breakfast
Complimentary Afternoon Tea
Non-Smoking
Within Walking Distance to Shops and Restaurants

Directions

From San Diego, take Interstate 8 west to El Cajon, then head north on Highway 67 through Ramona to Highway 78 east, which will bring you straight into Julian. At the four-way stop, turn right onto Main Street. The inn is located just down the road on your left.

Credit Cards Accepted

Visa, MasterCard, American Express.

ORCHARD HILL COUNTRY INN

2502 Washington Street
Julian, San Diego County
Tel. 800/716-7242 or 760/765-1700
Fax: 760/765-0290
Web Address: www.orchardhill.com
E-mail: information@orchardhill.com
Rates: $185-285
3pm check-in
Year Opened: 1994
Innkeepers: Pat and Darrell Straube

Profile

Orchard Hill, with its contemporary lodge and quartet of vintage Craftsman cottages, resembles more of a compound than an inn. With four acres of flower-lined paths replete with swaying hammocks, wooden picnic tables, secluded reading benches and hidden gardens, guests have little reason to venture far.

Just down the hill is the town of Julian, known for its **apple pie** and slow pace. In recent years it's become quite a tourist attraction, probably because it is so vastly different from anything Southern California has to offer. This former mining town boasts four mild seasons (expect some snow in the winter) along with a main road boasting false-front stores, wooden sidewalks and historic buildings. Once you've had your fill of homemade apple pie and cinnamon ice cream, a Julian staple, head back to the quiet of Orchard Hill Country Inn.

Accommodations

There are 22 guest rooms, 10 in the two-story lodge and the rest divided among the hillside cottages. The mood is contemporary country with an almost minimalist approach. Walls are coated in muted tones of apricot, honey, sage and cream with a collection of uncluttered appointments that may include fireplaces, plantation shutters, plump sofas and chairs, iron beds and wicker rockers. Televisions and VCRs are also placed in each room.

While the main lodge feels more like a hotel, the surrounding cottage rooms have that bed and breakfast feel. These snug annexes offer an array of amenities such as private porches or patios, wet bars, window seats, whirlpool tubs, and dual fireplaces that heat both the boudoir and bathroom. The setting, among the groves of Julian, is also unbeatable.

Amenities

The **Great Room**, situated in the main lodge, is a lofty retreat and a great setting for afternoon wine and snacks. A full breakfast, served in the inn's dining room complete with treetop views, is ultra-gourmet. With a flair for presentation, rotating entrees include egg strata with gruyere cheese, stuffed French toast, artichoke frittata and other items that you can easily walk off with a trek into town. Other noticeable touches included with your stay are Belgian chocolates, splits of wine and freshly baked cookies.

The inn also serves dinner in the **Julian Room**, available to both guests and the general public. The $30 prix fixe menu includes a four-course dinner with such offerings as stuffed chicken featuring spinach, prosciutto and gruyere cheese; pork tenderloin drizzled with a balsamic vinegar and raisin sauce; and seasonal roasted vegetables.

A **game room** is available to all guests and is located in the upper level of the lodge. Here you'll find a selection of board games and books along with a television and VCR. The inn also has an extensive **video library** with a list of classic, drama, comedy, family and foreign flicks.

At-A-Glance Features

22 Rooms
Children Welcome
Complimentary Breakfast
Complimentary Afternoon Refreshments
Full-Service Restaurant
Non-Smoking
Within Walking Distance to Town

Directions

From San Diego, take Interstate 8 west to El Cajon, then head north on Highway 67 through Ramona to Highway 78 east, which will bring you straight into Julian. At the four-way stop, cross over Main Street and proceed straight up the hill. The inn will be two blocks up on your left.

Credit Cards Accepted

Visa, MasterCard, American Express.

LA JOLLA

Served by San Diego International Airport (SAN).

BED AND BREAKFAST INN OF LA JOLLA

7753 Draper Avenue
La Jolla, San Diego County
Tel. 800/582-2466 or 858/456-2066
Fax: 858/456-1510
Web Address: www.innlajolla.com
E-mail: bedbreakfast@innlajolla.com
Rates: $159-379
3pm check-in
Year Opened: 1984
Innkeeper: Ron Shanks

Profile

This 15-room inn, consisting of the original home and a garden annex, is brimming with history. Architect Irving Gill, known for his Cubist-style designs, built this lovely home for the Kaust family in 1913. Kate Sessions, who is credited with turning nearby Balboa Park's desert terrain into a botanical showcase, created the inn's tranquil gardens. The house once belonged to patriotic composer John Philip Sousa, who resided here with his family for most of the 1920s.

If all this isn't enough, the La Jolla location puts it over the top. This seaside village, popular with socialites and celebrities, is among the best San Diego has to offer. Sloping streets and narrow passageways offer up a European flair, and the well-heeled passersby are just as lordly. The inn is within walking distance to La Jolla's quaint shops, galleries and bistros. Simply park the car and explore the town on foot.

Accommodations

Situated on a side street and within an ocean spray of the beach, the Inn at La Jolla is an idyllic retreat. There are nine rooms in the original awning-draped home with the remaining six housed in the garden annex.

Rooms are named for influential San Diegans, former residents of the estate, or the natural wonders that bless La Jolla. From the smallest room on the second floor to the most elaborate penthouse, all rooms are exquisitely appointed with period-style antiques, homey touches, graceful artwork and fresh flowers throughout. Many rooms have ocean and garden views and, as expected, no two rooms are alike. What you can expect are billowy Laura Ashley fabrics, lots of wicker and rattan and handsome antiques.

Celebrate in the **Holiday Room**, offering a swank setting with a white-on-white color scheme and cream and beige accents. The plump four-poster bed is draped in an ecru canopy and positioned in front of the fireplace. There's also lounging chairs, a double soaking tub and gracious views. The **Pacific View** room offers a vintage nautical motif, while the **Shores**, located off the library, resembles an English cottage.

Thoughtful touches are found behind the door of every room with fresh fruit bowls and flowers, sherry aging in crystal decanters, and plush terry robes for lounging.

Amenities

Join fellow house guests every morning for a bountiful gourmet breakfast properly served on bone china and antique silver. This meal can be enjoyed in the formal dining room or more casually amid the gardens. The same setting applies for afternoon wine and cheese, and fruit, coffee and baked goods are available throughout the day. The innkeeper will also prepare a picnic basket to be enjoyed at the beach or park; just be sure to make your request at least a day prior.

At-A-Glance Features

15 Rooms
Complimentary Breakfast
Complimentary Evening Wine and Hors d'oeuvres
Not Appropriate for Children Under 12
Picnic Basket Lunches Available
Within Walking Distance to Shops, Restaurants and Attractions

Directions

From Downtown San Diego, travel north on Interstate 5 and exit at Ardath Road west. Proceed straight, and Ardath Road will become Torrey Pines Road. Take a right on Prospect Place, and proceed to Draper Avenue near the Museum of Contemporary Art. Turn left on Draper, and the inn will be to your left about half a block down.

Credit Cards Accepted

Visa, MasterCard, American Express.

LA QUINTA

Served by Ontario International Airport (ONT).

LAKE LA QUINTA INN
78-120 Caleo Bay
La Quinta, Riverside County
Tel. 888/226-4546 or 760/564-7332
Fax: 760/564-6356
Web Address: www.lakelaquintainn.com
E-mail: stay@lakelaquintainn.com
Rates: $189-349
3pm check-in
Year Opened: 1998
Innkeepers: Tim and Cecilia Ellis

Profile
Set against the burnished Santa Rosa Mountains, among the tumbleweeds and geckos, you'll find the rambling estate of Lake La Quinta Inn. Desert and waterview seem hardly compatible words unless, of course, you're talking about a room overlooking one of Palm Springs' Olympic-size swimming pools. Yet Lake La Quinta Inn, formerly known as Two Angels Inn, offers chlorine-free liquid vistas on a dreamy lakefront setting.

The French-style chateau goes against the desert grain of red-tiled roofs and stucco facades; but, then again, Lake La Quinta Inn strives to be unique. A stay here can be likened to being a house guest at someone's estate – there simply is nothing commercial about it. If you prefer a very hands-on approach to innkeeping, then you'll embrace the philosophy practiced here. If, however, you prefer to come and go unnoticed, this may not be the place for you.

Accommodations
Behind the pitched roof and fleet of balconies are 11 rooms, two of which are located in the boathouse annex, offering varying themes such as **La Mancha, Safari, Tally Ho** and **Lotus**. Each room is a capsule of luxury with gas fireplaces, discreetly placed television sets and phones, private patios and Juliet-style balconies offering views of the lake and sprawling Coachella Valley.

Marrakech is an exotic room boasting a Moroccan-style entryway, while **Lotus** strives for feng shui harmony within its boathouse confines. Though its name is a bit hokey, **Memoirs** offers a beautiful sleigh bed and vintage touches typically found at a more traditional bed and breakfast. The other rooms, like **St. Andrews, Desert Spirit** and **Captain's Quarters**, speak for themselves.

Amenities

A hearty country breakfast is served each morning in the formal dining room or adjoining terrace, a tranquil spot to find yourself before temperatures start to rise. In the afternoon enjoy those spectacular desert sunsets while sipping wine with fellow guests.

An inviting **swimming pool** and **spa** are nice reprieves from the sweltering desert sun. Sometime during your stay you can visit the massage room for a rubdown or have the therapist pay a visit to your room. As for where to dine and enjoy some evening entertainment, the innkeepers can assist in making those arrangements. Nearby are some of the best **golf** and **tennis** venues in Southern California, and the **Coachella Valley** also offers some wonderfully hidden hiking trails.

At-A-Glance Features

11 Rooms
Complimentary Breakfast
Complimentary Afternoon Wine and Refreshments
En Suite Massage Therapy
Evening Turndown Service
Near to Shops and Restaurants
Not Appropriate For Children
Swimming Pool and Spa

Directions

From Los Angeles, take Interstate 10 east passing through Palm Springs and exit Washington Street. Turn right onto Washington Street and continue approximately five miles across Highway 111 to Avenue 48. Turn left on Avenue 48 and take an immediate left on Caleo Bay. The inn will be on your right-hand side.

Credit Cards Accepted

Visa, MasterCard, American Express, Discover.

LAGUNA BEACH

Served by John Wayne/Orange County International (SNA).

CASA LAGUNA INN

2510 South Coast Highway
Laguna Beach, Orange County
Tel. 800/233-0449 or 949/494-2996
Fax: 949/494-5009
Web Address: www.casalaguna.com
E-mail: info@casalaguna.com
Rates: $150-500
3pm check-in
Year Opened: 1935
Innkeepers: Francois Leclair

Profile

Laguna Beach is one of California's most enchanting seaside hamlets brimming with galleries, boutiques and al fresco bistros. While there is no shortage of hotels and motels, Casa Laguna Inn is just one of three bed and breakfast establishments in town.

Layered into a hillside with stunning ocean views, this lovely Mediterranean-style inn was actually part of a much larger estate, the Villa Rockledge, located across the street. The estate's owner used this annex as a guest house before it was transformed into a small inn during the mid-1930s. Towering palms and colorful bougainvillea create a lush setting among the red-tiled roofs, and the mood among guests is decidedly relaxed.

If you're in the market for a quaint seaside getaway, you can't do much better than Casa Laguna Inn.

Accommodations

Ascending up an embankment are a collection of 21 villas framed by colorful bougainvillea, swaying palms and leafy banana trees. Doors coated in Mykonos blue are the portals to the past, revealing period furnishings collected from the '20s, '30s and '40s. Hints of modernism can also be found with cable television, phones and refrigerators mostly used for cooling bottles of wine and designer water. Random acts of craftsmanship are evident throughout with vintage stained-glass adornments, bas relief carvings and a rare collection of Catalina tiles placed throughout the gardens and fountains.

There are six categories of rooms priced according to their size and views. The **Courtyard Rooms** and **Ocean View Rooms** are among the least expensive, but nonetheless charming with shared terraces and patios. The **Deluxe Ocean View Rooms** have all been recently remodeled to offer larger bathrooms with Jacuzzi tubs, CD players and VCRs plus complimentary fruit, bottled water and liqueurs. The **Ocean View Suites** are likened to individual compounds with living and dining areas, full kitchens and one to two bedrooms. The **Mission Suite**, part of the original estate, is vintage chic with hardwood floors, a cozy fireplace and an ample bedroom.

Trying to reserve the **Cottage** can be a challenging task. Freestanding and fabulous, it's a study in beachside luxury and offers all the elements of home: living room, dining room, kitchen and fireplace. Late 19th century stained-glass windows grace the bedroom, and a private patio provides ocean panoramas. For those who don't wish to be bothered, the Cottage offers total seclusion.

Amenities

Animal lovers are smitten with Casa Laguna Inn and for very good reason – they allow pets. Actually, Laguna Beach is a very dog-friendly town and well-behaved pooches are given carte blanche.

Guests are treated to a buffet breakfast each morning along with afternoon wine and cheese served in the library or outdoors in the garden. Coffee and teas are also available throughout the day. The inn's bell tower is a splendid refuge for observing California sunsets and ocean views. There is also a **refreshing swimming pool** for plunging, but most guests prefer the short walk to either **Victoria Beach** or **Moss Point**, where tide pools and coves can be explored.

At-A-Glance Features

21 Rooms
Children Welcome
Complimentary Breakfast
Complimentary Wine and Hors d'oeuvres
Pet-Friendly
Swimming Pool
Within Walking Distance to Shops, Restaurants and Beach

Directions

From Los Angeles, take the 405 Freeway south to the 73 Freeway south heading towards Corona del Mar/Newport Beach. Take the MacArthur Boulevard exit towards Bison Avenue, and then merge onto MacArthur Boulevard. Travel MacArthur until you reach Coast Highway and turn left. Travel on Coast Highway through the village of Laguna Beach, and turn left at Upland Road. The inn is located near Upland and Coast Highway.

Credit Cards Accepted

Visa, MasterCard, American Express.

LONG BEACH

Served by Los Angeles International Airport (LAX) or John Wayne/ Orange County International Airport (SNA).

DOCKSIDE BOAT AND BED

Dock 5 – Rainbow Harbor
Long Beach, Los Angeles County
Tel. 562/436-3111
Fax: 562/436-1181
Web Address: www.boatandbed.com
E-mail: boatandbed@yahoo.com
Rates: $175-240 - Parking Additional
2pm check-in
Date Opened: 1999
Innkeeper: Kim Harris

Profile

Dockside Boat and Bed has given new meaning to the term waterfront view. With its fleet of private yachts, which remain firmly anchored in the Long Beach Harbor, guests are at the helm of a most unique experience.

The location, in the **Downtown Long Beach Marina**, is within walking distance to shops, restaurants and attractions. Within walking distance is the new state-of-the-art **Long Beach Aquarium of the Pacific and Shoreline Village**, a bustling seaside marketplace flanked with shops, restaurants and amusements. The **Queen Mary**, a former 1930s Art Deco ocean liner, is just across the harbor and is open daily for on-board tours, dining and shopping.

The Long Beach Passport, a shuttle service that darts back and forth between the marina, downtown and the outlying neighborhoods, makes getting around convenient. For those who wish to venture out farther, the Metro Blue Line travels daily between Long Beach and Downtown Los Angeles.

Accommodations

Slumbering aboard a yacht is an adventure in luxury. Dockside Boat and Bed offers five vessels to choose from. The fleet is rather straightforward with a 50-foot sailboat, a 44-foot motor yacht and a pair of 50-plus foot cockpit sailboats.

The exception is the **Mei Wen Ti**, a 53-foot authentic Chinese Junk. Built in China around 1990, this striking vessel is easy to detect in the harbor. The exterior wood is stained the color of brown sugar, and Asian symbols in hues of red, green and yellow adorn oval panels set into the outer railings. A grinning tiger, looking fierce, is painted against the bow of the ship, and the elevated deck, with its wicker chairs, provides an excellent observation area for admiring the Queen Mary's silhouette. Below deck, the mood is snug but comfy with a sitting area, bedroom and galley. If this is what is meant by a slow boat to China, you'll want to book passage now.

Each vessel boasts ample deck space, eating areas, on-board restrooms with showers, CD players, televisions with VCRs, and everything else you'd expect to find ashore. The private dock also has a grill for warm weather barbecues, and galley refrigerators are large enough to store a bottle of wine and some beer.

Amenities

Dockside Boat and Bed provides the vessel, the view, the ambiance and a few other surprises. While there is no afternoon wine and cheese, goodie baskets left below deck fill such voids, and bottled water is always chilling in the galley's refrigerator. In the morning, a continental breakfast, consisting of muffins, croissants and fresh fruit and juice, is delivered in a basket and placed deckside. On-deck **spa treatments** can also be arranged, and pets and kids are welcome too.

At-A-Glance Features

5 Yachts
Children Welcome
Complimentary Continental Breakfast
Complimentary Snacks and Bottled Water
On-Board Spa Treatments
Pet-Friendly
Within Walking Distance to Shops, Restaurants, Beach
    and Attractions

Directions

From Los Angeles International Airport, head south on the 405 Freeway to the 710 Freeway south. Continue on the 710 Freeway until the end, and follow the Shoreline Drive exit. At Pine Avenue, turn right and park in the turnaround. At the end of the turnaround is the Pine Avenue Pier, and the first dock to the right will be Dock 5, where the check-in area is located.

Credit Cards Accepted

Visa, MasterCard, American Express, Discover.

FINE DINING IN LONG BEACH

In recent years, Long Beach has gained a reputation for its eclectic mix of dining venues. While nesting at Dockside Boat and Bed, you may want to pour yourself into a table at one of these restaurants; the area code for all is 562.

E.J. Malloy's, located on Broadway near the corner of Redondo, is a local pub serving up delicious sandwiches, burgers, chicken, pasta and the best fish and chips this side of England. Tel. 433-3769

La Opera, located on Pine Avenue at First Street, this elegant Italian ristorante provides a nice backdrop for special occasions. Tel. 491-0066

The Queen Mary Champagne Sunday Brunch, located aboard the famed ocean liner in the elegant Grand Salon, this weekly feast features foods from around the world and includes a free self-guided tour. Tel. 435-3511

The Sky Room, located on Ocean Boulevard just east of Pine Avenue, offers a time travel experience with Art Deco luxury, an elegant menu, a lounge for enjoying oversized martinis and a floor for dancing cheek to cheek. Tel. 983-2703

Super Mex, located at the corner of Alamitos Boulevard and First Street, this local landmark offers authentic Mexican food at reasonable prices. Tel. 436-0707

The Yard House, located at Shoreline Village overlooking the marina, this popular eatery features American Fusion cuisine along with 250 tap handles of beer. Tel. 628-0455.

MONTECITO

Served by Los Angeles International Airport (LAX).

SAN YSIDRO RANCH

900 San Ysidro Lane
Montecito, Santa Barbara County
Tel. 800/368-6788 or 805/969-5046
Fax: 805/565-1995
Web Address: www.sanysidroranch.com
E-mail: reservations@sanysidroranch.com
Rates: $375-3750
3pm check-in
Year Opened: 1893
Innkeeper: Janis Clapoff

Profile

Hidden in a flowering hillside and steeped in celebrity lore, San Ysidro Ranch is perhaps California's best offering. Life at this homestead is luxe and leisurely, but the ranch's humble beginnings tell a different tale.

During the early 1700s, the ranch's foothills were a way station for Franciscan monks. Around 1825, Tomas Olivera, one of many owners, built an adobe which served as the ranch's main house and is the only original structure to have survived. In 1883, John Harleigh Johnston and Taylor Goodrich purchased the property to harvest high-quality oranges and lemons; although mountain fires nearly claimed their groves, the men persevered. Sensing a growing popularity among the area resorts, Johnston transformed the working ranch into a small stylish hotel that could accommodate up to 40 guests and, in 1893, San Ysidro Ranch opened. It was an instant magnet for the wealthy, attracting its share of well-heeled bluebloods.

In 1935, actor Ronald Colman and his partner Alvin Weingand purchased the 540 acres from the Johnston family. The pair operated the resort as an exclusive hideaway for their clique of actor friends, and soon it became a pied-á-terre of sorts for Hollywood's elite. Little has changed at the San Ysidro Ranch during the past century. Its rustic charm and sprawling gardens still beckon the rich and famous with names like Sophia Loren, Heather Locklear, Phil Collins and a host of other familiar faces checking in almost daily.

Accommodations

There are 37 sublime rooms and suites set amid 21 rustically chic cottages. Dotted throughout the grounds, each chamber is a study in elegance with hardwood floors, wood-burning fireplaces, fine antiques, handmade quilts or down comforters, stocked refrigerators with a supply of complimentary goodies, plush terry cloth robes and, in some cases, French doors opening onto private decks where bubbling spas are revealed.

The inn offers a number of lodging options, from the least expensive **Canyon Rooms**, poised atop the property, to the one-bedroom **Premium Cottages** to the exclusive **Willow Tree Suite**, just to name a few. The ranch's layout is simple, and you'll always know which cottage is yours as surnames are spelled out in chunky blocks and then hung from cottage doors. Beyond the raised porches and portals is a botanical masterpiece of vivid flora, citrus, herb and vegetable gardens.

Amenities

Amid this hillside compound are a pair of tennis courts, swimming pool, bocce ball, horseshoes, a sculpture garden and endless acres of trails. There are two critically acclaimed restaurants: the provincial-style **Stonehouse Restaurant**, the ranch's original citrus packing house, serving casual lunches and more formal dinners; and the **Plow and Angel Pub** offering a limited menu and libations. In-room dining is available 24 hours, and seasonal poolside dining is also offered.

Even without all the subtle and not so subtle touches – fresh flowers on the nightstand, a candle shaped yellow rubber ducky floating in two-person tubs, surnames spelled out in wooden blocks and hung by cottage doors – the staff is truly schooled in the art of hospitality. When my husband and I arrived for our stay to celebrate a special occasion, a crock of warm chocolate, lady fingers and a bottle of fine champagne was delivered to our room as a congratulations. As we were checking out, I inquired about purchasing the hand-knitted *do not disturb* sign that hung from our door. I was told I could keep mine as a remembrance of my stay at the ranch. Such service is impressive.

Dogs are also well treated with the ranch's **Privileged Pets** program. It begins with a pawing of the pet guest register along with a neatly packaged welcome gift that includes a bowl, toys, Pawier water and treats. Come evening an attendant arrives for turn-down service, where comfy beds resemble a steak or milk bone, and a gourmet dog biscuit is left on the cushion. A special doggie menu is also available with such choices as New York steak, chopped beef or baked salmon. If your pet prefers something a bit lighter, there is canned or dry dog food, hickory-smoked bones, rawhide chews and other treats to choose from.

After running through the trails with their owner, a dog may need to unwind. Pets and their owners can enjoy an en-suite massage. **Dog masseurs** offer either a slow and gentle massage for relaxation or an authentic reiki rub which focuses on a dozen specific body points. Human guests are rewarded with a discount on their massage when they pamper their pet with a treatment. There is a $75 non-refundable per pet cleaning fee, and massages run $65 for a half hour.

And, while the inn's rates, both human and otherwise, certainly qualify as expensive, this is the type of place that would turn an ordinary getaway into something spectacular.

Directions

From Los Angeles, take Highway 101 north. As you approach Santa Barbara, exit San Ysidro Road and turn right. Follow San Ysidro Road up into the hills, and turn right onto San Ysidro Lane. The ranch's driveway will be to your left.

At-A-Glance Features

38 Rooms
Children Welcome
En-Suite Spa Services
Evening Turndown Service
Full-Service Restaurant and Pub
In-Room Refrigerators With Complimentary Soft Drinks
Nightly Turndown Service
Pet-Friendly
Swimming Pool
Tennis Courts

Credit Cards Accepted

Visa, MasterCard, American Express.

CELEBRITY WEDDINGS & HONEYMOONS AT SAN YSIDRO RANCH

*San Ysidro Ranch is a haven for celebrities and has been a hideaway for Hollywood's elite for decades. **Vivien Leigh** and **Laurence Olivier** were secretly wed in the ranch's Wedding Garden in 1940 and, in 1953, **John and Jackie Kennedy** spent the last leg of their honeymoon here. In fact, the cottage they occupied has been named in their honor.*

OJAI

Served by Los Angeles International Airport (LAX).

BLUE IGUANA INN

Highway 33 at 17794 North Ventura Avenue
Tel. 805/646-5277
Fax: 805/646-8078
Web Address: www.blueiguanainn.com
E-mail: innkeeper@blueiguanainn.com
Rates: $95-179
3pm check-in
Year Opened: 1997
Innkeeper: Julia Whitman

Profile

Billing itself as an artisan villa, the Blue Iguana Inn is among Ojai's newest escapes. Built in 1997 and reminiscent of a southwestern pueblo, the inn is affordably priced without sacrificing any comforts. Designed by local architects in the vintage mission style, flair for detail is evident beneath arched entryways, terra cotta roofing, and rugged outpost railings. Flagstone pathways trail through the quaint property, and guests are greeted with the presence of a mosaic sculpture and fountain in the shape of, what else, a blue iguana.

Located in Ojai, a charming hamlet located above Ventura and big on spiritual healing, the Blue Iguana Inn can be found on the fringes of the village. There's plenty to do up here, from nature hikes and equestrian outings to gallery browsing and spa hopping. Most of all, a trip to Ojai guarantees a peaceful and tranquil getaway.

Accommodation

Funky and fabulous are two words that come to mind when describing the Blue Iguana Inn. Each stylish room is adorned with hardwood floors, imported rugs, Mexican pine furniture and original artwork created by local artisans. The roomy casita suites are private and plush, the type of place that provides inspiration if only an easel and canvas were readily available. Adding to the comfort are televisions, phones, refreshment bars and coffee makers.

If you happen to admire the artwork, which seems a given, most of it is available for purchase. The inn serves as a mini-gallery showcasing the talents of local artists who reside in town.

Amenities

Amenities are somewhat limited at the Blue Iguana Inn. A complimentary continental breakfast is served only on weekends, and there is no evening wine or cheese. What you do get, however, are in-room mini bars stocked with snacks and drinks, a refreshing **swimming pool**, en-suite **spa treatments** by request, and the privilege of staying in what many people call Shangra-La.

At-A-Glance Features

11 Rooms
Children Welcome
Complimentary Continental Breakfast on Weekends Only
Pet-Friendly
Swimming Pool
Within Walking Distance to Shops, Restaurants and Galleries

Directions

From Los Angeles, travel Highway 101 north to Highway 33 heading towards Ojai. After passing the traffic light leading to Lake Casistas and Santa Barbara, the inn will be a half-mile up ahead on the right-hand side of the road at the corner of Loma and Highway 33.

Credit Cards Accepted

Visa, MasterCard, American Express, Discover, Diners Club.

THE FABULOUS SPA AT OJAI VALLEY INN

Director Frank Capra based his mythical Shangra-La in the film **The Lost Horizon** *on the beauty of Ojai. These days the new spa at the* **Ojai Valley Inn** *resembles a modern-day version of Shangra-La. Spanning 31,000 square feet of total luxury, guests are ushered into private treatment rooms and meditation lofts where both body and soul are treated to a good cleansing. In keeping with the inn's glorious 1920s architecture, the spa evokes the same relaxed Spanish village feel. There are 28 well-appointed treatment areas – some with fireplaces – offering sunbathing loggias, saunas and more. Skilled attendants cradle aching muscles while applying aroma oils to soothe any aches and pains. If you do one thing and one thing only while in Ojai, make it a visit to the Ojai Valley Inn's spa.*

PALM SPRINGS

Served by Ontario International Airport (ONT).

KORAKIA PENSIONE

257 South Patencio Road
Palm Springs, Riverside County
Tel. 760/864-6411
Fax: 760/864-4147
Web Address: www.palmspings.com/hotels/korakia
E-mail: none
Rates: $119-395
3pm check-in
Year Opened: 1992
Innkeeper: Melissa McDaniel

Profile

A hint of vintage Palm Springs glamour awaits those who nest at the Korakia Pensione, a heavenly fortress located in the town's exclusive Tennis Club area. Built by Scottish painter Gordon Coutts in 1924, the architecture found throughout this exotic villa was an attempt by Coutts to recreate his earlier life in Tangier.

By the time Douglas Smith, a leading California architectural preservationist, purchased the home in 1989, it offered none of the allure it once possessed. Astroturf and linoleum blanketed the original stamped concrete floors, cheap tile concealed the high ceilings, and the grand entrance, which was graced with a pair of carved wooden double doors, was boarded up. Determined to return the house to its original splendor, Smith infused the villa with Grecian influences and christened it Korakia, which means 'crow' in Greek.

With a passion for preserving relics, Smith took on the task of renovating a neighboring Mediterranean villa. The home, one owned by forgotten screen goddess J. Carol Nash, became part of the compound in 1997.

Accommodations

Going completely against the desert grain, Korakia Pensione is as exotic as anything you'd find in Morocco. Guests are lulled to sleep by the sound of a mosaic fountain in the distance, and then awake to the scent of citrus blossoms and hibiscus wafting through open windows.

Set against the San Jacinto Mountains on 1.5 acres, the two homes, united by a breezeway, recapture the literary and artistic ambiance that Palm Springs once enjoyed. Both estates boast the charm of southern Europe coupled with North African accents with a collection of antiques, featherbeds and Oriental rugs set against gleaming wood and stone floors.

In the **Moroccan Villa**, the **Garden Room** is one of the least expensive and most fetching rooms. Located in the courtyard adobe, it offers an arched entryway, queen-size built-in feather bed, sitting area and private patio. Across the way at the **Mediterranean Villa**, the **North Pool Bungalow** is a find with its private setting, lofty floor plan and French doors leading to the pool. Many of the suites contain full kitchens, and light cooking is permitted. But why slave over a hot stove when you're living life like a sultan?

Amenities

Korakia Pensione isn't the chatty kind of bed and breakfast where guests linger over cups of coffee making nice talk to everyone within earshot. Instead, it attracts those seeking seclusion and privacy – think honeymooners, deal makers and screenwriters hoping a weekend in the desert will remedy any creative blockage.

Breakfast can be enjoyed among a variety of settings at Korakia. Dine poolside, on the flagstone garden terrace beneath a crop of blooming fruit trees, or behind closed doors in the privacy of your room. There are **two pools** to lounge by, nightly turndown service, and in-room **spa treatments** available at guests' requests.

At-A-Glance Features

22 Rooms
Complimentary Full Breakfast
En Suite Spa Services
Evening Turndown Service
Near Shops and Restaurants
Not Appropriate For Children
Room Service and Poolside Dining
Swimming Pool

Directions

From Los Angeles, take Interstate 10 to Highway 111, which will eventually turn into Palm Canyon Drive. At Arenas turn right and proceed four blocks towards the mountains, turning left on Patencio. The entrance to the inn will be located about a block up on the right-hand side (the inn is located on both sides of the street).

Credit Cards Accepted

None.

CELEBRITY GUESTS AT KORAKIA PENSIONE

No one might remember silent screen star J. Carol Nash, but those who come to stay at her estate are certainly household names. Recent guests have included Laura Dern, Andy Garcia, Peter Coyote, Tom Ford, Gina Gershon, Debbie Mazar, Randy Quaid, Chris O'Donnell, Jennifer Jason Leigh and Alicia Silverstone. But even such status doesn't always guarantee a room. Try telling Al Pacino there's no vacancy.

ORBIT IN

562 West Arenas
Palm Springs, Riverside County
Tel. 877/996-7248 or 760/323-3585
Fax: 760/323-3599
Web Address: www.palmspings.com/oribitin
E-mail: mail@orbitin.com
Rates: $189-249
3pm check-in
Year Opened: 2001
Innkeeper: Christy Eugenis and Stan Amy

Profile

Neat-o and swell are hardly part of today's lexicon, but let's just say the Orbit In does justice to these almost forgotten words. Built in 1957, this 10-room resort has just recently been returned to its classic mid-century existence. One look around, and it's easy to imagine Dean and Sammy sipping martinis poolside or Lucy and Ethel plotting one of their kooky schemes.

In all its retro glory, the Orbit In is a virtual time capsule and the latest in a string of hip hotels to open in the Palm Springs area. Putting the groove back in groovy are such postwar features as Eiffel Tower-style chairs and funky Formica butterfly tables illuminated by flexor lamps.

What's even more nifty is that Orbit In is located in the historic Tennis Club District, just a just a few blocks off Palm Canyon Drive, near all the shops, restaurants and nightlife.

Accommodations

Modernism is alive and well at this vintage inn. The names of the rooms are a real hoot: **Martini**, the **Albert Frey Lounge**, **Rat Pack Suite**, **Atomic Paradise**, and the **Cha Cha Room**, just to name a few. Furnishing by renowned mid-century designers, such as Isamu Noguchi and Ray Eames, are blended with today's contemporary talents. Some fab '50s touches include white enamel kitchenettes and pink-tiled bathrooms.

In this age of technology, nostalgic journeys can only travel so far. Modern twists, such as data ports, VCRs and CD players, hardly go unnoticed. And, for those who have to be connected every minute of the day, there are also modems placed poolside.

Amenities

Palm Springs is the swimming pool capital of the world and, of course, the Orbit In has a great poolside setting. Complimentary refreshments are served beneath the cloudless skies, and the **Boomerang Bar** mixes some mean libations as well as some non-alcoholic beverages like the lemonade and iced tea "Arnold Palmer."

Other amenities include a **whirlpool** saddled alongside a raised firepit, as well as bicycles and helmets plus complimentary breakfast.

At-A-Glance Features

10 Rooms
Complimentary Bicycles
Complimentary Breakfast
Complimentary Poolside Snacks
Near Shops and Restaurants
Not Appropriate For Children
Swimming Pool and Hot Tub

Directions

From Los Angeles, take Interstate 10 to Highway 111, which will eventually turn into Palm Canyon Drive. At Arenas turn right towards the mountains. The inn will be up ahead on your right-hand side.

Credit Cards Accepted

Visa, MasterCard, American Express, Diners Club.

THE WILLOWS HISTORIC PALM SPRINGS INN

412 West Tahquitz Canyon Way
Palm Springs, Riverside County
Tel. 800/966-9597 or 760/320-0771
Fax: 760/320-0780
Web Address: www.thewillowspalmsprings.com
E-mail: innkeeper@thewillowspalmsprings.com
Rates: $225-550
4pm check-in
Year Opened: 1995
Innkeeper: Drs. Tracy Conrad and Paul Marut

Profile

A pair of silk lounging pajamas, a sterling cigarette holder, and a throaty Billie Holiday record is how you should come armed to The Willows. Never mind that the inn has a plush terry robe for you to slip into or that smoking is thankfully prohibited. As for the Billie Holiday tunes, the inn has a number of diva recordings that waft through the public rooms and tumble out onto the terrace.

But there is no denying the 1920s Hollywoodesque ambiance that belongs solely to The Willows. Maybe it's attributed to the fact that Marion Davies, the former screen siren who was as well known for her acting as she was for her dalliances with newspaper mogul William Randolph Hearst, lived here briefly during the 1950s. Or perhaps it has something to do with Clark Gable and Carole Lombard having reportedly spent a few nights of their honeymoon here as the guest of the original owner, former U.S. Secretary of the Treasury Samuel Untermyer. Untermyer, the first attorney in the United States to make a million dollar fee for a single case, entertained many of the nation's leading artists and public figures from the era, including close friend Albert Einstein and his wife Elsa.

Built in 1927, the two-story Italian-style villa features curved archways, wrought-iron balustrades, vaulted ceilings plus natural hardwood and slate flooring throughout. Its piéce de resistance is the gushing, hillside waterfall that flows two-stories through the center of the dining room. Adding to the allure is the fact that the inn, which is seemingly molded into the hillside, is located in the Old Palm Springs Village area. From here you can walk to all the shops, restaurants and entertainment venues that line the palm-studded streets.

Accommodations

The Willows, with its eight incredible rooms, retains the grandeur and elegance from a bygone era. Each stunning chamber joins the past with the present as a fleet of antique furnishings creatively masks such modern amenities as telephones and cable television. The rooms are spacious, offering private bathrooms and unique appointments such as sumptuous linens, handmade tiles, stone fireplaces, private balconies, garden patios or separate outside entrances. Picturesque mountains and colorful gardens are framed by windows and French doors, and the faint sounds of the courtyard waterfall can be heard from nearly every alcove. Two of the eight guest rooms – **Einstein's Garden Room** and the **Marion Davies Room** – are named for their famous occupants, while others, such as the **Rock Room**, are named for distinguishing features.

Though the villa looks somewhat different from Marion Davies' tenure, it's easy to see why the newspaper mistress fled the vastness of Heart Castle for the undeniable beauty of The Willows.

Amenities

The Willows has all the bells and whistles of a big resort – concierge service, room service, en-suite massage, swimming pool – with all the intimacy of a private estate. People usually come to Palm Springs with three things in mind: swimming, golf and tennis. Tennis clubs and golf courses are a dime a dozen in this desert community, and the innkeeper can help with making arrangements at nearby facilities. But why venture from the inn at all when you can lounge by the swimming pool all afternoon, enjoying tasty snacks and beverages? Each stay also includes a gourmet breakfast, enjoyed beneath the dining room's frescoed ceiling or on the expansive terrace.

After getting your morning fill, wander along the stone footpaths that traverse the hillside garden. It's been said that frequent visitor Albert Einstein claimed a secluded corner for himself in which to enjoy his daily ritual of meditating. End the day with a **massage** administered in the privacy of your room, or enjoy a private poolside dinner catered by the neighboring Le Vallauris restaurant.

At-A-Glance Features

8 Rooms
Complimentary Evening Wine Reception
Complimentary Full Breakfast and Poolside Refreshments
Concierge Service
En-Suite Spa Services
Near Shops and Restaurants
Non-Smoking
Not Suitable for Children Under 16

Room Service and Poolside Dining
Swimming Pool

Directions
From Los Angeles, take Interstate 10 to Highway 111, which will eventually turn into Palm Canyon Drive. At Tahquitz Canyon Way, turn right and the inn will be located about a block up on the right-hand side.

Credit Cards Accepted
Visa, MasterCard, American Express, Discover, Diners Club.

MARION DAVIES' KITCHEN ... I MEAN, BAR
When Marion Davies occupied the estate in 1955, she was said to have a penchant for alcohol. It's rumored that one of her first remodeling ventures included completely gutting the kitchen and installing a state-of-the-art bar.

PLAYA DEL REY

Served by Los Angeles International Airport (LAX).

INN AT PLAYA DEL REY

435 Culver Boulevard
Playa del Rey, Los Angeles County
Tel. 310/574-1920
Fax: 310/574-9920
Web Address: www.innatplayadelrey.com
E-mail: playainn@aol.com
Rates: $165-345
3pm check-in
Year Opened: 1995
Innkeepers: Donna Donnelly and Lauren Cresto

Profile

The Inn at Playa del Rey is a secluded haven located close to all coastal Los Angeles has to offer, yet completely tinsel-free. The Eastern Seaboard-style inn, built in 1995, skirts the Ballona Wetlands, one of the few remaining sanctuaries left in Southern California. Sadly, it has been approved for commercial development, but local residents and environmentalists have pledged to fight until the very end.

The inn is just a sandal toss from the beach, offering distant views of the marina, and is close to some of the area's best restaurants. Not only are couples finding their way to this idyllic hideaway, but business travelers, yearning for a place with a little more personality, are checking out of their high-rise hotels and into the Inn at Playa del Rey.

Accommodations

The Inn at Playa del Rey is what every person imagines L.A. living to be. As you sit on the edge of your bed, cool breezes rippling throughout, it's hard to believe you're in a major metropolis. The rooms look like spreads from a Pottery Barn catalogue: clean, crisp and without a trace of ordinary – the kind of ambiance we strive for in our own homes, but rarely achieve.

Standard rooms are anything but ordinary with such appointments as Jacuzzi jet tubs, fireplaces and French doors leading to balconies. There is also a family suite available, but this is the type of place you really don't want to bring the kids. Not because the inn doesn't allow it, but because this just simply isn't the setting for tikes.

The **Romantic Suites** are sublime and sexy; couples won't want to venture outdoors, let alone out of bed. These rooms are simple elegance at its best with oversized four-poster beds and huge soaking tubs illuminated by candles and an adjacent fireplace. An armoire conceals a television and VCR, but chances are you'll never even touch the remote control; there's really no reason to with digs like these.

Amenities

The inn's living room is exceptionally cozy with impressive French doors pushed open to reveal cool sea breezes. Stocked with books, classic movies and a few games, all available to take back to your room, guests are made to feel welcome and at ease.

Mornings begin with a sumptuous beach-style breakfast, and afternoons are social as guests unwind with a glass of wine or freshly squeezed lemonade and a wedge of cheese. There are complimentary **bicycles** available, probably the best way to enjoy a sunny afternoon along the strand, and **limited spa services** are offered with prior arrangement. For the business traveler or workaholic, the inn also houses a traveler's **business center** with all the necessities – fax machine, printer, copier – that can be wheeled to your room.

Just a three-block pedal from the inn is a 30-mile bicycle path leading to **Venice Beach** and other seaside towns. There's also fishing opportunities along the jetty, as well as nearby shopping, dining and simple gallivanting. Or you could retreat to the inn's back porch, stake claim to a white rocker, and let all your cares melt away with the mist.

At-A-Glance Features

21 Rooms
Children Welcome
Complimentary Bicycles
Complimentary Breakfast
Complimentary Afternoon Wine, Cheese and Refreshments
En Suite Spa Services
Near Shopping, Restaurants and Beach
Non-Smoking

Directions

From Los Angeles International Airport, take Century Boulevard to the 405 Freeway north. Heading towards Los Angeles, exit on the 90 Freeway west towards Marina del Rey, where the Freeway ends at Culver Boulevard. Turn left onto Culver Boulevard and proceed west for two miles.

Credit Cards Accepted

Visa, MasterCard, American Express.

SAN DIEGO

Served by San Diego International Airport (SAN).

CRYSTAL PIER HOTEL
4500 Ocean Boulevard
Tel. 800/748-5894 or 858/483-6983
Fax: 858.483-6811
Web Address: www.crystalpier.com
E-mail: none
Rates: $125-350
3pm check-in
Year Opened: 1936
Innkeeper: Jim Bostan

Profile
The cluster of white clapboard cottages neatly lining the pier provide fodder for those lounging on the beach. Built in 1936, nearly a decade after the pier went up, newcomers aren't sure whether they're summer homes or private residents. Locals, of course, know they are neither.

The vintage bungalows are dressed in cobalt blue accents and flanked with white picket fences and window boxes. Some may scoff at the high price to stay here, but it's one of Southern California's most unique settings. Though mornings start early, with noisy passersby strolling out onto the pier, the evenings belong to those who stay here as the wharf is closed to everyone but guests of the Crystal Pier Hotel.

Accommodations
Except for a half dozen cottages, the bulk of bungalows are located over the ocean. The whitewash interiors, though snug, are lofty and airy with hardwood floors, whitewashed exposed beam ceilings, sliding glass doors leading to rear decks flanked with umbrella-shaded tables, small tiled kitchens and living areas. Things get pricey when you leave the confines of a studio for the more elaborate one and two bedroom units. A parking space is also provided next to each cottage.

The cottages are separated by a low-lying white picket fences, so you might find yourself chatting with your neighbor to either side. However, most people staying at the Crystal Pier Hotel are at a loss for words once they lay eyes on the panoramic ocean vistas just outside their doors.

Amenities

Crystal Pier Hotel offers none of the amenities you might expect at a bed and breakfast inn, but you're welcome to provide your own. Stock your kitchen and prepare your own gourmet breakfast, or chill a bottle of wine and drink in the seascape at sundown. With a setting this spectacular, you can forgo the chocolates at bedtime and instead enjoy the sound of crashing waves as you're lulled to sleep.

Pacific Beach, one of San Diego's laidback surf ghettos, is right at your doorstep. Here you'll find fun and funky dining, as well as shopping and low-key entertainment. You're also just north of Mission Beach, home to the Giant Dipper Roller Coaster and SeaWorld; and Downtown San Diego's Gaslamp Quarter, located about 10 minutes by car, offers a thriving shopping, dining and jazz-infused entertainment district. If you want a two-nation vacation, head to Tijuana, Mexico, for the afternoon.

At-A-Glance Features

28 Cottages
Children Welcome
Close to Downtown San Diego
Located on Crystal Pier
Near Shops, Restaurants, Attractions and Beach
Non-Smoking

Directions

From Downtown San Diego, take Interstate 5 north to the Grand/Garnet exit. Follow Garnet Avenue west to the pier entrance. The cottages are located on the pier.

Credit Cards Accepted

Visa, MasterCard, Discover.

SANTA BARBARA

Served by Los Angeles International Airport.

CHESIRE CAT INN

36 West Valerio Street
Santa Barbara, Santa Barbara County
Tel. 805/569-1610
Fax: 805/682-1876
Web Address: www.cheshirecat.com
E-mail: cheshire@cheshirecat.com
Rates: $140-300
3pm check-in
Year Opened: 1984
Innkeeper: Christine Dunstan

Profile

Childhood memories are brought to life at this Alice In Wonderland-inspired bed and breakfast inn. Aside from a grinning cat or two, the theme is reflected in the name of the rooms only. The compound consists of a pair of 1894 Victorian homes and two suites situated in the decade-old Coach House with a trio of 1930s-era cottages and an additional stunning Victorian manor located across the street.

Owner Christine Dunstan brings a touch of her native England to laid back Southern California. From the selection of antiques to the manicured gardens to the impeccable service bestowed on guests, Dunstan has created an elegant English retreat. Located just above downtown, the inn is still within easy walking distance to Santa Barbara's many shops and restaurants.

Accommodations

With its collection of buildings and various settings, it's safe to say that a stay at the Cheshire Cat is a completely different experience for each guest. The neighboring Victorian homes, joined together by a common courtyard, offer all the bygone elegance you'd expect. Both homes contain six rooms each and offer a touch of whimsy with such chamber names as **Mock Turtle**, **Queen of Hearts** and **Mad Hatter**. In here the decor is classic with carpeted rooms, English antiques, Laura Ashley furnishings and spacious sitting areas.

The **Coach House** accommodations, located on a second level above the parking garage and overlooking the gardens, are quite charming.

Though built a little more than a decade ago, the pair of suites, Tweedledee and Tweedledum, do a nice job of complementing the original homes. Extremely private and primed for romance, the rooms are elegantly furnished. The **Tweedledee** is a studio suite painted in soft garden shades complete with wet bar and farmhouse table. It's roomier counterpart, **Tweedledum**, is a two-room Jacuzzi suite situated under a veil of oak beams complete with hardwood floors, wet bar and gas-burning fireplace. The Coach House is the only area on the premises where infants can be accommodated, but a crying baby will likely spoil any romance afoot. Try to escape sans children.

Across the street are a triad of 1930s-era cottages, **The Woodford**, **Prestbury** and **Mobberly**, named for the lovliest villages in Cheshire. From the outside they look rather plain with their neutral wooden shingles and shrouds of shrubbery, but the interiors are quite sophisticated. Cloaked in hardwood floors and warmed by gas fireplaces, these cottages are reminiscent of an American country home. Cozy touches, such as built-ins, casement windows and French doors, are found in the living room, dining nook, full-size kitchen and bedroom. Each bungalow's master suite opens onto a large private redwood deck where a bubbling Jacuzzi has been readied for your arrival.

The **James House**, situated behind the cottages, was acquired by the inn in 1999. With just four rooms, it is ideal for individual guests or those traveling with an entourage. **The Lion** chamber is located on the main level, while the **White Queen**, **White King** and **Unicorn** share the second floor. My favorite room, the Unicorn, features a large sunroom overlooking the front yard – a perfect place to enjoy morning meals.

Amenities

With the exception of the cottages and the Coach House, the three Victorian mansions each have their own parlor. However, the butteredcolor corner mansion is where guests gather in the evening for wine and cheese. If weather permits, and it usually does, this daily ritual takes place outside in the courtyard. An ample selection of local wines, chunks of cheese, crudités and fresh fruit are displayed near a trickling fountain.

Breakfast is strictly gourmet with a host of savory selections including frittata, homemade muffins and breads, fresh fruit and juice, and robust pots of coffee. The dining room table is set each morning with Wedgewood china, or you can choose to dine on the flower-filled brick patio. Most guests seem content to have breakfast delivered to their rooms.

The manicured gardens contain a white-lattice pergola concealing a steaming spa for guests' use. As for spa services, there is a full menu of massages, facials and body treatments that can be administered in the pair of spa therapy rooms at the James House or behind your chamber doors.

At-A-Glance Features

21 Rooms
Bicycles, English Lawn Croquet and Beach Equipment
Children Welcome
Complimentary Breakfast
Complimentary Evening Wine and Hors d'oeuvres
En Suite Spa Services
Within Walking Distance to Shops, Restaurants and Attractions

Directions

From Los Angeles, head north on Highway 101, exit Arrellagla Street to Chapala. Turn left on Chapala, the inn is one block up on Valerio.

Credit Cards Accepted

Visa, MasterCard, American Express, Discover.

SIMPSON HOUSE INN

121 East Arrellaga Street
Santa Barbara, Santa Barbara County
Tel. 800/676-1280 or 805/963-7067
Fax: 805/564-4811
Web Address: www.simpsonhouseinn.com
E-mail: reservations@simpsonhouseinn.com
Rates: $195-500
3pm check-in
Year Opened: 1985
Innkeepers: Glyn and Linda Davies

Profile

Imagine something spectacular, then multiply it a hundred times. Now you have a basic idea of what a getaway to the Simpson House Inn is like. Touted as North America's only AAA Five-Diamond Bed and Breakfast Inn, the Simpson House has all the wondrous trappings of a country manor. This is one of my favorite bed and breakfasts in all of California.

Scotsman Robert Simpson built this lovely Victorian home in 1874, and his family resided here for many years. By the time Glyn and Linda Davies stumbled upon it in 1976, the Simpsons had long since moved on and hardly a trace of elegance could be detected. The Davies immediately went to work restoring the 19th century home to its original splendor, finally welcoming their first overnight guests in 1985. To label this historic inn stunning would be like calling the Statue of Liberty tall. While the description is accurate, it doesn't even hint at the wondrous experience that lies ahead. Positioned atop a sloping knoll, the Simpson House Inn is shielded from the outside world by sandstone walls and a cloak of tall hedges. The English garden is shaded by mature oaks and swaying magnolias, which provide a natural umbrella for loungers.

One of my favorite afternoon rituals here is to sit on the wisteria-draped back porch sipping a glass of Chardonnay and losing myself in a good book. But there are many other places on the grounds to escape, including the pergola tucked away in a corner of the garden. There are also a pair of gregarious black Labrador Retrievers ready to play fetch with whomever will throw a ball in their direction. If you're not a dog lover, the innkeepers are quick to send them on their way. Within walking distance are all of the great shops and restaurants belonging to downtown Santa Barbara; just hop aboard one of the inn's bikes and pedal away

Simply put, the Simpson House Inn is the epitome of gracious living.

Accommodations

The inn has a trio of dwellings in which to slumber, including the main house, the old barn and a collection of cottages. No matter where you stay, you'll enjoy the convenience of having a television and VCR, air conditioning (though it's rarely needed in Santa Barbara), and telephone with voice mail.

The **main house**, one of the oldest wooden structures within the city limits, is an inviting enclave featuring lovely antiques, Oriental carpets and hand-printed Victorian wallpaper. The Davies have added their own personal touches by displaying family portraits along the walls, and a photo album in the parlor gives visitors an added appreciation for this home with a collection of before and after snapshots. The six rooms are named for the Simpson family, and each has a private bath.

Behind the Victorian home is the original **1878 barn**, which has been transformed into four magical suites. The two-story structure houses a set of suites on each floor and provides the ultimate in luxury with fireplaces, French doors leading to private garden decks, original pine floors, wet bars and antique armoires concealing television sets and VCRs.

Added to the property in recent years are three **garden cottages**, the **Abbeywood**, **Greenwich** and **Plumstead**. These are the creme de la creme of comfort, offering the ultimate in privacy with canopied featherbeds, fireplaces, whirlpools and private courtyards offset by trickling fountains.

Amenities

Not only is the Simpson House Inn a great place to sleep, it's a great place to satisfy your hunger. Breakfast is transformed into a culinary event and served on either the wrap-around verandah overlooking the grounds or on a cluster of garden tables surrounding an ornate terra cotta fountain. If you are nesting in either the barn or a garden cottage, you also have the option of enjoying the first meal of the day on your private deck.

During the afternoon, an extravagant spread so pleasing in presentation it's worthy of a magazine cover, is laid out on the formal dining room table for everyone to sample. You'll enjoy an assortment of local wines, tea and sherry. If you're planning on sampling one of the local restaurants for dinner, you may be wise to eat light at this gathering, a challenge I'd rather not accept since the selection is so tempting.

The Simpson House Inn offers so much more than the typical bed and breakfast getaway. Should you feel the need for some pampering, a professional **spa therapist** can be summoned to the privacy of your room for a facial, massage, aromatherapy treatment or reflexology. During the early evening, a chambermaid provides turndown service along with a delivery of fresh chocolate truffles. And guests also enjoy membership privileges at a nearby health club and pool.

At-A-Glance Features

14 Rooms
Children Welcome
Complimentary Breakfast
Complimentary Evening Wine and Hors d'oeuvres
Concierge Service
En Suite Spa Services
Gratuity-Free Service
Within Walking Distance to Shops, Restaurants and Attractions

Directions

From Los Angeles, head north on Highway 101; exit Garden/Laguna Street and turn right onto Garden Street. Travel one block to Guitierez and turn left. Go another block to Santa Barbara Street and turn right, continuing for 13 blocks to Arrellaga. Turn left on Arrellaga. The Simpson House Inn is located on your right.

Credit Cards Accepted

Visa, MasterCard, American Express, Discover.

STAY IN A MONASTERY FOR SOMETHING DIFFERENT

*If you've been praying for a completely different kind of travel experience, you might find exactly what you're looking for at **Mount Calvary Monastery and Retreat House**. Nestled in the Santa Ynez Mountains on a heavenly ridge overlooking Santa Barbara, this sanctuary was established in 1947 by the Order of the Holy Cross, a Benedictine monastic community. Though you don't have to be a monk to enjoy its tranquillity, you are expected to observe a few house rules, including being punctual for meals, observing silence from 8:30pm on most evenings through the next day's breakfast, and paying close attention to the early curfew. Rates, which include meals, are $70 per person, per night. For information, call 805/962-9855 extension 10, or visit www.mount-calvary.org.*

TIFFANY INN

1323 De La Vina Street
Santa Barbara, Santa Barbara County
Tel. 800/999-5672 or 805/963-2283
Fax: 805/962-0994
Web Address: tiffanyinn.com
E-mail: innkeeper@tiffanyinn.com
Rates: $135-285
3pm check-in
Year Opened: 1982
Innkeeper: Jan Martin Winn

Profile

The Tiffany Inn is a stately Victorian mansion built around the turn of the century. I'm partial to this retreat mainly because my husband and I rented the entire inn on the eve of our wedding for family and friends. Aside from having fond memories, we have returned on several occasions simply because we enjoy the understated elegance The Tiffany Inn provides.

Originally built as a single family home, the three-story manor was transformed first into an antique shop and then into a bed and breakfast inn. The family that started both ventures lived in what is now the Penthouse Suite, while operating their home-based businesses. They eventually moved out, added the additional room, and created one of Santa Barbara's best inns.

After nearly 20 years as innkeepers, the couple decided to sell The Tiffany Inn to the proprietor of the Upham Hotel, another charmer located just across the street. Though the inn has taken on the air of a country house, it could never escape its Victorian roots.

Accommodations

The Tiffany Inn is located on a busy avenue, as are most of Santa Barbara's accommodations, but street noise is quickly remedied once inside.

There are seven rooms spanning three floors, each its own capsule of luxury. The **Honeymoon Suite** is the only room located on the first level, but it has the advantage of having its own outside entrance, wood-burning fireplace, and sunken double whirlpool tub. A lovely staircase leads to the second level where five additional rooms open up to a common hallway including my personal favorite, **Victoria**. Tucked away in a corner and overlooking the back garden through a pair of French doors, this room is one of the most romantic. Resting atop the inn and occupying the entire third floor is the **Penthouse**, a more contemporary hideaway than those rooms below. Appointments include a sprawling bedroom with fireplace, refrigerator, television and VCR, sitting area and double whirlpool bath. If you wish, breakfast can be served on the private treetop terrace.

When I first started coming to The Tiffany Inn, phones and televisions were nowhere to be found. Since then, telephones have been installed in every room with the majority of chambers outfitted with televisions and VCRs.

Amenities

The inn's dining room, which once held a common table, has now taken on a pub-like existence. Breakfast is now served in either the antique-filled parlor or, more preferably, on the outside terrace overlooking the rear gardens. Breakfast is often lavish, and definitely filling with a continental variety offered for light eaters from 7:30am or a full breakfast served from 8-10am. Coffee and tea are available throughout the morning. Come evening, sample Santa Barbara's wines paired with a display of snacks. To satisfy any last minute cravings, a plate of cookies are usually left out at bedtime.

The innkeeper can arrange for an in-room **spa treatment** and fulfill just about any other whim. Another plus about staying at The Tiffany Inn is its close proximity to **State Street**, Santa Barbara's thriving downtown district, where a rash of shops and restaurants are all within walking distance.

At-A-Glance Features

7 Rooms
Children Welcome
Complimentary Breakfast
Complimentary Evening Wine and Cheese
En Suite Spa Treatments
Non-Smoking
Within Walking Distance to Shops, Restaurants and Attractions

Directions

From Los Angeles, travel Highway 101 north to the Arrellaga Street exit. Proceed straight following Arrellaga Street to De La Vina. At De La Vina, turn right; the inn will be on your right-hand side.

Credit Cards Accepted

Visa, MasterCard, American Express, Discover.

VILLA ROSA INN

14 Chapala Street
Santa Barbara, Santa Barbara County
Tel. 805/ 966-0851
Fax: 805/962-7159
Web Address: none
E-mail: apuetz@jetlink.net
Rates: $110-230
3pm check-in
Year Opened: 1982
Innkeeper: Annie Puetz

Profile

The Villa Rosa Inn, in all its Spanish glory, promotes a casual elegance a mere 84 steps from the beach. Upon opening its doors in the 1930s, it provided shelter to American seniors; as the decades passed, it became a popular refuge for local students attending city college and the University of California, Santa Barbara. In the 1980s the Spanish hacienda was sold to its present owners. It was quickly renovated and reopened to become one of the city's most sought-after retreats.

Located just blocks from the beach, the Villa Rosa offers a reprieve from Santa Barbara's more common Victorian bed and breakfast inns. Though it's a bit of a hike to the main part of town, Santa Barbara operates a wonderful shuttle system that will have you to the city center within 10 minutes.

Accommodations

If you have a hankering for seaside living, an escape to Villa Rosa is in order. There are 18 spacious rooms located on the upper level, each offering the comforts of home. The interiors are a blend of California mission and Santa Fe chic with windows framing ocean, harbor or mountain vistas. Some offer fireplaces and kitchenettes, while others are graced with wrought-iron balconies. Fall asleep listening to the strains of crashing waves, and awake to more of the same.

Amenities

It would be quite easy to throw on a swimsuit and head to the beach, but it's even more convenient to roll out of bed and make your way to the **courtyard pool** for a morning dip. The French doors leading to this snug oasis are always open, and guests wander in and out throughout the day. A continental breakfast is served each morning, which can be taken poolside or enjoyed in the lobby area. Come evening, sip wine beneath the living room's exposed beam ceiling, and return again for a port or sherry nightcap.

Many of Santa Barbara's seaside restaurants are located within walking distance, including a pair of eateries located on the historic wharf. There are also places to rent bikes nearby, and the hub of downtown is within a five-minute drive.

At-A-Glance Features

18 rooms
Children 14 and Older Welcome
Close to Downtown Shops
Complimentary Continental Breakfast
Complimentary Evening Wine and Cheese
Complimentary Port and Sherry

Swimming Pool and Outdoor Spa
Near Beach and Restaurants
Non-Smoking

Directions
From Los Angeles, take Highway 101 north to the Laguna Street/
Garden Street exit. At the fork in the ramp stay to your left, and turn left
onto Garden Street. At East Cabrillo Boulevard turn right, and right onto
Chapala Street.

Credit Cards Accepted
Visa, MasterCard, American Express.

SANTA BARBARA'S ARTS & CRAFTS SHOW
*If you're staying at The Villa Rosa Inn, you'll have the advantage of
being near the Arts & Crafts Show, a weekly marketplace situated along
the oceanfront. For the past 35 years, local artists have gathered every
Sunday from 10am to dusk to display their wares, which run the gamut from
landmark paintings to sculptures to cloth teepee tents for kids. You'll also
find funky pottery, wind chimes and oddly-shaped wine holders. The show
is located along a one-mile stretch of Cabrillo Avenue east of Stearns Wharf.
This event also takes place on Memorial Day, Fourth of July and Labor
Day.*

SANTA MONICA

Served by Los Angeles International Airport (LAX).

CHANNEL ROAD INN

219 W. Channel Road
Santa Monica, Los Angeles County
Tel. 310/459-1920
Fax: 310/454-9920
Web Address: www.channelroadinn.com
E-mail: channelinn@aol.com
Rates: $160-335
3pm check-in
Date Opened: 1988
Innkeepers: Heather Suskin and Christine Marwell

Profile

Los Angeles is known for its glamorous hotels replete with cabana-lined pools and star-studded guest lists. But when it comes to more intimate accommodations, such as a bed and breakfast inn, the spotlight is usually on Channel Road Inn.

Built in 1910 along Second Street in Santa Monica for Thomas McCall and his family, the home has the distinction of being a rare West Coast architectural example with its shingle-clad Colonial Revival style. The home remained with the original family until 1962, when it was purchased and moved to its present rustic canyon location. The new owners begun to add a third story, but the construction was halted and the house abandoned. For the next 12 years it stood empty, invaded only by the elements and vagrants, before being purchased and restored by its present owners.

Accommodations

As you pass through the expansive pair of Colonial Revival doors concealing the essence of Channel Road Inn, you suddenly feel as if you're back in the 1920s. The cozy living room is flanked with a collection of vintage photos and trinkets, and the aroma of coffee seems to waft through the room.

There are 14 splendid guest rooms offering romantic touches with soft down comforters, Amish quilts and private bathrooms. Some offer sitting areas, jutting balconies, ocean views and antique tubs. **Room #9** is a favorite with an antique wicker bed, sunny sitting area and oceanview deck – a perfect setting for enjoying the day's first cup of coffee. Even if you choose a small, simpler room, you can't go wrong. All rooms feature telephones with voice mail, televisions, VCRs and data ports.

Amenities

One of the inn's best amenities is its location. In recent years Santa Monica has enjoyed a revival with the development of **Third Street Promenade**, the opening of an amusement center at the end of the pier, a crop of trendy restaurants, and a fleet of fashionable boutiques and al fresco restaurants along Montana Avenue. Of course the beach is another of Santa Monica's many assets.

Back at the inn, guests are treated to a full breakfast with such offerings as egg soufflé and apple French toast. In the afternoon, guests empty the sand from their shoes just in time to take tea and enjoy a batch of homemade cookies. Evenings consist of wine and cheese, fresh lemonade and iced tea. In between bites, borrow one of the inn's **bicycles** and follow the 30-mile bike path that meanders along the beach, or get a real workout with a climb up the famous **Santa Monica Canyon Steps**. If you need a massage or facial afterwards, the innkeepers can arrange to have one administered in your room.

At-A-Glance Features

14 Rooms
Children Welcome
Complimentary Bicycles
Complimentary Breakfast
Complimentary Afternoon Tea and Cookies
Complimentary Evening Wine and Cheese
En Suite Spa Services
Near Beach, Shopping and Dining
Outdoor Whirlpool

Directions

From Los Angeles International Airport, take the 405 Freeway north to Interstate 10 west. Follow the freeway until it ends at Pacific Coast Highway (PCH). Take PCH north for about two miles, then take a right on West Channel Road. The inn will be up about two blocks on your left.

Credit Cards Accepted

Visa, MasterCard, American Express.

CELEBRITY RESTAURANTS IN SANTA MONICA

*If you want to see how some stars moonlight – as restaurateurs – you might want to visit some of Santa Monica's celebrity-owned restaurants. Among those doing double time are **Arnold Schwarzenegger** and **Maria Shriver**, owners of Schatzi's on Main, Tel. 310/399-4800, and **Bob Weir** of Grateful Dead fame who is a partner of the popular Reel Inn, Tel. 310/ 395-5538.*

SEAL BEACH

Served by Los Angeles International Airport (LAX) or John Wayne/ Orange County International Airport (SNA).

SEAL BEACH INN & GARDENS

212 Fifth Street
Seal Beach, Orange County
Tel. 800/443-3292 or 562/493-2416
Fax: 562/799-0483
Web Address: www.sealbeachinn.com
E-mail: hideaway@sealbeachinn.com
Rates: $165-350
3pm check-in
Year Opened: 1977
Innkeeper: Majorie Bettenhausen-Schmaehl

Profile

When this small hostelry first came to life in the early 1920s, it was known simply as The Seal Beach Inn. Wealthy visitors, including silent screen stars, flocked to the inn to enjoy the nearby rococo bath palaces, the pier, and the thrills of The Derby roller coaster. Except for the pier and the inn, all the other landmarks from that bygone era have vanished.

When present owner Marjorie Bettenhausen-Schmaehl purchased this historic 1923 property more than two decades ago, the years had not been kind to it. The property resembled more of a flop house than a quaint country inn, and it took several years to transform it from ragged to regal. Armed with determination and perseverance, Bettenhausen-Schmaehl managed to transform this former beast into a raving beauty. The inn's collection of antique furnishings and artifacts were hand selected during her many travels across the United States and abroad.

Today the Seal Beach Inn & Gardens is a lovely Victorian fortress located just steps from the charming shops and expansive shoreline belonging to this quaint coastal town. Though Jodie Foster, Leslie Ann Warren and Bo Derek are among the famous guests, the inn possesses none of the pretense associated with a celebrity haunt.

Accommodations

This seaside inn, with its striking wrought-iron balustrade and brick courtyard, would have easily provided Tennessee Williams with some novel inspiration. Each room bears a floral name and some offer whirlpool spas and fireplaces. A selection of guest rooms showcase hand-painted walls in floral motifs by Bulgarian artist Yollie Hagland, and 14 suites have sitting areas and 1920s-style kitchenettes. The inn recently acquired a freestanding cottage next door, which provides complete privacy for those guests who desire it.

The inn is furnished with various antiques ranging from Belgium lace curtains and clocks to classic beds purchased from the estate of actor John Barrymore. Other noteworthy pieces you're likely to encounter include intricate 19th century iron gates, an 1800s oak Hoosier china cabinet, a church altar from Chicago, and an impressive Parisian fountain made of iron measuring eight feet tall and weighing 2,000 pounds.

Amenities

Near the courtyard, flanked with blooming flora and countless varieties of trees, vines, shrubs and plants, is the quaint library. Beyond a pair of French doors is where a lavish daily breakfast and afternoon tea are served. There is a secluded outdoor **swimming pool** to enjoy, and plush embroidered bathrobes to wear to and from your room. Time is best spent amid the aged **gardens** laced with its benches, trickling fountains, ivy trellises, and tables for two. Sit beneath the fleet of oversized moss flower baskets suspended from the ornate iron balcony and enjoy an afternoon of **bird watching**. Experts have spotted more than 50 rare and common species fluttering through the grounds in recent years.

Just a few blocks away is the charming town of **Seal Beach**, where fine shops and restaurants await; the beach and pier are within walking distance, too. However, once you sign the inn's guest register, you may find it difficult to pull yourself away from its illustrious confines.

At-A-Glance Features

24 Rooms
Not Appropropriate for Children
Complimentary Continental Breakfast
Complimentary Afternoon Tea
Near Shops, Restaurants and Beach
Non-Smoking Rooms
Swimming Pool

Directions

From Los Angeles, take the 405 Freeway south and exit Seal Beach Boulevard. Go south approximately three miles, and turn right on Pacific Coast Highway. Drive about a mile, and turn left on Main. Take Main to Central Avenue and turn right onto 5th. The inn is located on the corner of Central and 5th Avenue.

Credit Cards Accepted

Visa, MasterCard, American Express, Discover.

ELEGANT ARTIFACTS AT THE
SEAL BEACH INN & GARDENS

The owner's passion for unique treasures is evident throughout the property. Items of particular interest are the 200-year-old Parisian fountain, the Victorian cast-iron window boxes and newel posts, an iron fireback circa 1794, turn-of-the-century street lamps, Pre-Civil War beds once belonging to a southern plantation, furnishings from actor John Barrymore's estate, and much more. Ask the innkeeper for an impromptu tour.

SOUTH PASADENA

Served by Los Angeles International Airport (LAX).

THE BISSELL HOUSE
201 Orange Grove Avenue
South Pasadena, Los Angeles County
Tel. 800/441-3530 or 626/441-3535
Fax: 626/441-3671
Web Address: www.bissellhouse.com
E-mail: info@bissellhouse.com
Rates: $115-160
3pm check-in
Year Opened: 1994
Innkeepers: Russ and Leonore Butcher

Profile
The Bissell House is located on what is commonly known as Millionaire's Row, named so for the grand houses that once lined the street during the late 19th century. Many of the homes are still standing, including this charming three-story Victorian mansion. Built in 1887, the house was named for the third owner, Anna Bissell McCay, who resided here from 1903 until the 1950s. Mrs. McCay was the daughter of Melville Bissell, a midwesterner who made his fortune designing and manufacturing carpet sweepers. Anna was one of the area's most respected philanthropists and often had the honor of hosting prestigious guests at her home, including genius Albert Einstein.

Romantically Victorian and a great place to pucker up, the inn's South Pasadena location makes it convenient for exploring Southern California. Downtown Los Angeles is just 12 minutes away, though you'd never suspect it, and attractions like **Santa Anita Racetrack** and the **Norton Simon Museum** are equally close. **Old Town Pasadena**, a favorite destination for shopping, dining and strolling, is less than five minutes away.

Accommodations
Gabled and glorious, the Bissell House boasts landmark status, an accolade well deserved. A towering hedge creates a makeshift fortress, leaving guests feeling completely isolated from the outside world.

The three-story estate offers five guest rooms, each individually decorated with an elegant hand. Vintage touches include leaded-glass windows, claw-foot tubs and pedestal sinks placed alongside a handful of modern conveniences. British overtones are reflected in the room names, such as **Prince Albert** and **English Holiday**.

Amenities

The formal dining room is the backdrop for weekday continental breakfasts and full gourmet breakfasts are served on weekends only. The aroma of freshly brewed coffee signals that it's time to dine, and the display of just-baked breads and sweets create added temptation. Rooms are stocked with complimentary wine, beer, juice, soft drinks, bottled water plus cookies, crackers, fruit and other edibles. It's impossible to starve while staying at the Bissell House, though you can still keep a svelte silhouette by doing laps in the pool.

If you're planning on coming for the annual Tournament of Roses Parade and the annual Rose Bowl that follows, this is an excellent alternative to the area's big chain hotels. Just be sure to make reservations early – say by January 2!

At-A-Glance Features

5 Rooms
Complimentary Breakfast
Complimentary In-Room Refreshments
Near Shops, Dining and Attractions
Not Appropriate for Children
Swimming Pool

Directions

From Downtown Los Angeles, take the 10 Freeway east to the Orange Grove exit. Turn left onto Orange Grove, making a left at Colombia. The first driveway on your left will be the inn's. The inn is located on the southwest corner of Orange Grove and Columbia.

Credit Cards Accepted

Visa, MasterCard, American Express.

ANTIQUE HUNTING IN PASADENA

If you enjoy antique hunting, Pasadena offers a pair of monthly marketplaces. The **Pasadena City College Flea Market** *takes place the first Sunday of every month and is a favorite haunt of junk-collecting celebrities. Taking place in the parking lots, the market houses more than 450 vendors selling mostly vintage furniture and collectibles, and includes one of the area's best record swaps. Admission and parking are free. Tel. 626/585-7906 for information.*

The second Sunday of every month you're sure to find most of Los Angeles milling around the makeshift stalls at **The Rose Bowl Flea Market** *in Pasadena. More than one million unusual items can be found along the stadium's outer perimeter, including antiques and collectibles mingled in with some occasional junk. Prices vary, but the dealers are always willing to knock a few bucks off the so-called asking price. This market has a modest admission fee and limited parking. Tel. 323/560-7469 for details.*

SUNSET BEACH

Served by Los Angeles International Airport (LAX) or John Wayne/
Orange County Airport (SNA).

RANCHO BOLSA CHICA INN
17101 Pacific Coast Highway
Sunset Beach, Orange County
Tel. 800/366-1064 or 562/592-4332
Fax: 562/592-4332
Web Address: none
E-mail: none
Rates: $100-120
3pm check-in
Year Opened: 1981
Innkeeper: Patsy Brodine

Profile
Pacific Coast Highway is both picturesque and functional, depending
on what part of the state you're traveling through. In Sunset Beach it's
strictly functional. Lining both sides of the thoroughfare near the Los
Angeles-Orange County line are al fresco restaurants, roadside motels,
antique stores and plenty of aquatic shops. This is also the same stretch
of highway where the Rancho Bolsa Chica Inn is situated.

When I first stumbled upon the 1946 motel-cum-bed and breakfast
inn a few years back, I never expected to find such a treasure. From the
street it appears charming enough with its Spanish-tiled roof, vivid blue
trim and rounded awning draped above the entrance. But beyond the
paned-glass door that leads to the collection of garden rooms, it's as if
you've stepped from a black and white existence into a Technicolor
dream. Because there are no public rooms, such as a parlor or dining area,
privacy gets high marks from the many returning guests.

Accommodations
Behind the fleet of French doors, graced with tiny brass crab
knockers, another reminder that you're within a sandal-toss of the beach,
are the suite-like chambers. Each room is a capsule of comfort with
Mexican paver tiles, hand-made quilts, antique furnishings and cozy
fireplaces. There is also a small, nicely appointed efficiency equipped with
a little stove, dishware and cooking utensils for added convenience. The

inn is also pet-friendly, and one suite can accommodate families with children.

Amenities

With the recent arrival of a nighttime prowler, in this case a harmless possum, breakfast baskets are no longer left at the door. Instead, guests simply pick up their parcel of pastries and muffins the prior evening to enjoy the following morning. Firewood is stored in each room, and a small whirlpool is located along the brick path. A public room contains a coin-operated washer and dryer, a stash of menus from area restaurants, and additional firewood should you happen to visit during a cool spell. A small courtyard patio is where you'll find lounge chairs and barbecues.

As for location, it's doubtful you'll find such a quaint and affordable inn located so close to the **beach**. As for what to see and where to go, take your pick. About a 45-minute drive south are tony **South Coast Plaza**, **Fashion Island** and **Laguna Beach**. Head north and you can be at the **Long Beach Aquarium of the Pacific** or the **Queen Mary** in about 15 minutes. As for the beach, try a 5-minute walk...if that.

At-A-Glance Features

10 Rooms
Barbecues on Premises
Children Welcome
Complimentary Continental Breakfast
Pet-Friendly
Within Walking Distance Restaurants and Beach

Directions

From Los Angeles, take the 405 Freeway south and exit Seal Beach Boulevard. Go south approximately three miles, and turn left on Pacific Coast Highway. Drive about three miles, and the Rancho Bolsa Chica Inn will be on your right side. If you hit Warner Boulevard, you've gone too far.

Credit Cards Accepted

Visa, MasterCard, American Express, Discover.

VENTURA

Served by Los Angeles International Airport (LAX).

THE VICTORIAN ROSE

896 East Main Street
Ventura, Ventura County
Tel. 805/641-1888
Fax: 805/643 – 1335
Web Address: http://victorian-rose.com
E-mail: victrose@pacbell.net
Rates: $99-175
4pm check-in
Year Opened: 1999
Innkeepers: Richard and Nona Bogatch

Profile

For many guests who find themselves slumbering beneath the roof of the Victorian Rose, it's a near religious experience. Not surprising when you consider this inn is actually a 113-year-old Gothic church, the last of its kind in the area, complete with a 96-foot steeple and a fleet of magnificent stained-glass windows.

The interiors are a melange of Victorian, Gothic, Eastlake, Norwegian and Mission splendor with carved beams looming 26 feet above and angelic cherubs perched throughout. The public rooms, scattered with trunks full of cherubs and vintage collectibles, offer several inviting sitting areas. While they may not be misted with holy water, the sound of trickling fountains still brings about a sense of peace to visitors.

Accommodations

Each of the five rooms, which open onto a common area where parishioners once worshipped, is its own delightful sanctuary with varying antiques.

The inn's namesake corner bedroom is outfitted with a hand-painted Italian Bombay queen bed, a 200-year-old map chest, a 10-foot-high and a century-old gas burning fireplace. An angel-laden banister leads from the verandah to the safety of the **Fleur-de-lis** chamber, where a four-poster French brass bed dominates the room. The **Wisteria Garden**, a tranquil hideaway that once served as the minister's study, is not only the inn's least expensive room but also the most charming.

Perhaps the most intriguing boudoir is that of the **Emperors'
Bedroom**. This former choir's loft is a heavenly delight with a spiral
staircase ascending 12 feet to a private interior balcony. Once on solid
ground, an assembly of stained-glass windows and dragons complete the
dynasty decor.

Amenities

Guests break bread each morning over a delightful gourmet breakfast, followed up each afternoon with a selection of wine and cheese.
There is an outdoor verandah and a **Jacuzzi** to enjoy, and guest room
soaps are handmade on the premises.

Ventura is an affordable beach town packed with plenty of shops,
restaurants and recreation. The inn is located on Main Street, and just a
few blocks down is the pulse of downtown **Ventura**, where a weekly
farmers' market takes place and rows of tidy antique stores are found.

At-A-Glance Features

5 Rooms
Complimentary Breakfast
Complimentary Afternoon Wine and Cheese
Not Appropriate for Children
Outdoor Jacuzzi
Within Walking Distance to Beach, Shops, Restaurants
     and Attractions

Directions

From Los Angeles, head north on Highway 101 and exit California
Street and turn right. The inn is located four blocks near the corner of
Kalorama Street.

Credit Cards Accepted

Visa, MasterCard, American Express.

9. VISITOR RESOURCES

For statewide travel information, contact:
California Division of Tourism
P.O. Box 1499, Department 1
Sacramento, CA 95812
Tel. 800/862-2543
www.gocalif.ca.gov

For information on California Bed & Breakfast Inns, contact:
The California Association of Bed & Breakfast Inns
2715 Porter Street
Soquel, CA 95073
Tel. 831/464-8159
www.cabbi.com

For regional information, contact these centers for visitors' assistance:
Amador County Chamber of Commerce
PO Box 596
125 Peek St.
Jackson, CA 95642
Tel. 209/223-0350
www.cdepot.net/chamber

Anaheim/Orange County Visitor & Convention Bureau
800 West Katella Avenue
Anaheim, CA 92803
Tel. 714/999-8999
www.anaheimoc.org

Eureka/Humboldt County Convention & Visitors Bureau
1034 Second Street
Eureka, CA 95501
Tel. 707/443-5097
www.redwoodvisitor.org

Fort Bragg-Mendocino Coast Chamber of Commerce
PO Box 1141
Fort Bragg, CA 95437
Tel. 707/961-6300
www.mendocinocoast.com

Half Moon Bay Chamber of Commerce and Visitors Bureau
520 Kelly Avenue
Half Moon Bay, CA 94019
Tel. 650/726-8380
www.halfmoonbaychamber.org

Lake Tahoe Visitors Authority
1156 Ski Run Boulevard
South Lake Tahoe, CA 96150
Tel. 916/544-5050
www.virtualtahoe.com

Long Beach Area Convention & Visitors Bureau
One World Trade Center, Suite 300
Long Beach, CA 90831
Tel. 562/436-3645
www.golongbeach.org

Los Angeles Convention and Visitors Bureau
633 West Fifth Street, Suite 6000
Los Angeles, CA 90071
Tel. 213/624-7300
www.lacvb.com

Monterey County Convention & Visitors Bureau
PO Box 1770
Monterey, CA 93942
Tel. 888/221-1010
www.gomonterey.org

Napa Valley Conference & Visitors Bureau
1310 Napa Town Center
Napa, CA 94559
Tel. 707/226-7459
www.napavalley.com

Nevada County Chambers of Commerce
132 Main Street
Nevada City, CA 95959
Tel. 800/655-6569
www.ncgold.com

Palm Springs Convention and Visitors Bureau
69-930 Highway 111, Suite 201
Rancho Mirage, CA 92270
Tel. 760/770-9000
www.desert-resorts.com

Pasadena Convention & Visitors Bureau
171 South Los Robles Avenue
Pasadena, CA 91101
Tel. 626/795-9311
www.pasadenacal.com

Russian River Region Visitors Bureau
14034 Armstrong Woods Road
Guerneville, CA 95445
Tel. 800/253-8800
www.russianriver.com

Sacramento Convention & Visitors Bureau
1421 K Street
Sacramento, CA 95814
Tel. 916/264-7777
www.sacramentocvb.org

San Diego Convention and Visitors Bureau
401 "B" Street, Suite 1400
San Diego, CA 92101
Tel. 619/232-3101
www.sandiego.org

San Diego North County Convention and Visitors Bureau
720 North Broadway
Escondido, CA 92025
Tel. 800/848-3336
www.sandiegonorth.com

San Francisco Convention & Visitors Bureau
201 Third Street, Suite 900
San Francisco, CA 94103
Tel. 415/391-2000
www.sfvisitor.org

San Mateo County Convention & Visitors Bureau
111 Anza Boulevard, Suite 410
Burlingame, CA 94010
Tel. 650/348-7600
www.sanmateocountycvb.com

Santa Barbara Convention and Visitors Bureau
12 East Carrill Street
Santa Barbara, CA 93101
(805) 966-9222
www.santabarbaraca.com

Santa Cruz County Conference & Visitors Council
701 Front Street
Santa Cruz, CA 95060
Tel. 831/425-1234
www.santacruzca.org

Santa Rosa Conference and Visitors Bureau
637 First Street
Santa Rosa, CA 95404
Tel. 707/577-8674
www.visitsantarosa.com

Sonoma County Tourism Program
5000 Roberts Lake Road, Suite A
Rohnert Park, CA 94928
Tel. 800/576-6662
www.sonomacounty.com

Tahoe North Visitors & Convention Bureau
PO Box 5578
Tahoe City, CA 96145
Tel. 800/824-6348
www.aminews.com/tahoenorth

Tuolumne County Visitors Bureau
PO Box 4020
55 West Stockton Street
Sonora, CA 95370
Tel. 209/533-4420
*www.mlode.com/inn-sierra/*visitor

Twain-Harte Area Chamber of Commerce
PO Box 404
Twain Harte, CA 95383
Tel. 209/586-4482
www.twainhartecc.com

Ventura Convention and Visitors Bureau
89 South California Street, Suite C
Ventura, CA 93001
Tel. 805/648-2075
www.ventura-usa.com

Yosemite/Sierra Visitors Bureau
40637 Highway 41
Oakhurst, CA 93644
Tel. 559/683-4636
www.yosemite-sierra.org

FEATURES INDEX

Adults Only

All-Inclusive

Coastal Locations

Inns With Less Than 10 Rooms

COUNTY CROSS-REFERENCE INDEX

B&Bs BY DESTINATION INDEX

ALPHABETICAL INDEX

TRAVEL NOTES

TRAVEL NOTES

TRAVEL NOTES

TRAVEL NOTES

TRAVEL NOTES

TRAVEL NOTES

OPEN ROAD PUBLISHING

U.S.A.

America's Cheap Sleeps, $16.95
America's Grand Hotels, $14.95
America's Most Charming Towns &
    Villages, $17.95
Arizona Guide, $16.95
Boston Guide, $13.95
California Wine Country Guide, $12.95
Colorado Guide, $17.95
Disneyworld With Kids, $14.95
Florida Guide, $16.95
Hawaii Guide, $18.95
Las Vegas Guide, $14.95
Las Vegas With Kids, $14.95
National Parks With Kids, $14.95
New Mexico Guide, $16.95
San Francisco Guide, $16.95
Southern California Guide, $18.95
Spa Guide U.S.A., $14.95
Texas Guide, $16.95
Utah Guide, $16.95
Vermont Guide, $16.95

MIDDLE EAST/AFRICA

Egypt Guide, $17.95
Israel Guide, $17.95
Jerusalem Guide, $13.95
Kenya Guide, $18.95

UNIQUE TRAVEL

Celebrity Weddings & Honeymoon
    Getaways, $16.95
The World's Most Intimate Cruises, $16.95

SMART HANDBOOKS

The Smart Home Buyer's
    Handbook, $16.95
The Smart Runner's Handbook, $9.95

LATIN AMERICA & CARIBBEAN

Bahamas Guide, $13.95
Belize Guide, $16.95
Bermuda Guide, $14.95
Caribbean Guide, $21.95
Caribbean With Kids, $14.95
Chile Guide, $18.95
Costa Rica Guide, $17.95
Ecuador & Galapagos Islands Guide, $17.95
Guatemala Guide, $18.95
Honduras & Bay Islands Guide, $16.95

EUROPE

Austria Guide, $15.95
Czech & Slovak Republics Guide, $18.95
France Guide, $16.95
Greek Islands Guide, $16.95
Holland Guide, $16.95
Ireland Guide, $17.95
Italy Guide, $19.95
Italy With Kids, $14.95
London Guide, $14.95
Moscow Guide, $16.95
Paris Guide, $13.95
Portugal Guide, $16.95
Prague Guide, $14.95
Rome Guide, $14.95
Scotland Guide, $17.95
Spain Guide, $18.95
Turkey Guide, $18.95

ASIA

China Guide, $21.95
Japan Guide, $19.95
Philippines Guide, $18.95
Tahiti & French Polynesia Guide, $18.95
Tokyo Guide, $13.95
Thailand Guide, $18.95
Vietnam Guide, $14.95

To order any Open Road book, send us a check or money order for the price of the book(s) plus $3.00 shipping and handling for domestic orders, to: **Open Road Publishing**, PO Box 284, Cold Spring Harbor, NY 11724